BLOOD
RELATIONS

BLOOD
RELATIONS

John Greenya

Harcourt Brace Jovanovich, Publishers

San Diego   New York   London

Library of Congress Cataloging-in-Publication Data

Greenya, John.
Blood relations.

1. Benson, Steven. 2. Benson family.
3. Crime and criminals—Florida—Biography.
4. Murder—Florida.
I. Title.
HV6248.B457G7   1987   364.1'523'19974   [B]   87-8413
ISBN 0-15-113217-8

Designed by G. B. D. Smith

Printed in the United States of America

First edition

A   B   C   D   E

For Gertrude K. Greenya
who, by her example,
taught me to love books

Author's Note

In February of 1986, I received a call from Boston attorney "Ric" Cirace. He introduced himself as a friend of Wicki Bailey, whom I knew, and said that she'd recommended he call me. He said he had a client in a most unusual situation, and on her behalf he was being contacted by writers, agents, and publishers, and even people who claimed to represent motion picture and television interests. He identified his client as Carol Lynn Benson Kendall and, briefly, told me her story.

He also mentioned that he and I had met some years earlier, when I was in Boston doing research for a book I was doing with F. Lee Bailey on the Patty Hearst case, and I had worked for a week or two in the law offices of J. Albert Johnson, Lee Bailey's long-time friend and co-counsel in the Hearst case. I had a vague memory of having met Ric Cirace, but a clear one of having met his mother, Fran, a charming and irrepressible woman who then worked in Al Johnson's office. I'd had the great pleasure of spending an evening in the apartment of Fran and her equally charming husband, Ernie, and had remembered that evening with pleasure ever since.

At the end of our conversation, Ric Cirace asked me if I could advise him, unofficially on how to deal with the people who were making the various offers he'd mentioned. He also asked if I might be interested, "down the road," in writing about the case, should Mrs. Kendall decide to get involved in a book project after the murder trial of her brother, in which she was slated to testify for the State.

We discussed the fact that his client should make no decision on any book or movie deal before she testified against her brother, as that might jeopardize his rights, either in fact or just in appearance. I asked him to let me know when a firm trial date was set, as I found the case intriguing.

After the trial—which I covered on a free-lance basis for the Style Section of the Washington *Post*—I met Carol Lynn Kendall for the first time and discussed working with her on an "authorized" book. Six weeks later we signed an agreement, of which this book is the result.

Our agreement was that I would write an objective account of her family and of the trial, based on my research, her exclusive cooperation, and the access she would provide me to family and friends. In return for that exclusive cooperation, I agreed to give her a share in the book's royalties. When I was finished, Carol Lynn Benson Kendall would have the right to read what I had written, to correct errors of fact, but only to *suggest* other types of changes. She would have no control over my interpretation of the facts.

I have made the decision, unilaterally, to protect the privacy of certain individuals. As a result, Scott's natural father, whose name I know, is identified only as "Brett," which is not even his correct first name. I could see no valid journalistic reason for including his name. In several other cases, I have given people different names, because they asked that I protect their identities, and I did so. In my opinion, who they are—as opposed to what they have said or done—is not the central issue. If readers are bothered by this, I am sorry. But I would do it again.

I have included certain anecdotes and information that may be repugnant to some, but the genesis of this book is a horrible crime. To have sanitized that material would have been to suggest that the crime was not, somehow, as serious and grisly as it most definitely was.

Toward the end of the trial, a newspaper reporter said to me, "This family is a bunch of sleazeballs. This whole case is about sleazeballs." I didn't agree then, and I certainly do not agree now, having spent seven or eight months "studying" them. To me, the Benson family is one in which what may well have begun with the very best of intentions went very horribly awry. They are an American family, for better and for worse. And I think we should be careful lest we judge them *too* harshly, and so learn nothing from their tragic experience.

John Greenya
Washington, D.C.
April 1987

On August 7, 1986 Steven Benson was convicted of the murders of Margaret Benson, Scott Benson, and the attempted murder of Carol Lynn Benson Kendall. As this book goes to press, only the formal notice of appeal has been filed by the defense in the case of Florida vs. Steven Wayne Benson.

Prologue

July 9, 1985. It was only a quarter after nine in the morning, but the sun was already baking southwestern Florida. Even the trash men moved slowly—in deference to the heat, but also to the affluence of the neighborhood. Quail Creek, a fairly new subdivision at the north end of Naples, offers sprawling, well-built homes in a variety of styles, all of them priced well beyond the quarter-million range.

The street names suggest tranquility—and the kind of quiet money, both old and new, that has made Naples a contender for the title of richest town in America. There are Foxtail Path and Snowberry Lane, White Violet Drive and Butterfly Orchid Lane, plus Pond Apple Drive and two more Lanes, Coco Plum and Bald Cypress. Valewood Drive leads residents, and visitors who can get by the guard station, into this enclave of sun-drenched comfort, where one is seldom far from the sight of a golf cart or the sound of a tennis ball being sent back across a taut white net.

It is not a community inhabited by young couples with two

incomes and big jobs; there are few BMWs and Saab Turbos in evidence. Most garages and driveways feature Cadillacs and Lincoln Town Cars. Many families also own an unfashionable, all-purpose utility vehicle—like the seven-year-old Chevrolet Suburban wagon that was parked, on that particular July morning, in front of 13002 White Violet Drive.

Behind the wheel was Scott Benson, a handsome youth in his twenties, looking sleepy and bored. Next to him, Margaret Benson, a well-kept, sixtyish blonde. Another attractive blonde, Carol Lynn Benson Kendall, in age approximately halfway between the other two passengers, came out of the house and got into the back seat on the driver's side. She later recalled the scene:

I was the last one out, so by the time I got there Scott was sitting in the driver's seat, and I remember thinking to myself, "What in the world is Scott doing in the driver's seat?" Logically, in my mind, Steven, the older brother, would do the driving, not Scott. . . .

Mother, at this point, was sitting in the front seat at the passenger side. Now normally I would have sat there because I tend to get carsick. I was going to say something to her, but I thought, oh heck she's already in, and we're not going that far, so I'll just sit in the back. And Steven was behind her on the passenger side, and he had something sitting on the top which I think was coffee. I wasn't paying that much attention. . . .

I have in my mind that he helped her in. As I was walking out [of the house] he had helped her in and had shut her door. . . .

And then his door, his door was open there, and I started around on the other side of the car to get in. Because since Steven was getting in on the passenger-side back seat, the only seat left for me was on the other side. So I went around on that side. And Scott must have had his door closed because I don't remember walking around it. But I opened the door, and the windows were open because the air conditioning wasn't working. . . .

Steven walked around the back of the car, and I was in the process of getting myself in . . . and by that time Steven must have been next to me, because he gave me a kind of boost up into the car. I had my car door open, because it's always so hot. . . .

Somewhere along the line, my mother said, "Who's got the keys?" Steven either was out of the car or got out and walked around the car to give the keys to Scott. So I was in the car at that point, and Scott was in the driver's seat, and my mother was in her side with her door shut and I'm sure she had her seat belt on because she always kept her seat belt on.

And so Steven then turns around to start back to the other side of the car to get in, and just as he turns he says, "Oh dear, I forgot . . . or, just a minute, I forgot . . ." something, "I'll have to run in the house and get it." And mother said, "Fine.". . .

I was reaching over to get my glass. I wanted to make sure it didn't spill, because my mother would have got upset if I had spilled my Coke all over the car seat. . . .

I think I must have been reaching for the glass, and just, just suddenly, it was like there was this big orange thing all around me, and holding me down, and my reaction was that I was being *electrocuted*, because in my mind the only thing I could think of was pictures on television where people can't move and they're all stiff . . . like when they're being electrocuted. And I called out, "I'm being electrocuted. Somebody please help me, I'm being electrocuted!"

And I felt myself being pushed, pushed down in this big orangey thing, kind of surrounding me . . . one moment it wasn't there and one moment it was there. I called out for somebody to help me, and nobody was doing anything. So I guess my self-preservation took over. . . .

I remember squinching my eyes open just a little bit, maybe this one, and out of the corner of my eye, and I can't say whether my door was there or whether there wasn't any door there, but all I remember seeing is my brother Scott's body lying on the ground, and I just knew instinctively that he was dead. . . .

But then in that same second I could see . . . creeping around the seat between where the seat would be and the frame . . . there were flames starting to come out. And I suddenly realized that the car was on fire and that I had, that I had, had to get out.

So I, I started to get out of the car, and I looked out and I couldn't see my hands, and I thought [they had] burned off. . . . I remember thinking, how am I going to roll on the ground if I don't have anything to catch myself with? . . . So I forced myself out of the car on, on the ground, and I started trying to remember all the things that you're taught when you're growing up about what you're supposed to do, and I . . . I remembered you were supposed to roll on the grass.

So I rolled myself onto my back, and then my shoulder was still really hot, and I didn't, didn't know what to do about it because I wasn't sure I had any hands. Or whether, if I touched it, it would make them burn or anything. But I managed to do it.

And I took my shirt, a little shirt that came up to my waist, a pullover, and I managed to pull my shirt up over myself, and, and to get it off of me. And then by that time I think I was yelling to somebody to come help me, help me.

And then about this time I saw Steven come out of the house and stop on the driveway, and he, he just looked, he was terrified, and it was almost like he was going to be mad at me. . . .

Steven just had a look of absolute horror on his face, as if the world had just blown up or something, I don't know, I don't know how to describe it. And I think I called for him to help me, and he turned around and he ran back into the house. . . .

> Carol Lynn Benson Kendall
> Police interview
> Burn and Trauma Center
> Massachusetts General Hospital
> July 25, 1985

A short, intense man with a fierce love for his profession, especially its adversarial aspects, attorney E. Richard Cirace had been on his own for less than two years when on July 24, 1985, he received a phone call from a mutual friend of his and Carol Lynn Benson Kendall's, asking him to go to her hospital room at the Burn and Trauma Center at Mass General. She was the survivor of a horrible tragedy, said the friend, and had been advised by a lawyer in Florida that she needed local counsel in her place of residence, Boston.

"Look, I've got a client who's already on the way in, but as soon as we're finished, I'll get right over and see her. Okay? Say an hour from now?"

"Fine," said the friend, "I'll tell Carol Lynn. She'll be very relieved."

Prior to establishing his own practice, Ric Cirace (pronounced *sir-ah-see*) had been in the law offices of John Albert Johnson. A Boston legal fixture for more than three decades, Johnson has a wide-ranging general practice. He is also a close personal and professional friend of criminal lawyer F. Lee Bailey. Johnson and Bailey have worked together on many cases, and a young Ric Cirace did legal legwork for them on the Patty Hearst case in the mid-1970s.

In his apprenticeship, Cirace had experienced a wide variety of legal work, criminal and civil, personal and procedural, but it

would be hard to imagine any law practice that could have prepared a single attorney fully for the range and complexity—in
human as well as legal terms—of what came to be called, simply,
the Benson case.

As he walked down the twelfth-floor corridor of the White Building, where the Burn and Trauma Center of Massachusetts General Hospital is located, Cirace passed two orderlies. One was
saying to the other, "Did you see the woman in 1219? She looks
like French toast." Room 1219 was where he was headed.

The woman propped up in bed had very little hair. What had
not been burned off was close-cropped and it stuck out from the
side of her skull like uneven stalks of blond wheat. Long black
patches of zinc ointment lined her right arm and shoulder and
contrasted sharply with the pinkness of nearby unburned skin
and the new grafts on her face. Incongruously, she smiled, though
it seemed a smile of embarrassment at having to receive a caller
in such a state.

For Carol Lynn Kendall, one look at the man she was to hire
as her attorney was enough to reassure her. "When Richard walked
into my hospital room—and I can still remember the suit and
even the shirt and tie he was wearing—I could sense his confidence. I felt immediately that here was a man I could trust completely." She would even say, "I don't think of Richard as my
attorney. I think of him as the man who takes care of me." Later,
that relationship would change.

Cirace's recollection, while not quite as precise, is equally vivid.
"I didn't know what to expect when I walked into that hospital
room, but one look at her told you something horrible had happened. She had hardly any hair, and her arm, which was outside
of the sheet, and her shoulder were covered with black ointment.
I remembered the orderly's description, and realized that as cruel
as it was, it was also rather accurate."

At Cirace's request, Mrs. Kendall began to tell him about herself and her family. She told him that both her father and her

mother's father had been in the tobacco business, first in Baltimore and then in Lancaster, Pennsylvania, and that both had done quite well. Her life story was one of considerable comfort, if not—as was then being claimed in the first full burst of media attention to the crime that had so mutilated her—immense wealth on the scale of a Rockefeller or a Kennedy.

She sketched the family history. Her father and mother had three children, herself and two boys. She was forty-one, her brother Steven had just turned thirty-four, and her youngest brother, Scott, was twenty-one.

She went on. Her father had died five years before, leaving a sizable estate. Her mother, Margaret Benson, had been living in Naples, Florida, since 1981, the year after Mr. Benson died. Scott had been living with her mother. Steven, who lived with his wife and three young children in nearby Fort Myers, was, according to Carol Lynn, the head of a number of small companies he had set up with his mother's money. As for herself, she was divorced and lived with her two teenage sons in Chestnut Hill, a suburb of Boston.

She told Cirace that on the morning of July 9, less than three weeks before, while she was visiting her mother in Florida, the whole family had climbed into their 1978 Chevy Suburban wagon to drive out and take a look at a lot on which Margaret Benson planned to build a huge new home. The wagon blew up, killing her mother, her brother Scott, and almost killing her. Steven Benson, the elder of her two brothers—the one who had arranged the trip and even the seating—had gone back into the house at the last moment for something he said he'd forgotten.

Cirace's meeting with Carol Lynn Benson Kendall took place on Wednesday, July 24, fifteen days after the tragedy. On Thursday, he canceled all his appointments, went back to the hospital, and had her tell him the story again. "I've learned the hard way that clients don't always tell you the truth, but by the end of the day I was convinced she was being totally honest. It was also clear to me that she was a tragic victim."

The next day, when two police officers were due to arrive from Florida, he had her tell him the story yet another time. "There were still no inconsistencies. It was a terrible story, and one of the most terrible parts of it was that the chief suspect was her brother Steven."

Cirace could see that Carol Lynn was having great difficulty dealing with the possibility that her brother had committed this monstrous crime. But there were two incidents that made the lawyer fear his new client might still be very much in danger.

Although two and a half weeks had passed since the bombing—weeks in which Carol Lynn remained in serious condition, first in the Naples Community Hospital and then in Mass General—except for one brief visit in the hospital in Boston, while on his way to the funeral, there had been no communication from her brother Steven. He and she were the sole survivors, but there had been no phone call, no card. Steven had, however, according to Carol Lynn, attempted to make contact of a sort, and not once but twice.

Within hours after the bombing, while lying in her hospital bed in Florida, she looked up and out the open door, and caught a glimpse of the nurses' station. There stood Steven.

"What was your reaction?" Cirace asked.

"Total fear. I thought he had come to kill me. But then he turned and disappeared without coming into my room."

The second incident happened only several days before the police arrived. A very upset Travis Kendall, at fifteen the younger of Carol Lynn's sons, called the hospital to report that he had just received a phone call from Uncle Steven—who wanted to know how packages were delivered to Carol Lynn's hospital room. On hearing this, Cirace immediately called both Mass General security and the bomb squad of the Boston Police Department.

The two Florida law-enforcement personnel—George Nowicki of the Bureau of Alcohol, Tobacco, and Firearms and Wayne Graham of the Collier County Sheriff's Office—arrived on Thursday, July 25, at the hospital to question Carol Lynn. After Cirace had established that his client was in no way, then or in the foreseeable future, a suspect in the case, he told the police he would advise her to cooperate fully.

After a long and emotionally draining day of interviews, the doctors insisted Carol Lynn be given a day of rest. On Sunday, after they finished questioning Carol Lynn, the two detectives took Cirace aside and told him there was something they thought he ought to know. "Ric," said Nowicki, "we've got people in Lancaster right now investigating the family, and they're turning up a lot of information. The majority of it has to do with Steven, things like the fact that Steven basically left Lancaster in disgrace because he had failed in so many different jobs and businesses. And it turns out that young Scott was not exactly a model youth, and not exactly unacquainted with drugs. But we are hearing things about Carol Lynn, too.

"One of them is rather important, and could have a bearing on the case, especially if the day should come that she has to get up on a witness stand to testify against her brother. Wayne and I agree you should be told what that is."

Cirace nodded for the special agent to continue.

"As you know, Carol Lynn always refers to Scott Benson as 'my brother.' 'My brother Scott this,' and 'my brother Scott that,' but apparently Scott Benson was not Carol Lynn's brother—Scott Benson was Carol Lynn's *son*.

"She got pregnant in her first year of college, had the baby, and her parents adopted him. If she persists in calling him her 'brother,' and if she ends up being a witness against Steven and gets up on the stand and calls Scott her brother, and the defense knows he was not, then it could destroy her credibility entirely."

The next day Cirace saw his client alone. "Carol Lynn, you know I appreciate all that you've been through, and you know I would never cause you any additional pain or distress unless it were absolutely unavoidable and I had an excellent reason. I'm afraid I have to ask you a very hard question: was Scott Benson your son?"

Her eyes widened. She was momentarily stunned. It was the first time she had ever been asked that question. In a small voice, Carol Lynn Benson Kendall answered, "Yes."

Forty-four days after the explosion—on the morning of Thursday, August 22, 1985—three men set out in an unmarked car belonging to the Collier County Sheriff's Office. They were George Nowicki; Wayne Graham; and Graham's boss on the Benson case, Lieutenant Harold Young.

At the office of attorney Barry Hillmeyer, they arrested Steven Wayne Benson for the first-degree murder of Margaret Benson and Scott Benson, and the attempted murder of Carol Lynn Benson Kendall.

After the police had processed Benson's arrest at the Lee County Jail, they put him in the back of their car and began the half-hour trip back to Naples. A few miles outside of Fort Myers, Steven Benson fell asleep.

BLOOD
RELATIONS

One

The Clan

The Patriarch

In the beginning there was Harry Hitchcock. Born in Baltimore at the close of the nineteenth century, Harry Hitchcock grew to become a wealthy man in the tobacco business, the father of two daughters, and a born-again Christian long before anyone heard of that term. But all of Harry Hitchcock's pride of accomplishment, and what was left of his dreams, were shattered on the morning his daughter Margaret and his great-grandson Scott Benson were murdered.

"What do I have now?" the highly successful eighty-eight-year-old retired tobacco executive asked in a 1986 interview. "Years ago, I gave my money away to my children in the expectation that it would make their lives easier, so that they could enjoy it while they were still young. Yet this is what happened. Every night I go to bed praying that I will wake up in the morning and find that it was just a very bad dream, a nightmare."

The heroes of Horatio Alger offer pale comparison to the real-life story of Harry Hitchcock and his father; for that, one must turn to Dickens. Walter Hitchcock was a skilled carpenter and cabinetmaker until the age of twenty-five, when he went blind. Harry was two at the time. Blessed with a good singing voice, a fierce urge for survival, and a wife who could play the piano, Hitchcock *père* went into vaudeville as "Professor Walter T. Hitchcock, Baltimore's Blind Singer."

He took his act—and any others he thought could bring in money—to vaudeville, minstrel, and carnival tent shows. One, two, and three things led to another, and Walter Hitchcock found himself with a theatrical booking agency among his many ventures, few of which were profitable. One of the acts he booked was little Harry Hitchcock, who sang and danced. "I was a male Shirley Temple," Hitchcock says, "before anyone had ever heard of her. I used to sing songs with titles like, 'I Want to Be a Soldier'—I didn't want to, but I sang it anyway. One night my father got sick and I had to fill in for him. That night I sang, 'Smarty, Smarty, Thought You Had a Party.' "

Harry Hitchcock's father had scores of irons in the show-business fire, from slide shows to a short-lived *female* minstrel show, but the living he made was still marginal. Harry remembers eating "fried bread—slices of stale bread dipped under the spigot and then fried."

Later, with the help of an uncle—"The only one in the family who had any money," recalls Harry Hitchcock—Walter bought an Edison motion picture machine and got an early start in the movie business. Baltimore didn't even have theaters at the time. Walter took his shows to halls, or to big rooms at places like St. Mary's Industrial School, where one of the young delinquents was George Herman (later known as "Babe") Ruth. Harry Hitchcock says, "He was an 'inmate' there because he was too young to go to jail." Not only was Harry part of all these endeavors, he was also the one who led his father from place to place—"That was 'way before they had guide dogs," he explains.

When Harry Hitchcock was twelve years old, his mother died, and he quit school to take her place in his father's office, thus ending his formal education in the sixth grade. At sixteen, he went to work for the Baltimore Bargain House, a mail-order catalog business, where he began as a clerk and ended as a bookkeeper. By that point the First World War had begun, and although he was of prime fighting age, his new job as the assistant paymaster for the contractor that was building Camp Meade, Maryland carried with it a deferment from active duty.

After the war ended, Hitchcock was once again counting and disbursing other people's money, as opposed to making his own. Still several years away from the tobacco business in which he was to make his mark and his fortune, he worked in the accounting office of the Bethlehem Steel Corporation at its Sparrows Point plant on the Chesapeake Bay outside of Baltimore, a job he left in 1919.

Harry Hitchcock was married that same year, to Charlotte Brown, a second-generation Irish girl who was also from Baltimore. Three years later, their daughter Margaret was born in that city, but then it was more than a decade before the birth of their second child, Janet Lee. The difference in their ages was to affect the girls' relationship in curious ways, just as Margaret's decision to adopt Scott, many years later, was to change forever her relations with her own children, Carol Lynn and Steven.

In 1921, the ambitious young man who became the much-loved patriarch of the Benson family, switched jobs again. He had entered the tobacco business, but he had not yet found his proper niche within it. He went to work for the W. H. Winstead Company, a Baltimore division of the huge Universal Leaf Tobacco Company of Richmond, Virginia. He began as an assistant bookkeeper and eventually became head bookkeeper.

After about five years in that position, Hitchcock made what today is called a "career move," giving up the safe, if limited, pay scale of a bookkeeper for the potentially more lucrative but uncertain field of sales. It was, he says, "the best decision I ever made, from a financial standpoint, but it was one that would take a great toll on my family."

Hitchcock's new job also involved buying tobacco. Universal

Leaf had long coveted the lush southeastern Pennsylvania farm-
ing country populated by Mennonite and Amish families, and it
sent Harry to the Lancaster area to open up that territory for
W. H. Winstead. He continued to live in Baltimore and work out
of Winstead's offices downtown on East Redwood Street, but with
increasing frequency he was on the road.

He taught himself to be an excellent salesman and eventually
learned enough about tobacco to be a skilled buyer as well. But
in the beginning, he had to do a bit of faking, something he'd
picked up while hawking for his father. "It was a quirk of fate
that I got into the tobacco business because I never used it and I
wasn't a salesman. I was driven not by the lust for money or the
power that money can bring, but solely by a fear of failure. I
would make it clear to customers that the little I knew about
tobacco did not extend beyond what was on the tags, and my
naïveté convinced customers that I was genuine. I sold myself
rather than the tobacco."

Early on, Hitchcock decided that his fortune did not lie in the
more expensive tobaccos and the cigars made from them. "I tar-
geted my selling to makers of lower-priced cigars—because I recognized that there were more Chevies than Cadillacs—and my
buying to the kind of tobacco they used. The company grew during the Depression when lack of money forced cigar makers to
produce lower-priced cigars."

Eventually the people in the home office of Universal Leaf
decided that Hitchcock must have concealed a wide knowledge
of tobacco, because he was doing so well. "They said," he recalls
half a century later, " 'You know a lot more than you let on,' but
the truth is, I didn't."

In 1940, Universal Leaf formally recognized Harry Hitchcock's
value by asking him to head a brand new subsidiary, Lancaster
Leaf. If the move was a gamble, it was an inspired one.

"Universal Leaf had had an earlier and unprofitable experience
with cigar leaf tobacco, and they were reluctant to get back into
that aspect of the tobacco business. But they did allow me to

restart a tobacco leaf department, and, starting from scratch without any cigar leaf business, I, along with the help of many others, developed what became the largest cigar leaf tobacco company worldwide. That was Lancaster Leaf."

Throughout the thirties, Hitchcock had continued his peripatetic ways, traveling from Baltimore to Lancaster and points north, south, and west in search of the best buys in leaf tobacco. He logged, he estimates, "an average of fifty thousand miles a year, calling on cigar manufacturers across the country. And this was all done by car or train, because I never liked to fly."

He covered the East Coast from Connecticut to Key West, Florida and journeyed even as far west as Texas. "I called on one man in Tampa for twenty years before he finally gave me an order. He had his desk in the back of the room, and he'd see me come in and he'd wave his hand and yell, 'Hitchcock, I don't need any tobacco!' But eventually he gave in."

By his own admission, he was gone from home far too much in the days he built his company and his fortune. "I neglected my family. My job became not only the most important thing in my life, but my whole life. The only vacations I ever took were short ones, and if I was home I was always on the telephone, talking business."

It wasn't as if Hitchcock had not been warned about the price he was paying in human terms because of his obsession with work and the company. "My wife used to say that we were happier when I was making twenty-five dollars a week."

Hitchcock's growing wealth was hidden from public view. He likes to brag that he never made more than fifteen thousand dollars a year in salary from Lancaster Leaf. But that fails to take into account the stock he was piling up year after year, as part owner of the company.

Not only did he not flaunt his wealth, but he lived as if he did not have it. "I was never really conscious of being wealthy. My wife insisted on doing her own housework and the only car I had was a company car. People in Lancaster were surprised when the newspaper disclosed that Lancaster Tobacco Company was such a prosperous company and that I owned part of it. I didn't live rich."

Harry Hitchcock did a most unusual thing at the time that Lancaster Leaf was formed. He gave away a significant part of his potential fortune to his two children. "I don't want to get into dollar amounts, but when the company was set up I let my daughters have some of the stock. At the time I gave it to them [1940] it had relatively little value. The value of it developed later."

Why did he make this gesture, one that is hardly common in American business—or American families? "I didn't want them to have to wait until I died to enjoy whatever benefits came from my activities." And it was this decision, clearly one based on good intentions, that made Janet Lee Hitchcock Murphy and Margaret Hitchcock Benson rich women. For better and for worse.

Although Hitchcock will not reveal the percentage of ownership he had in Lancaster Leaf, and therefore the amount of stock he had to divvy up among his family, he admits that he split it three ways. In addition to giving one-third to each of his daughters, he gave the same portion to his wife, in the belief that she would outlive him. As it happened, she did not, dying in 1980. Her money was the principal source of the trust funds for the five grandchildren: Carol Lynn, Steven, and Scott Benson, and Janet Lee Murphy's two daughters, Sheryl and Brenda.

Not long after Harry Hitchcock had reached fifty, something happened to change his life. "I was born again in Jesus Christ. It happened at the Belvedere Hotel in Baltimore. I was what the Protestant Christians call 'born again.' It changed my whole outlook on life—my whole perspective, my whole sense of values. I was invited to attend a prayer breakfast at the Belvedere Hotel, and that's where it happened. You'd have to experience it yourself to understand it. I had climbed the ladder of what people called success, but I had lost contact with the Lord until 1950, when I returned."

By this point, Margaret had married Edward Benson, also of

Baltimore, and the son-in-law had been brought into Lancaster Leaf as soon as he was discharged from the Air Force. In 1950, it was already clear that he was a fine addition to the company, and Harry Hitchcock began to relax his own work schedule and channel more of his efforts and energy into religious activities, particularly prayer breakfasts. He has attended the Presidential Prayer Breakfast in Washington, D.C., for thirty-five of its thirty-six years, missing only the first one.

In 1959, after six decades as a Baltimore resident, Hitchcock finally moved to Lancaster (where both of his daughters and their husbands were already living). Although he had never been one to make a public display of his wealth—indeed, one much younger Lancaster businessman said, "Harry Hitchcock never realized what money was"—when he got to Lancaster he bought a large stone residence on Center Road in the tony School Lane Hills area. But the address was unimportant to Hitchcock; what mattered was the fact that his backyard abutted that of his daughter Margaret and Edward Benson, on Ridge Road, and was around the corner from where Janet Lee and her family then lived.

Increasingly, Harry Hitchcock let Edward Benson run Lancaster Leaf while he tended, literally, to his flowers and became more and more involved in religious philanthropy. His home is situated on its two-acre lot in a way that allows ample room in both the front and rear yards for his thousands of tulips, azaleas, and flowering bushes. Each spring, Hitchcock, who is by all accounts a civic and charitable institution in Lancaster, opens the grounds of his home to visitors so that they can admire the flowers and trees at close range. "In 1986," he boasts, "six thousand people signed the guest book. And, remember, many of those are couples and only one person signs."

In the thirties and forties, when he "invaded" Lancaster as a fledgling tobacco man from Baltimore, Harry Hitchcock was the quintessential outsider. Today, by dint of character, extreme hard work, and the application of innate business skills that he honed to perfection, Harry Hitchcock is a pillar of the community, and it would be difficult if not impossible to find a knowledgeable professional or businessman in Lancaster who would say anything negative about him.

Yet he remains in certain essential ways an outsider still. He does not belong to the Lancaster Country Club, *the* country club, though he can go there at virtually any time he wants as a guest. He has never joined the Hamilton Club, the most influential downtown professional and businessman's club. His church is not the ne plus ultra St. James Episcopal, but the far less socially prominent First United Methodist. It is to his church, to the Lancaster Bible College, and to the Messiah Bible College that he has given very substantial sums. To the former, he gave a classroom building, Hitchcock Hall, and to the latter, he gave a major portion of their athletic complex.

What it is essential to understand about Harry Hitchcock is that he does not care about his position in Lancaster society, or that his church is not the one truly acceptable church, socially speaking. And he has been just as oblivious to the actual amount of money he had piled up over the years.

In many ways, his attitudes toward Lancaster society and its marks of social and financial acceptability were at variance with those of his daughters—or at least his daughter Margaret—and their families. And in the case of Margaret Hitchcock Benson and her husband and their children, that may have been what has made the tragic difference.

In Harry Hitchcock's own mind, there is another possible reason for the tragedy that engulfed his family. It is a sin that he himself committed, a sin most unchristian and uncharitable. In 1985, Hitchcock's church named a new minister, a black man, who happened to have a white wife. This mixed marriage so upset Hitchcock that he, along with others, resigned from the church. Just two days later, his daughter and his great-grandson were blown to death in Naples, Florida, by his grandson Steven.

Some parishioners have never returned. Today, Harry Hitchcock is back in the fold, an obedient servant of the Word as preached by the black minister. He has sought forgiveness for his sin and made his peace. But he cannot shake the feeling that it was that sin, at least in part, which doomed his family.

Margaret and Benny

She was always, right up to the end, bright, quick, attractive, and a little nervous. As a child, Margaret Hitchcock was a proper and a studious girl, anything but assertive. She would have to *learn* to be assertive, and that would take years. Even then, she only managed it within her immediate family.

For more than a quarter-century, Margaret had the undivided attention of her husband, Edward Benson. In fact, so undivided was his attention, and so great her appreciation of it, that friends say they never heard the couple argue. One friend mentioned that when they were in a room together, "There was an innate sense of being comfortable with one another." Clearly, Margaret reveled in this new experience. When Edward Benson died, in 1980, the center fell out of Margaret's life. Five years later, by which time she was finally beginning to gain control over her own life and enjoy her newly discovered independence, she was murdered in circumstances so bizarre as to strain credibility.

During Margaret's formative years the family lived in a substantial stone house on Hillen Road in Baltimore's Lake Montebello area. Although her father was away a great deal, his growing success as a buyer and seller of tobacco meant that life back at home in Baltimore was increasingly comfortable. Neither of the Hitchcock girls grew up worrying about money.

Margaret did well in school, first at Eastern High School and then at Baltimore's Goucher College, a school with a solid academic reputation, then and now, but also a school whose students liked to have a good time, and some girls didn't mind if people knew it. (Young men in Baltimore still use an old saw to compare the school with Notre Dame, a local Roman Catholic girls' college: "Dame to wed, Goucher to bed." But, clearly, Miss Margaret Hitchcock was not one of *those* Goucher girls.)

Located in the western suburb of Towson (and coed since 1986), Goucher had been in downtown Baltimore from 1885 to 1952. Sara Haardt, the young woman who was to become the wife of H. L. Mencken, one of Baltimore's most famous sons, was an instructor in English at Goucher when she met the great man in 1923. As fate would have it, he was delivering his annual lecture to Goucher girls on what he felt should be their favorite topic, "How to Catch a Husband."

In Margaret Benson's day, twenty years later, there was, however, a distinct difference. The Second World War, both impending and then actual, sharply reduced the number of available young men. What's more, Margaret, while she loved to have a good time (and especially to dance), also had a serious side.

Her major was the difficult field of biology. On the way to her B.A. she took such courses as embryology, two semesters of genetics, and physiological histology. When the school bought the property on which it now stands, Margaret Benson, at the request of her botany professor, went out to the new campus area and cataloged all the trees.

In the summer of 1942, she was accepted for study at the Marine Biological Laboratory of the prestigious Woods Hole Oceanographic Institute in Falmouth, Massachusetts. There, according to her daughter, she left her mark in the way of specimen contributions to the institute's famous algae collection. Carol Lynn recalls her mother's account—Margaret was apparently an excellent storyteller—of herself and some other Woods Hole students getting stranded on Cape Cod after dark. It being the summer of 1942, they were checked out by the Coast Guard to make sure they hadn't just come from a German U-boat.

In her last year at Goucher, the Biology Department recommended her for special honors. Her father says she was "inches away from making Phi Beta Kappa." Somehow, in addition to her academic work, Margaret Benson found time to study piano at the nearby Peabody Institute, to belong to the Ramsay Street Players, and to study dance at the Carol Lynn Fetzer Dance School, which so impressed her that she named her daughter after its founder.

In her third year of college, Margaret Hitchcock met a young man to whom she was instantly attracted. Tall, with arresting dark eyes and a sense of presence unusual in one so young, his name was Edward Hughlett Benson. He was two years older than Margaret and worked as a clerk in the menswear section of Hutzler's Department Store in downtown Baltimore. His quiet demeanor was in direct contrast to her vivacity.

There were other differences too. Although he was not from a poor family, Edward Benson's background was clearly different from that of Margaret Hitchcock. An only child, he lived with his parents in what his daughter Carol Lynn describes as "a houseful of women. I'm not sure exactly how they were all related, and to whom, but there were about five women in the house while he was growing up."

In his youth, Edward Benson had spent months in bed, recovering from polio, and as a result was not a particularly athletic young man. Years later he told friends that he owed his recovery to his Aunt Pauline, who spent hours massaging his legs. By all accounts he was a serious young man, which may simply have been his personality, but might also have been the result of his childhood illness and his family circumstances. According to the family, he was mature and responsible far beyond his years.

As his daughter tells it, he had wanted to be a doctor, and after graduating from Baltimore's highly regarded City College High School he had started college with that goal in mind. But he had to drop out of school almost immediately and go to work because his father, a railroad employee, had been injured on the job and could no longer support his family. Apparently, Grandfather Benson was an alcoholic. Carol Lynn remembers her mother saying that when she and Edward Benson were dating, he would regularly call home to see if he were needed to pick his father up someplace. This problem drinking, it was felt, hastened the death of Edward's mother. "As I understand it, my father was always a grown-up," she says.

A mutual friend introduced Edward to Margaret Hitchcock in 1941. On their first date he told her he intended to marry her. That same type of single-minded pursuit also marked his business career, according to several people who worked with him and knew him over a period of years. "Benny was an incredible worker," said one business friend.

By 1942, the United States was at war, and Edward Benson was in the Air Force, eventually earning a commission and an assignment training pilots. He asked Margaret to marry him, and in early December 1942—a year and a few days after the Japanese attack on Pearl Harbor—she flew to Lackland Air Force Base in San Antonio, Texas and they were married. After a brief honeymoon, she returned to Baltimore to finish her senior year at Goucher.

That spring she learned that she had won a scholarship to Wellesley to pursue a master's degree in botany. She turned it down. At least that was the story she told her daughter. (While Carol Lynn recalls hearing the story several times, Wellesley College, which did have a graduate program in biology at the time, does not keep the names of people who turned down scholarship offers.)

For the next three years, the newly married Bensons lived a typical—for World War II—stateside military life on a succession of Air Force bases across the country. From San Antonio to Kansas, with stops in between, Benson taught more able-bodied men to fly off to war overseas. Carol Lynn was born in Enid, Oklahoma (site of the Vance Air Force base) on July 8, 1944.

The young couple's military travels became family legend. "I particularly remember," says Carol Lynn, "my mother telling us about Mrs. Britten's rooming house in Liberal, Kansas. The woman had a genius for making things last. Each week every boarder got one towel, which had to last you the week. Mrs. Britten, who would make one ham or one roast stretch the full week, said she had one dress and couldn't understand why any woman thought she needed more than one."

On the day before Edward Benson was to be shipped overseas, the war ended. He was discharged a captain, and he and Margaret returned to Baltimore where he went to work for his father-in-law, Harry Hitchcock, who was by then the president of Lancaster Leaf Tobacco.

Hitchcock had no qualms about hiring "family." In later years he was to hire Martin Murphy, then Janet Lee's husband, plus several of Carol Lynn's boyfriends. None had the success of Edward Benson. Harry says one of the home office executives used to kid him by asking, "Whenever one of the girls gets a new boyfriend, do you check him out to see if he'll make a good tobacco man?"

Harry Hitchcock remembers his initial impression of young Edward Benson. "He didn't know anything about the tobacco business, but that didn't concern me because I hadn't known anything about it either when I began. I knew his background, and I knew he was smart. I figured he would work hard, and I was right. It didn't bother me to hire my own daughter's husband. If I could give him a good chance, why not? It was up to him whether he made it or not."

Within a few years it was obvious that Hitchcock's trust was not misplaced. He made Edward Benson a vice-president of Lancaster Leaf, and later its president. About 1947, the Bensons moved to Lancaster from Baltimore. Steven was not yet born, and Carol Lynn, then three, was in Miss Downey's all-day kindergarten. They bought their first house in Lancaster and prepared to blend into the social fabric of their new home town.

As things turned out, however, they were not exactly welcomed with open arms. There were several reasons. First, like so many other American towns with a long, proud history, Lancaster had its leading families and its social pecking order. While newcomers were, from time to time, invited into the inner circle, it was not common practice to do so, unless their genealogy was locally acceptable—although working for Armstrong Cork was sometimes deemed sufficient qualification. And second, the Bensons were in the tobacco business, which meant they were in competition with some of these same families.

Norman Rockwell would have been a little nervous in Lancaster. While the area is undeniably "American" and wedded to the old virtues, it is hardly typical of the kinds of communities that the beloved artist liked to memorialize. For one thing, it is much richer, beginning with the land. Justifiably called "America's Garden Spot," Lancaster County, which covers 952 square miles in a triangular portion of the southeast corner of the state, was originally settled by farmers, in particular the so-called "plain people"—the Amish and the Mennonites. Their considerable efforts have brought forth a rich abundance of crops and great personal wealth.

While the Amish remain on their farms and within their own enclosed social orders, the Mennonites are more adaptable and blend into the business, professional, and even social lives of their surrounding communities, of which the city of Lancaster was and is the largest. Today, much of old Lancaster has Mennonite roots.

In the mid-fifties, Richard Gehman, a popular writer who lived in the Lancaster area but normally worked in and wrote about happenings in New York City, turned his attention to his own neighborhood. In his book, *Murder in Paradise,* about the trial and conviction of a young World War II veteran from the area who murdered a pretty cashier at Franklin and Marshall College, he gives this description of Lancaster:

Not all of the wealth comes from the soil; in the County seat, the city of Lancaster, there are large manufacturing plants— Armstrong Cork and Hamilton Watch have their headquarters there, and there are branches of Radio Corporation of America and Aluminum Corporation of America. Despite these relatively new industrial developments, the County has remained primarily agricultural in character. For years it was known as the second richest farm section in the United States, and it always led all other counties in the nation in production of tobacco. . . . The County is as beautiful as it is rich. Its fertile soil is distributed over gently sloping hills, crossed by swift, clear little brooks and leisurely creeks. . . . The majority of the gray stone and white frame farmhouses are very old, and so are their attendant barns, silos and outbuildings. Many of these rural estates have been in the same families for generations, and aspiring farmers from the city have always had a difficult time prying land from the natives. There is a wonderfully serene quality about this countryside, and a picture shot at random almost anywhere could stand as an idealized, stylized representation of agrarian scenery. Appropriately enough, some early landowners named one Lancaster County hamlet "Paradise."

That was the lay of the land, literally and figuratively, when Edward Benson moved his family from Baltimore to Lancaster to work for Lancaster Leaf Tobacco Company. It was bad enough for a businessman to be employed by a company other than Armstrong Cork or Hamilton Watch or RCA, three companies whose executives were apt to find instant acceptability in Lancaster society. But to have the bad taste to be employed by an upstart, outsider *tobacco* company like Lancaster Leaf was simply asking to be excluded. Also, it probably did not help the Bensons that Harry Hitchcock showed so little interest in the approval of Lancaster society.

To the credit of Edward and Margaret, they hardly seemed bothered when they weren't courted by old Lancaster. They both shrugged it off and went about their own business. He was far too preoccupied with the buying and selling of tobacco to be much concerned with social acceptance, and Margaret was a pragmatist. Instead of joining *the* dance club, the Bensons and a group of other young people their age went out and started their own— the Quadrille Dance Club. Its seasonal dances were quite popular formal affairs, with the women in ball gowns and the men in tuxedos. Their friends were others like themselves, relatively young couples who were trying to manage careers and raise families now that the uncertainties of the war years were a thing of the past.

Mary Miller Glose, RN, was a member of the Quadrille and remained a good friend of Margaret and Edward Benson until both of them died. Her memories of the Bensons stretch back over thirty years. Most vivid is her recollection of the fun they all had. "Margaret loved to have a good time and she loved to dance. She especially loved to dance. While Benny"—the name used by all who knew him socially or in business—"was not *that* outgoing, he loved to see Margaret have a good time. He wasn't without a sense of humor of his own, but he was essentially a quiet, and a rather formal, man. But he loved to see Margaret have a good time, and he loved to be able to provide for her."

Mary Miller Glose also recalls that in the early 1960s Edward Benson, by then the president of Lancaster Leaf, hired a young Dutchman by the name of Willem van Huystee, and soon the Bensons and the younger van Huystees became friends.

"I didn't warm to Edward Benson right away," said Willem

van Huystee in 1986. "He was a rather formal, even stiff, man until you got to know him or he decided he liked you. I was hired on August 1, 1963, and sent immediately to the Philippines. I was given three months' time in which to make money, to show a profit. This was right after the original U.S. Surgeon General's Report on smoking and health and everyone in the industry was petrified. At the time in the Philippines we were exporting about twelve thousand to fifteen thousand bales a year, and by the end of twelve months, I had that up to eighty thousand bales.

"As a result, I became Edward Benson's boy. We founded Philippine Lancaster, Inc., which worked out well for all of us."

It was during this period that Lancaster Leaf was capping its most ambitious international growth, an accomplishment for which Harry Hitchcock gives Edward Benson full credit. Van Huystee was a part of that growth. In 1966 he was sent to Europe, with a base in Antwerp, Belgium, and did so well there—helping to found Lancotab, N.A., a tobacco exporting company that, like the one in the Philippines, still exists today—that in March 1968 he was returned to Lancaster to be, as he put it, "Edward Benson's main aide." Benson made sure that van Huystee got a small financial interest in the company.

"From that point on," says van Huystee, "my wife and I became quite good friends with the Bensons. We even went on vacations together. I believe we were the ones who interested them in skiing, and I know we were responsible for their interest in quality foreign automobiles. Until I came with the company, Benny always drove the biggest Fleetwood Cadillac you could get, just like Harry Hitchcock's."

Once he'd seen the top of the automotive mountain, Edward Benson's taste in cars was never the same. Before long he had two Mercedes—a 250 sedan for Margaret to drive and a 230 SL sports model for himself—and in the late 1970s there was a Jaguar XJS and even a Citroën SM, an intriguing combination of a French body and a Maserati engine that gained some devotees in the United States at the time. He began to collect classic cars—

at one point he owned a Stutz roadster—and at the time of his death there was a small collection of interesting marques and models in the family warehouse in Lancaster.

Van Huystee points out that much of this increasingly conspicuous consumption came about only after 1967, when the Benson family fortunes had improved dramatically. Until then, no one would have called Edward Benson underpaid—by the midsixties, his salary reportedly ranged from eighty thousand to one-hundred-twenty thousand dollars per year—but after that point there was a noticeable upgrading of the family's already comfortable standard of living.

The event that transformed the Bensons from well off to wealthy involved the Lancaster Leaf stock that Harry Hitchcock had divided into thirds in 1940. More than a quarter-century later, Universal Leaf, the parent company, replaced Lancaster Leaf stock with its own on a one-to-one basis.

Suddenly, what had been stock in a privately held company, was now of the blue-ribbon variety. That meant the stock was as good as cash, for it could be sold or traded or borrowed on or used as collateral for a major purchase. Unlike the smaller company's stock, that of Universal Leaf was publicly held and listed on one of the big boards, the New York Stock Exchange. Aside from the small inconvenience of the time it would take to convert it, the stock was as real as money can get. And it did not take the Benson family long to demonstrate their appreciation of that reality.

Soon there was a ski lodge in Sainte Adèle, in Quebec, Canada, along with a large house on the Atlantic Ocean in Ventnor, New Jersey, in addition to the main family home at 1515 Ridge Road in Lancaster. In later years, while Edward Benson was still alive, they owned a moderate-sized house near the Franklin and Marshall campus (when Steven was first married and a student there), a house around the corner from Ridge Road, where Carol Lynn and her boys lived most of their time in Lancaster, and, later, two houses directly across the street from them on Ridge Road, one for Carol Lynn and her children, and one for Steven and his wife (homes the children once traded). Just before his death, in 1980, Edward Benson and Margaret bought their first home in Naples, Florida, a magnificent canalside property in Port Royal, Naples's most exclusive area.

The senior Bensons were never strangers to indulgent spending, especially where their children were concerned. One of Carol Lynn's first boyfriends, who came to know the family well, when asked if the Bensons overindulged their children said, "If you call giving a kid an eighteen-foot inboard motor boat for his tenth birthday an indulgence, then I guess you'd have to say they did." Carol Lynn takes issue, and points out, "You have to understand how unusual that ten-year-old kid [Steven] was. He knew enough to pass the Coast Guard safe-boating course, having read and memorized all their manuals. It *wasn't* that indulgent a gift."

Carol Lynn received her fair share of gifts. When she turned sixteen, a brand new, bright red Ford Sunliner convertible showed up in the driveway. But that kind of gift was, as she once put it, "when you consider the circumstances in which I grew up, a 'given.' "

Harry Hitchcock now says that he was concerned about the way his daughter Margaret and her husband spent money on their children. "But when I would mention it to Margaret, she would look at me and say, 'But what am I going to do? They're my *children*.' " And sister Janet Lee adds that their mother used to say, " 'Janet Lee, you'll go out and buy a can of beans, but Margaret will buy a whole *case*.' "

"This was not extravagance," points out Carol Lynn. "My parents both understood the economy of buying by volume."

Margaret Benson was always interested in possessions, especially furniture, and Edward was increasingly proud of his ability to give her the wherewithal to buy those things. He was, as all of their friends attest, devoted to Margaret, and if acquiring things made her happy, then it made him happy to enable her to do so. One friend recalled a particularly electric auction in Lancaster: "The auctioneer was my friend, and when I arrived he had just stopped for a break. 'What's going on?' I asked, and he told me, 'Carolyn Steinman [daughter of the man who founded the department store and one of the newspapers, and indisputably one of the richest women in Lancaster] is buying everything in sight. I can run her up on anything. Just watch.' And he did. He'd offer an item—an antique lamp or a Persian rug—and she'd bid it out of sight. No one else had a chance.

"Just then Margaret and Benny came in, and Margaret asked what was going on. I told her that Carolyn Steinman was buying everything in sight and that nobody could keep up with her. 'Oh?' said Margaret.

"And with that she started to bid against Carolyn, and they just went at it, head to head, the rest of the night. The people had never seen anything like it. *I'd* never seen anything like it, before or since!"

As the years passed and the children grew older, there were other large purchases (boats, for example) and large outlays to help the children—a year of law school plus apartment rent for Carol Lynn, and various business opportunities for Steven—but the pattern of spending remained the same. If it would make Margaret happy, or if it would help the children, then it was done.

Willem van Huystee, looking back, says, "Benny had earned all the money, certainly, nobody gave him anything for nothing, and clearly he wanted to be happy; but it was as if he just couldn't relax. He just couldn't *enjoy* the money.

"He had an excellent reputation in the tobacco business, and he should have been able to relax, but in the last few years of his life he seemed to grow increasingly unhappy. My office was the first one you passed to get to his or Harry Hitchcock's, and I recall that when Harry would go past in the morning it was like a ray of sunshine. Then Benny would go by and it was instant gloom, like a big rain cloud."

Several people who knew Edward Benson well feel that one of

the reasons he was unhappy in the last few years of his life was that he was bitterly disappointed at having to face the inescapable conclusion that his son Steven was not going to carry on the Hitchcock-Benson tradition within Lancaster Leaf. Insiders also suggest that in his last years Edward Benson was increasingly somber because he could see the legacy of his and his father-in-law's years of effort being assaulted by the "outsiders" at Universal. Although some suggest that for all the opportunities Benny gave his son he could have given him more direction and some real authority, no one suggests that he did not give Steven almost every chance a father could give a son.

Carol Lynn adds, "My mother used to beg my father to give Steven a specific title and some business guidance, but his involvement with fighting the Universal faction was so total that he ignored her."

Steven himself, she says, came to his father and asked him to give him a specific job to do, some form of *training*. She says Steven wanted some tutelage, like that his father had received from Harry Hitchcock. But his plea was unsuccessful. "In effect," she says, "he wasn't there for Steven."

There was another problem: from the time Steven was fourteen, there had been another "son." In 1966, Edward and Margaret Benson, then forty-six and forty-four years old, respectively, adopted Scott Benson, the illegitimate son born to their own daughter, Carol Lynn, when she was nineteen years old. Although a number of close friends suspected that the baby was Carol Lynn's, the Bensons told no one—not even Janet Lee Murphy, Margaret's sister. And they proceeded to raise Scott as their own adopted child.

Carol Lynn says, "From the very beginning, my mother was obsessed with Scott to the point of irrationality." In a moment of reflection, Harry Hitchcock says that while Scott was always an affectionate child, Steven was not. "That was just his disposition. It didn't mean he loved us any less." Carol Lynn shakes her head:

"Steven was affectionate with me, my mother told me, and extremely affectionate with her—until she and my father adopted Scott."

"It was a most unusual family," says Willem van Huystee. "My wife used to say, 'Nothing normal ever happens in that family,' and she was right. Almost every day at the office there would be a phone call for Benny, and he'd say, 'Margaret is choking,' or 'Carol Lynn is bleeding.' There was always a crisis.

"I think that family was calling out, screaming out, for attention from each other, but they didn't know how to give it. They could only explain their feelings in dollars and cents."

Van Huystee feels Edward Benson was the main figure in the family drama: "Margaret never got a chance to blossom under Benny. He was strong, outspoken, the God-Father, but he had a wall around him, as if he were saying, 'Don't step in.' Control is a good word to hang on Benny. One thing is certain: the influence of Benny on the children is the source for what happened to the family."

Janet Lee Murphy, Edward Benson's sister-in-law for almost forty years, says of him, "He was an enigma. He was a good person, but came across as being aloof. He absolutely adored Margaret, and he took care of every problem, emotional and physical, that anyone had, especially Carol Lynn. She just looked up at him like he was a little god. He was the leader of the clan. And then he died, and things kind of fell apart after that."

Carol Lynn

" 'Whenever I tried to find you, you were always on somebody else's blanket.' " According to Carol Lynn Benson Kendall, that's how her mother described her as a young child, always exploring, independent. The immediate reference was to summers in Ocean City, Maryland, with the Benson family blanket spread out on the wide beach; but the idea seems to fit a larger frame of reference as well. Perhaps it was this adventurous spirit, among other things, that prepared Carol Lynn for her role as a survivor.

Today, Carol Lynn Benson Kendall may be forty-two years old, but it remains obvious that she was once a beauty-contest winner. Especially if you look at her from the left side. A friend of hers said recently, "If you sit on Carol Lynn's left, and look at her, she is still a beautiful woman. The skin on her hand is so lovely, almost translucent, that she could pose for Ponds commercials. But then she turns her head, and you want to cry."

A three-inch strip of angry-looking red skin hangs, wattlelike, from her jawline, and several large, red subdermal slashes streak her face. Her right ear, which is almost always totally covered by her hair, is brand new, having been rebuilt entirely. Since the explosions on July 9, 1985, that killed her mother and her son Scott, Carol Lynn has undergone five operations, two of which lasted two to three hours, and the others three to five hours each.

Says her chief surgeon, Dr. John Francis Burke, head of the Burn and Trauma Center of the Massachusetts General Hospital (and generally considered to be one of the top "burn men" not just nationally but in the world), "Mrs. Kendall came to us after being in the hospital in Florida for several days, but it was three weeks before her life was no longer in danger." Asked to describe, for a layman, the seriousness of Carol Lynn's injuries, Dr. Burke shakes his head. "No one who didn't undergo the same thing can really understand the severity." According to Dr. Burke, no household accident, no matter how terrible, can produce burns and injuries like hers.

How far has Carol Lynn Benson Kendall come since the explosion and her hospitalization? "I was determined," she says, "not to let this thing change my life." Today, while she awaits the last of her surgery—and the settlement of her mother's extremely complicated estate—she has been unable to complete her master's thesis, or go back to her volunteer job at a neighborhood television station. She supplements her two-thousand-six-hundred-dollar-a-month trust income (from her grandmother Hitchcock's estate) by substitute teaching math or science in a public high school in suburban Boston.

Although her parents lived in Baltimore briefly before moving to Lancaster after the Second World War, Carol Lynn does not recall it. Her earliest recollections are of the latter city. As far as she is concerned, Lancaster was home, the place where she grew up. But her memories of these early years appear to be somewhat mixed. And after a certain point they are decidedly negative.

"I went to James C. Buchanan [public] Elementary School until the fifth grade, and then I went to the Lancaster Country Day

School from sixth through twelfth. My memories of those years are not among my fondest."

She never found classwork a challenge and could get top grades without any effort. Insufficient incentive, however, was to plague her throughout her academic career, on all levels. She was undoubtedly reminded, by both her mother and her grandfather (and maybe even her aunt), that in junior high in Baltimore, her mother had received a five-dollar cash prize for having the highest marks in her class for a full year. Nevertheless, Carol Lynn transferred from public to private school precisely because of her academic performance. The principal of James Buchanan called in Margaret and Edward Benson and told them they had a very bright young girl on their hands and she would be far better off at Country Day.

For the most part, Carol Lynn—not yet a blonde—tolerated school and enjoyed life. More tomboy than prissy missy, she nonetheless recalls telling even grade-school friends that she wanted to grow up and marry a businessman and have twelve children—"six boys and six girls."

Once she enrolled at Country Day, life broadened and brightened for Carol Lynn. An excellent school then and now, it was coeducational, and that was just fine with Carol Lynn Benson. Also just fine was the fact that her classmates represented the social and economic upper crust of Lancaster.

She was not a snob or an elitist, but she was comfortable with people her own age whose families could give them the same things her family gave her and her brother Steven. (This is not to say, however, that she was not spoiled.)

"I had been brought up," she recalled recently, "in a situation where certain things were what I call my 'givens.' A certain way of life was the norm. I took piano lessons and dancing lessons, for example, but not riding lessons; they did that in Philadelphia. But one of the givens was that you belonged to the [country] club. That was normal. I mean, you belong to the club; you don't think about it. You belong to the club—doesn't everybody? Now that sounds horribly snooty, but it wasn't that you thought about it that way. Because certainly we were not superwealthy people and snobby and all, it was just that everybody around me, all the people I socialized with, lived the same way.

"We all belonged to the club. A lot of us went to the same piano teacher. We all went to cotillion—not *the* Cotillion. Every other Wednesday during certain months of the year we all went for ballroom dancing, and it was called cotillion. You wore your little white gloves, and the boys wore their little white gloves, and you lined up on one side of the room and the boys on the other, and you learned to do the Cha-cha and the box step. I went to the private school in town. It was that kind of life."

But "that kind of life" changed for Carol Lynn Benson in the autumn of her senior year of high school. What occasioned that change was one of those "givens"—*the* Cotillion.

"My entire upbringing, during my youth, from a social stand-point was geared around what would be the normal progression for everybody I associated with. And as part of that progression you anticipate certain things happening along the way. One of those things is Cotillion."

By this point in her life Carol Lynn was fully mature, physi-cally, and was, by all accounts, a strikingly beautiful young woman. While she knew all the boys her age from the right families, she dated their older brothers, who were already in college. She was most definitely one of the in crowd. The name Benson—that of Carol Lynn, at least—was mentioned along with those of the children of the old, established Lancaster families, such as the Hesses, the Manns, and the Rancks.

In 1961 it was to be Carol Lynn's year, and that of her girl-friends, to be presented to society. By late autumn of 1961, Co-tillion was the main topic of conversation. "We'd talk about it—'Who's coming out this year?' and 'Who's having this party?' 'Where are you going to get your dress?' and 'Where are you going to hold *your* party?'—because everyone who came out had a party, and all the other girls are invited to all the parties. The boys, of course, would have been going to the parties for a year or two, because there's always a shortage of boys."

Like the others, Carol Lynn had started to talk with her parents about making arrangements for her party. She was a bit disappointed to learn that they were not as enthusiastic as she was. "Maybe my parents didn't think about it as much as I did, because my mother certainly wasn't into that scene at all. My mother thought all of that stuff was totally ridiculous and unnecessary. But then she didn't socialize with that group; she had nothing to do with that group's parents, because, mainly, they wouldn't have anything to do with her. As my mother would say, 'The only time those people are even civil to me is when they want money from me.' "

Margaret Benson refused to accept the behavior of some of the social set. According to her daughter, she had done volunteer work for the Junior League at its thrift shop until she learned that the other women would go through the donated clothing and skim off the cream of the outfits before putting the rest out for sale.

"My mother felt that was being so hypocritical that she wouldn't have anything to do with it. She used to say that she could go back to doing laundry in the bathtub and have nothing and be happy. And I think my mother really could. She just had very simple tastes about things." But several of Margaret's friends disagree, suggesting that her lack of enthusiasm stemmed from her not being invited to join certain civic committees of high social visibility.

Her mother's lack of enthusiasm aside, Carol Lynn and all her friends—about a dozen girls, all of them classmates at Country Day—were getting increasingly excited as the time to receive their official invitations to the Cotillion drew near.

"The invitations came out in the beginning of November, but not everybody got theirs the first day. Then some got theirs, and then a couple more got theirs, but mine didn't come. And mine didn't come. And mine didn't come. And mine didn't come. And then suddenly everybody who had expected to get them, had received theirs. Except me."

It was understood by general consensus and a shared knowledge of how such things worked, that of the fourteen girls in Carol Lynn's class, there were three who would not be asked to join the Cotillion. One was Jewish (an automatic out); another was a scholarship student; and the third was the daughter of the headmaster. All of the others, including Carol Lynn Benson, were fully expected to be asked.

All ten of her friends were invited to join the Cotillion, to make their debuts, and Carol Lynn was not. No mistake had been made; she simply was not invited. "My mother tried to play the whole thing down: 'It doesn't matter, dear; it's not important; there are other things more important in life.' Well, for me, at that stage, there weren't! I was devastated. Not being invited was like being told, 'You are not acceptable.' . . . It was like being blacklisted. I was no longer to be invited to anybody's party, I was no longer to be included in anything because *I was not socially acceptable.*"

What this rejection meant, effectively, was that for the next three months, Carol Lynn Benson did not go out. At least, she did not go out with the same boys from the same crowd she'd grown up with—or with their elder brothers—because all the social events were related to the Cotillion, from which she'd been purposely excluded by her friends' parents (who drew up each year's list). The long-range implications were equally harsh; she would never again be included in the activities of the crowd she had grown up with.

Several other factors further complicated her life at this time. One was preexisting, and the other two new. The preexisting condition involved a young man, Charlie, whom Carol Lynn had met at summer school in Mexico. They had become, she says, deeply involved emotionally in a short period of time, and in the summer she turned seventeen she had flown to visit him at his home in Corpus Christi just before he left to start his freshman year at the University of Texas.

"I believe that if it had been a year later, if I had graduated from high school, then we would have been married. We were that crazy about each other, and that serious, but at the time we were just too young." Carol Lynn stayed in touch with Charlie throughout her senior year, by phone if less often by mail, and he was in her thoughts a great deal during the initial phases of her ostracism.

By early 1962, in part because of the absence of her Texan and also because of being blacklisted from her social group, she had begun to date another young man, Brett, who was a couple of years older than she was. They had met when her parents, who had become avid sailors, had bought a boat from a boatyard in Edgewater, Maryland. Brett, whose family was in the boat business, had already begun college at the University of Delaware, but before long he was spending most of his time in Lancaster.

"I didn't look at it that way then," says Carol Lynn, "but I guess I just sort of turned to him. And I'm sure that all of what was going on made me more dependent on him."

As this relationship was forming, a new situation developed that was also to have a significant effect on Carol Lynn's life.

"I had applied for early admission to Vassar, which was the only place I wanted to go. I had it all planned out: a degree in drama from Vassar and a career as an actress. I'd had high honor roll grades consistently and high college boards, so I figured I had a good chance to make it."

To Carol Lynn's surprise, Vassar notified her that her application had been deferred for regular Spring decision. By the time Vassar sent its letter of acceptance, an odd scenario had begun to unfold.

"I was told that I had actually been accepted for early admission, but that someone on the Country Day faculty, concerned that I would do even less work than usual if I knew I'd already been accepted—since the school work was so easy for me I was hardly exerting myself as it was—had asked Vassar not to notify me of my acceptance until the Spring."

Carol Lynn was so furious at this "interference in my life" that she turned down the acceptance. Despite her mother's warning that it would be a "big mistake," she enrolled at Goucher College. "It had been fine for my mother, because she was the type that liked to study, but for me it was a *disaster.*"

Carol Lynn's faculty advisor, and Math teacher, at Country Day was Albert Pomory—"and the only person then or since who called me 'Lynn.' " Although Mr. Pomory left teaching in the mid-1960s, and has been a businessman on the East Coast ever since, when contacted in early 1986, he readily remembered Carol Lynn Benson.

He does not, however, recall anything of this nature happening to Carol Lynn, though he adds, "It is not inconceivable that someone at Country Day, in an excess of concern for a student, might have done such a thing. What is important is that she seems to *believe* it happened, and that's almost equally unfortunate." Carol Lynn says, "I know the story sounds inconceivable, but it was what I was led to believe."

What Mr. Pomory does recall, and with apparent fondness, is "Lynn" Benson and her family. "I thought that she was an extremely bright, unusually bright, and capable student with a rosy future. I couldn't imagine anything but the best for her. She was a fantastically outstanding math student. You couldn't look for a better one."

Mr. Pomory, who says he had always assumed that Carol Lynn had done as well in her other classes, also mentioned that in his contact with her family, he found them to be warm and loving and seemed to have "an obvious intimacy."

He does recall, however, noticing a degree of isolation, that Carol Lynn might not have been totally accepted by the other students. "She was not what I would call a highly integrated individual in the extracurricular activity of the school. I sensed that she was isolated from more peer group interactions within the school, but I always attributed that to the fact that she was so smart. I figured that this kid was so bright and so competent that there may have been a certain amount of jealousy between her and the rest of her classmates."

Carol Lynn finished her senior year in something less than an idyllic mood. She continued to see the young man from the University of Delaware, Brett, and her senior yearbook contained a joking reference to him. Beneath her senior picture, that of a lovely young lady with a wistful look, it said, in the elliptical, mock-heroic style common to yearbooks: " 'Benny' From a 14 to a 7 with self-control . . . blonde or brunette? . . . boys, boys, men . . . long, long eyelashes . . . homework? . . . just advanced math . . . I just can't express myself in writing . . . why no French this year? . . . summers in the Southwest, and Mexican signors . . . Ford Sunliner convertibles do mix with Jaguars . . . June's the month . . . girls or coed, I just can't decide . . . saddle shoes . . . rings, jackets, sweatshirts, O. K., I've got everything . . . slumber party debates . . . I don't care, that's what I believe . . . no more F. and M. . . . nope!" Beside her picture it noted that she entered "L.C.D.S." in 1955, and then listed her activities: "J.V. Hockey, 1, 2; J.V. Basketball, 1, 2, 3; Hospital Work, 1, 2, 3, 4; Art Club, 1, 2, 3; Chorus, 1, 2, 3, 4; President of Chorus, 4; Bazaar, 1, 2, 3, 4; Class Treasurer, 4; Yearbook, 1, 2, 3, 4; Chairman of Typists for Yearbook, 4; Drama, 1, 2, 3, 4."

Each senior had two pictures on his or her special page. In the lower right-hand corner was a snapshot of Carol Lynn as an infant, with a puzzled look on her squarish face, and a spiky shock of dark hair. Shown a copy of that baby picture in 1987, both Carol Lynn's aunt and her grandfather had the same shocked reaction: "It looks just like Scotty!"

"Carol Lynn wanted me [Brett] and her parents said okay, because whatever Carol Lynn wanted, Carol Lynn got," says the man who twenty-five years ago filled a particular void and left an indelible mark on the life of Carol Lynn Benson. "We got engaged, but after she had gone off to college we just sort of drifted apart. She decided she was missing too much of the social life down there, so she broke off the relationship. We were simply too young, but still I feel that Carol Lynn and my wife were the only two great loves of my life. I think it was tragic for both of us."

The man remained in the Lancaster area after he and Carol Lynn broke up, and he has an affectionate, if mixed, memory of Margaret and Edward Benson. "They were a pretty domineering family, and they used their wealth as leverage with their kids— 'If you don't do this, then I won't give you . . .'—but they were very nice to me. Benny tried to become a father figure to me, because I was away from home. I have no animosities toward them. I feel they were *for* us, but our big problem was age."

Brett moved in with the Bensons, as he recalls it, even prior to the time Carol Lynn went away to school. He says, "We used to love it when Benny would go away on a trip because Margaret would let us sleep together. I have to say they treated me very well. They took me in like a son."

While living in the house, he says he shared a bedroom with Steven. More than twenty years later, his memories of Carol Lynn's younger brother are still vivid. "He was your typical spoiled rich kid. On his tenth birthday they gave him an eighteen-foot in-board motor boat, a six-cylinder Lyman Grey Marine. He had things handed to him. The companies he started in Lancaster were nothing but jokes."

Carol Lynn broke their engagement in March 1963, and he took it hard. "I started dating right away and within a very short time—weeks, I think—I got married. It was clearly on the rebound from Carol Lynn." He was moving out of his Lancaster apartment, two or three days after his wedding, when he got a phone call from Carol Lynn (who did not know he was married) in Baltimore.

"Guess what?" she said, "I'm pregnant."

The next day he got a call from Edward and Margaret Benson. "They asked for a meeting, and I agreed. They told me the child would be put up for adoption. That was the last time I ever saw them."

While agreeing in principle with Brett's account, Carol Lynn has a very different memory of certain details. For one thing, regarding their sleeping together while her father was away, she says, "I don't remember that at all." She continues, "I guess we got engaged around June, right before graduation, and then we got unengaged the next month. We had been dating during my senior year, though not too often, prior to my not being asked to join Cotillion. I suppose we drew together in part because of [Charlie] being away, and in part because of this estrangement from my whole social surrounding. We didn't get engaged until about June, I'm sure, because I had an engagement party near graduation, so that's how I can remember. And it wasn't too much later that I broke the engagement off."

In the summer of 1962, during the time she was engaged, Carol Lynn and her parents made a one month trip to Europe, and "It was while I was there that I decided I didn't want to be engaged. I'm sure we were only engaged for a few months. I don't remember him living in the same house when I was living there, but he *had* come up and worked for my father, and whether he was living in the house then, I don't know."

Carol Lynn's grandfather supplies an additional perspective on what took place during that trip to Europe in 1962. "After the engagement, Benny and Margaret began to hear things about [Brett] that they didn't like," he says, "so they took her to Europe and worked on her. They broke up the engagement."

Carol Lynn says she clearly remembers having broken off the engagement by the autumn, and that he was persistent in trying to get her to change her mind. He did succeed in getting her to join him for a "college weekend" in Delaware early in 1963. "I didn't want to go, but I finally gave in and went. We stayed together that weekend, in a hotel where a lot of the other kids stayed too, and I *know* that's when I got pregnant. It was clear to me then that it was never going to work between us, and I told

him so that weekend before I left. To think that I had gotten
pregnant on that weekend was almost unbelievable. It just never
even occurred to me that I could get pregnant."

Perhaps she should not have been so surprised. Her attitude
was anything but enlightened, even for the early 1960s.

"Why did I get pregnant? I got pregnant because my mother
had such a restrictive and Victorian attitude about sex that I was
totally uneducated. My mother's knowledge came from my
grandmother and it was even more archaic than mine. I think my
mother said she was thirteen or fourteen before she even knew
where babies came from. I got absolutely no sex education what-
soever from my mother. She had spent so much of her life telling
me that sex was bad, or that a person was bad if she did anything
without being married, that even had I wanted to use contraceptive methods, I had no knowledge of them at all. I wouldn't have
known where to go [to get them]. Even when I was older, and in
college, I believed everybody would think I was a *whore* if they
thought I was having sex without being married.

"At one point when I was [living] in Washington [after college]
I was able to get contraceptive pills—and I was twenty-two years
old, not some little kid—and then I moved to Texas and I ran
out of them. My girlfriend Joella's father became my doctor, but
I was embarrassed to ask him for pills. I was afraid that he would
think I was such an awful person. I was so geared from my mother's harping on me all those years about how evil it was to do it if
you weren't married . . . how people would just think you were
the scum of the earth.

"So when I got pregnant from Brett it was just stupid, because
I didn't know any better. I really didn't understand the whole
thing. I didn't understand that you could lose your virginity without sleeping with somebody. I didn't really understand what virginity *was*."

Carol Lynn has no memory of serious mother-daughter talks.
"There was no such thing. The few talks that there were, had
been: 'You just don't do it. Only *prostitutes* do it. You'd be an

evil, wicked person if you even think about doing it.' It is hard in today's world to realize how *stupid* I was. I had absolutely, really, no knowledge at all."

Her knowledge of sex in high school, such as it was, came from reading, especially *Lady Chatterley's Lover*. "I can remember hiding the book, because I was so afraid my parents would find out I was reading it. But actually I didn't learn all that much from reading. I'd have to say that even though Brett knew more about sex than I did, it was still like two kids groping in the dark."

Carol Lynn believes she was less knowledgeable about the facts of life than her friends because her mother was so extreme. Margaret Benson was so fanatical on this subject that once, in front of Carol Lynn's two teenage children, she said that their mother was no better than a prostitute because she had had sex before getting married.

Told that Brett had said her mother used to let the two of them sleep together in the house when her father was away on business, Carol Lynn Kendall looked stunned. "I have no recollection of that at *all*. I cannot imagine that at all. I have no recollection of that, and, knowing my mother, I just cannot picture that at all."

Another of his contentions with which she disagrees is that she had been pregnant before, and had had an abortion, and that her parents were afraid of the psychological effect on her of having another one.

"Absolutely not!" she says without hesitation.

Whatever the case, an eighteen-year-old Carol Lynn Benson found herself very much pregnant by the spring of 1963, and Scott was born on Christmas Day of that year.

Brett says her parents told him their plans for the baby—that he or she would be put up for adoption. What the Bensons told their daughter was quite different.

"The arrangement was that I would go to live with my Aunt Pauline in Baltimore. The people at school thought I had gone home to Lancaster because I had a bad case of mono, and the people in Lancaster thought I was in school. Putting the baby up for adoption was discussed, but I never really envisioned myself doing it. It was like the Scarlett O'Hara 'I'll-think-about-it-to-morrow' syndrome. After Scott was born, everyone kept at me, telling me I could not keep him. And then one day, while I was still in the hospital, I learned he was in a foster home. I returned to school basically not knowing what was going to happen to him. But my father promised me that they would take care of Scotty while I was finishing school, and then when I was out of school and could get a job, I would get him back and raise him myself, as my son.

"One day, my parents showed up at Goucher and, without telling me where we were going or why, took me to a little town somewhere in Maryland. I can recall a long hallway and an old man, a justice of the peace or something, and there was a paper they wanted me to sign. I didn't want to sign it. But my father insisted, told me it was better this way, that I could have him back when I got out of school. But I still didn't want to sign it. That would be like having part of me torn away. I only signed because I believed my father."

When her child was about two years old, Carol Lynn called Brett one day and asked him, as he remembers it, "if I would like to see my son. I said yes, and she brought him over to the business I was managing.

"My marriage had failed by then and I was happy to see them. She looked as beautiful as ever, and he was real cute. We had a good visit, and when they were leaving I asked her if I could call her, and see them again, and Carol Lynn said yes. I was pretty excited about the prospects of our getting back together, but the next day her father called me. Benny said he didn't think our getting together again would be a very good idea. That was the end of that."

About a year later, Carol Lynn finished college. When she went to her parents to reclaim her child, they said no. Her father took her aside and explained to her that while they knew they had made a promise to her, a promise which they'd had every intention of keeping, they now found that they simply could not give Scotty back.

"I can recall it as clearly as if it were yesterday," she remembers. "My father said to me, 'I'm sorry, but it would hurt your mother too much.' "

Steven

Harry Hitchcock still keeps a picture of his grandson Steven Benson in his living room. Other family members are not so kind. Says Hitchcock's daughter, Janet Lee, "That's a picture of a man who killed his own mother, my father's own daughter, and my own sister. I could never keep his picture in *my* house. But then my father is *such* a good man."

Outside the Hitchcock residence, flowers sprout everywhere. Inside, it's pictures. Bunches bloom on tables, mantelpieces, desks. A pictorial history of the family could be put together in short order.

There are pictures of Harry and his wife and of the two of them with their daughters, Margaret and Janet Lee. Then pictures of the girls at various stages of their lives. These are followed, in an eclectic though neat sequential order, by pictures of the Benson and Murphy children: Carol Lynn as Miss Ventnor; a thin-faced and handsome Steven at fifteen or so; Scott at various ages; and Janet Lee's girls, Sheryl and Brenda.

Buried somewhere is undoubtedly a picture of Carol Lynn's 1968 wedding, a straight line of beautiful young people, with neat hair styles and perfect smiles worthy of *Life* magazine. Standing slightly to the side and above are Margaret and Benny, the latter looking even more somber than usual, his dark eyes darker and more brooding. Tom Kendall, the water skier from Cypress Gardens, Florida, to whom Carol Lynn was briefly married, is a study in WASP handsomeness, 1960s style.

The third generation is also in evidence in "Boppa's" house, individually and in sets. There's Scott in a high school (Mc-Caskey, a public school, not Country Day) graduation photo, and Janet Lee's girls, the older one, Sheryl, and Brenda, a leggy beauty shown with two of her fellow Penn State cheerleaders two or three seasons ago. Finally, there's one of Sheryl and her husband Kevin, smiling hopefully as young married couples do, and then a photo of them with their first baby.

There is also a picture of the widow Margaret—the same one that was featured in *People* magazine—looking svelte and attractive in a cool summer dress. In the picture, one of her father's favorites, her jaw is set firmly as if she might be saying, "I'm all right. I can take care of myself now." But the eyes betray a certain nervousness.

Janet Lee Murphy has many of these same pictures in her home, in the living room and the dining room and in the small den on the west side of the house. But she has no pictures of Steven.

What she does have is books. And two whole shelves are taken up with volumes whose titles make interesting reading: *The Abnormal Personality, Personality and Other Behavior Disorders, Mental Hygiene*, and several with the word "criminal" in their titles. Janet Lee has a degree in psychology from the University of Maryland, and the titles of her old college textbooks read like a primer on how to detect, if not escape, a homicidal sociopath. One cannot avoid the irony of these books sitting in Steven Benson's aunt's bookcase.

"He inherited his grandfather's ambition, his father's somber mien, and talent from no one." That harsh-sounding evaluation of Steven Benson was offered by a man who worked with his father for many years and with Steven himself for a few. Unfortunately, it appears to be true, except perhaps for the talent. Nonetheless, others who have known Steven Benson for years say that, while he has some obvious abilities, there was seldom, if ever, a conjunction of talent, opportunity, and effort. As his first wife put it, "Steven had a lot of trouble getting things to come together the way he wanted them to."

It wasn't easy to follow Carol Lynn's act. Lancaster Country Day's yearbook from 1962, which features almost a dozen pictures of his sister in a variety of posts and poses, also includes two pictures of Steven Wayne Benson, fifth grader. In both, he looks less like a youth and more like a little old man.

In his class picture, Steven wears a full suit and a white shirt with a dark tie. His patterned socks suggest a flair for fashion, as do his two-tone buckskin shoes. His expression is one of seriousness and propriety. In a group shot of the Student Government Association in which he appears to be the youngest member, Steven is wearing a different suit and, again, a shirt and dark tie.

Was he as serious as these pictures seem to suggest? "No," says Tim Trexler, a close friend of Steven's since junior high school. He adds that this should not be taken to mean that Steven was ever gregarious or outgoing.

His grandfather, Harry Hitchcock, recalls that "Steven was aware, when he was growing up, that his grandfather and his father had been successful in business, and he wanted to be also. Unfortunately, he had rather grandiose ideas. He preferred starting from the top to starting from the bottom. I preferred that he start like me, from the bottom. But I never told him that, because he had a father living, and he got his guidance from his father."

Growing up, Steven was particularly taken with boating and

with electronics, and he spent many hours learning about and enjoying both interests. When Steven was ten years old, Brett helped him build his first radio, a Heathkit.

He was also interested in fireworks and other types of explosives.

Later, after the killing, when the media descended on Lancaster to find out about the family, the brother of a girl Steven knew in high school told a reporter he'd once found, in a closet in his own house, a box filled with wire, dry cell batteries, and electrical attachments known as alligator clips.

"I guess you'd call them bombs," he said, adding that his thought, on seeing the paraphernalia, was: "Oh, this is Steven Benson's stuff."

Clearly, Steven had ability in the field of electronics. His mother liked to brag that he had taken apart—and put together again—a television set before he was ten years old. Several years later he was able to do all the wiring for the alarm systems in the family's various homes.

He showed an early interest in "entrepreneurism," a word that both he and his mother liked. At the age of fourteen he started a lawn business. Somehow, he had access to a checking account, for his sister recalls that it got him into trouble.

"Steven was only about fourteen or maybe fifteen when my parents discovered he'd been kiting checks. According to my mother, my father took care of it quietly, and made the checks good."

Steven survived high school—having transferred from Country Day to J. B. McCaskey, a public school—though not without a certain amount of embarrassment for his lack of athletic skill. A physical education coach, tired of Steven's constant attempts to get out of gym by claiming he'd forgotten his shorts, made him participate wearing his underwear instead. That Steven cried in public as a result was recalled by several of his classmates years later when the media showed up to ask questions.

Obviously Steven was bright, and just as obviously his interests lay outside the classroom. He made no secret of his family's wealth, wearing a full-length leather coat to school and, not long after he turned sixteen, driving a 280 SL Mercedes.

"We met in high school," says Nancy Ferguson, the quiet girl who became his first wife. "Steven had asked me out a couple of times, but I hesitated. I guess, looking back on it, it was because I realized he came from a different class of people than I was accustomed to." Nancy's background was modest. Her father had a midlevel position at Lancaster Press. "Eventually we started going out, but even then it wasn't what I would call an exclusive relationship, though it did become one after a couple of months. We were in some of the same classes together in high school and I got to know a little bit about him and liked what I saw so I decided I would go out with him."

If Nancy was quiet as an adolescent, and she readily admits she was, then Steven was even quieter. Even his laughter was restrained. She says that while he did "cut loose" occasionally, for the most part his laugh was a "restrained, businessman's laugh, like his father's. He was always on the serious side," though not as serious as photos usually made him look.

Apparently, Steven's social life was rather limited. Nancy says she was aware of only one other girl that he had gone out with in high school. A close male friend who asked that his name not be used disputes this, saying that Steven probably gave that impression because he preferred to date one girl at a time. "As far as sex is concerned," he volunteered, "we were neither advanced nor superslow, probably somewhere in the middle of the bell curve." At any rate, Nancy and Steven were married early, during her second year of college.

The wedding was performed with all the pomp and circumstance befitting the scion of a successful Lancaster business family. It was held in Grace Lutheran Church with the reception at the Hamilton Club, and while the Bensons were not exactly thrilled at the prospect of Steven marrying so young or to someone so clearly outside the clan, socially and economically, they kept, according to one close family friend, "a stiff upper lip." That reservation aside, the family liked Nancy, something that could not be said about Debby, his second wife.

Tim Trexler was Steven's best man, and Nancy had her best friend, Deborah Abel, as her maid of honor. The rest of the party was made up of friends and relatives from both sides. Today, almost fifteen years later, one oddity leaps out of the wedding pictures. Nancy Ferguson was born with brown hair; and it was light brown to blonde when she and Steven met. But her wedding pictures show a trim, fair girl whose face peers out from a cascade of long, golden, almost white curls. According to Nancy, Margaret Benson thought it would be "nice" if she and Carol Lynn and Nancy all looked alike on that special day.

After a two-week honeymoon in Bermuda, the young couple returned to Lancaster and the business of their education. Nancy was then studying at Millersville State College and Steven was at Franklin and Marshall, just blocks from the pleasant three-bedroom house that Steven's father had bought for them in the west end of Lancaster. At least that's what everyone in his family, except for his wife, thought he was doing.

Their respective attitudes toward college could hardly have been more different. Nancy already knew that she wanted to pursue a career in special education and work with brain-damaged children. But Steven had few goals in mind, other than the fact that he wanted to be a successful businessman like his father and grandfather before him.

Nancy was organized, highly motivated. Her husband, by contrast, seemed to have no clear idea of why he was in college. As she put it, "He's smart, but, for whatever reason, he just wouldn't discipline himself to sit down and study."

She recalls that when he would drive down to pick her up for weekends—she was finishing her degree at a school an hour's drive from Lancaster—he would always have his books in the car. "But," she says, "the books would stay in the car all weekend." Eventually, he dropped out before he finished his second year, but he never told his parents he was no longer a student.

Carol Lynn says that she believes Nancy either never knew about Steven's subterfuge or was covering up for him, "like a good wife." According to Carol Lynn, it was not until Steven was scheduled to graduate that his parents learned he was no longer even enrolled at Franklin and Marshall. They were under this "misimpression" because Steven had, somehow, been able to arrange it so that they were receiving—or he was receiving and showing to them—report cards for all the years he was supposed to have been in college. And they were paying the tuition.

Carol Lynn says that years later her mother used this deception as an example of her son's "brilliance." "You must understand," says Carol Lynn, "that Steven had a whole different attitude about things. He had an entirely different attitude about money, about my mother's money. Steven *used* my mother's money. It was not that my mother manipulated Steven by the use of money. If anything, it was the exact opposite. It wasn't that no one in the family ever said anything to Steven about the way he [mis]managed businesses. My father did, my mother did, we all did, at some time or another. But Steven would just go ahead and do things, and then come and say, 'Get me out of it.' This was Steven's mode of behavior all along the way."

Nancy Ferguson saw this problem early on and knew that sooner or later it would destroy her marriage. For one thing, "Steven always seemed to have money. I don't know if his parents had him on an allowance or not. That was not the kind of information he shared. He liked providing for, and I think he would have been very insulted if I had asked, 'Where's all this money coming from?' "

The pattern that Carol Lynn described many years later was obvious to Nancy in the mid-seventies. "Steven never had to start a project, work it all the way through, and reach a goal. He would get part of the way through, and if he had difficulty, Daddy was

always there to bail him out. And he knew—he learned his lessons well—he knew that if he got into trouble, all he had to do
was to go to his parents and they would help him out."

Another point of irritation for Steven's first wife, though more
so in retrospect than at the time, was that she had been required
to sign a prenuptial agreement. Dated May 26, 1972, it states, as
"BACKGROUND" that "The parties hereto intend to be married in
the near future. Each is possessed of property, the nature and
extent of which has been fully disclosed by each to the other.
Both parties desire to define the interest which each shall have
with respect to the property of the other"—a polite way of saying, "who gets what in the event of a divorce."

The document continues:

IT IS THEREFORE AGREED AS FOLLOWS:
1. *Release of Marital Rights by Wife.* Nancy C. Ferguson hereby
waives and releases all right and interest, statutory or otherwise, including, but not limited to, dower, widow's allowance,
statutory allowance, distribution in intestacy, and right of elec-
tion to take against the will of Steven W. Benson which she
might acquire as the wife, widow, heir-at-law, next of kin or
distributee of Steven W. Benson, in his property, owned by
him at the time of the marriage or acquired by him at any time
thereafter in his estate upon his death.

A similar clause follows in regard to "Release of Marital Rights
by Husband," in which Steven gives up all of his present and
future rights to Nancy Ferguson's estate. What might make this
clause seem odd to the uninitiated is the list, appended to the
agreement, that breaks down their respective assets. The bride-
to-be's assets are spelled out as follows:

Nancy Carol Ferguson

1962 Oldsmobile Cutlass	$ 450.00
Trust fund	1,000.00

Furniture	750.00
Jewelry	1,850.00
Cash in banks	300.00
	$4,350.00 Total

Steven's assets were somewhat more impressive:

Steven Wayne Benson

Lancaster Landscapers	$12,850.00
Cash in banks	1,200.00
Stocks and Bonds	20,700.00
Jewelry	2,500.00
Tools and radio equipment	4,800.00
Automotive equipment	6,900.00
Furniture	1,500.00
	$50,450.00 Total

Steven's entry also included a significant postscript. Immediately under his total is a line that reads: "It is also noted that Steven Wayne Benson is one of the heirs in two sizable estates." So there.

As Nancy Ferguson recalls it, Steven did not even tell her what she was signing, but merely told her she had to go with him to a lawyer's office to sign "a paper." Frankly, she says, it made no difference to her, because she considered the whole thing a waste of time. She had not married Steven with plans for divorce in the back of her mind. "I was raised to expect that I would go to college, get married, and raise a family. I didn't know what I signed until later, and then I didn't care."

If the agreement itself sounds rather cold-blooded for such a wholesome, family-oriented, religious town as Lancaster, Pennsylvania, it is not, according to a Benson family friend and Lancaster businessman for forty years.

"Around here we have a lot of rich families, and their sons and daughters don't always marry people who also have money. So prenuptial agreements are quite common."

The "Lancaster Landscaping" listed in Nancy and Steven's agreement was what his first lawn business had grown into, but the size of its valuation was not an indication of its profitability. The business, which is still joked about in Lancaster today, was the first of Steven's grandiose efforts, to borrow the word his grandfather uses to describe it.

Given carte blanche, directly or by default, by his parents, Steven bought enough equipment for, as Harry Hitchcock puts it, "a company that had been in business for twenty years." An employee said, "If there was a right-handed edger, we had it; if there was such a thing as a *left*-handed edger, you can be sure that Steven would have bought that too."

When Steven gave up on the landscaping business and went to work at Lancaster Leaf in the early 1970s, the tens of thousands of dollars worth of equipment was put in storage, first in a barn outside of Lancaster and then in the family warehouse in the city. Years later, the equipment was still there, and until the time of her death, Margaret was still trying to figure out what to do about it. Amos Sands, who works part-time as a handyman for Harry Hitchcock, says, "I don't know how many trips I made to the airport to pick up Margaret and Steven when they'd come in and go to the warehouse to try and figure out what to do about that old stuff. I'm sure they spent more in air fare than they could ever get for the whole bunch."

Nancy Ferguson does not recall that the landscaping company ever made a profit, despite all the equipment and the financial support. But she had other things to worry about by that point. While fitting into the Benson family as Steven's wife was initially more difficult than she had anticipated—"I didn't realize that in marrying Steven I was also marrying Edward and Margaret Benson and Carol Lynn and even Scott too"—Nancy had made the adjustment.

What she had not been prepared for were the difficulties that arose after Steven went to work for his father at Lancaster Leaf. As Willem van Huystee pointed out, Steven was hampered by the fact that his father would give him neither a specific job nor a specific title. Carol Lynn remembers her mother raising this topic with her father at the dinner table from time to time. But Benny, who kept his own counsel about such matters, apparently preferred to keep Steven in that amorphous state. Clearly, the work force was not thrilled with this particular boss's son coming in and making grand suggestions, which was Steven's wont.

Years later, the family was to say that Steven's first marriage broke up because he and Nancy had no children, and they implied that it was because she was too much of a career woman. Nancy Ferguson bristles at the first suggestion—"We went to several doctors trying to find out why I couldn't get pregnant. We were *trying* to have a family"—and laughs at the second, though as much at the term as at the truth of it.

Not surprisingly, she and the Bensons came to different conclusions about the same events. For one thing, according to Carol Lynn, her family felt that when Steven got married he "dropped" them and "spent all of his non-holiday time with Nancy's family." Nancy says almost the opposite: "The Bensons wanted their children with them at all times, and for all occasions, especially holidays. After a few years it became customary for us to spend Christmas with them at their ski chalet in Canada, so I once said to Steven that because we spent every Christmas with his parents we should spend Thanksgiving with mine; but it was never easy."

They had been married about three or four years—Steven was working for Lancaster Leaf—when Nancy began to suspect that her husband was having an affair. She even had a pretty good idea who the woman was, an employee at one of the factories. Unable to confront Steven, she called his father, who verified her suspicion.

"How do you know it's true?" she asked.

"Because," Edward Benson replied, "I had him followed."

Armed with this knowledge, she accused Steven and he admitted it. And, in a scene redolent of a Theodore Dreiser novel, when Nancy said she would like to see the woman to figure out what she was up against, Steven took his wife to *meet* his girlfriend. The woman lived in a dingy flat above a movie theater in a small town outside of Lancaster. When she realized that Steven had just introduced her to his wife, she called him into another room, and Nancy got up and left.

Later, when she asked him what he saw in the woman, Steven said, "She doesn't represent the establishment."

While Nancy was trying to sort out her situation, she had to deal with unwelcome advice from the Benson family. Edward suggested that she was too interested in her own studies, and that what Steven needed to straighten himself out was a regular home life with his dinner on the table at five o'clock every night.

By this point, she had finished all her course work for her master's degree in special education, but she found it impossible to work up the energy to write her thesis. Soon it was apparent that she and Steven no longer had a marriage, and she moved out. Instead of pursuing her original career goal, she spent a couple of years working as a paralegal and then found a new one—after three more years of schooling she became a veterinarian's nurse.

In 1980, Nancy had her last conversation with Steven: "He was all excited about a new project. He had bought some farmland and was going to subdivide it and sell the lots for homes. I tried to sound enthusiastic for him, because he was so excited, but it just sounded to me like another one of Steven's projects that he would be interested in for a while and then it would fail. I could hear it playing all over again."

By the time his first marriage broke up, Steven had a record of failure that was known only to the family. Again and again, he had gone into deals or made extravagant purchases that required his father—or his mother without his father's knowledge, or vice versa—to bail him out and then cover for him lest his grandfather or someone in the Lancaster "establishment" would find out and write him off completely and forever.

Carol Lynn says that her parents didn't want her grandfather to think badly of Steven, so they always covered up whatever he did. "But it wasn't a matter of discipline. One has to understand that we are talking about a very private family—my mother's famous phrase was 'You don't wash your dirty linen in public.' It's a matter of family honor. Everything is done for family honor. There is the family name. You do everything for the good of the family as a whole. My whole life I've spent sacrificing for the family. I didn't come first. So it wasn't a matter of being permissive. And it wasn't a matter of a disciplinary situation. It was not as if there was a choice of what to do—because to not do it would reflect upon the honor of the family, so therefore it became a matter that had to be taken care of. That attitude tends to be, I know, more medieval; today most people would simply say, 'The hell with it,' but in those times families covered for family members. You protected your own, you did whatever was necessary for the protection of the family as a whole."

But would Carol Lynn Benson Kendall protect her own children if it meant covering for them the way her mother and father covered for Steven? "I would," she says without hesitation, and then adds, "fortunately I'm not faced with the same situation."

Later, Nancy Ferguson recalled a conversation she and Steven had shortly before their marriage broke up. "In trying to figure out what had gone wrong, I asked what it would take to make him happy, and he said, 'To be a millionaire by the time I'm thirty.'

" 'But Steven,' I asked, 'how would you feel if that didn't happen?'

"He looked at me, and he said, 'I guess it wouldn't be so bad; I've never really been happy anyway.' "

Scott

"My problem with Scott is that I have to grieve for him twice."

CAROL LYNN BENSON KENDALL

DECEMBER 1986

Some years ago, the popular phrase teenagers screamed at their parents in the middle of a heated argument was: "I didn't ask to be born!" Scott Benson was one teenager who might have been justified in making that statement, and yet apparently he never did. If he knew that Carol Lynn was his real mother—and there is very little credible evidence that he did—then he never confronted her or Margaret with that fact. As difficult, and even dangerous, as he could be, there was always one bottom line with Scott: he loved life and did his best to enjoy it.

Only a handful of people knew that the baby Margaret and Benny had adopted was really their grandson. The Bensons were so resolute about keeping Scott's parentage a secret that Margaret's sister, Janet Lee Murphy, did not know the truth for seven years. "And my former husband found out before I did. I was almost hurt."

Other close friends said that Benny told them Margaret's doctors had said adopting a child might help her get over a "nervous condition" she'd been suffering. According to Willem van Huystee, "They never admitted whose baby it was, even though my wife asked her. While we were in the Philippines with them Benny said the doctors had said it would be good for them."

Federal Judge Clarence Newcomer, then an attorney in Lancaster, and his wife were good friends of the Bensons. He remembers, "We were with Margaret and Benny on a boat trip, in the Chesapeake Bay, I think, and they were very concerned about Carol Lynn. They kept calling her every day, stopping just to call her. Years later, we figured that must have been the period of time when she was pregnant with Scott. But they never told us it was her baby, and we were as close to Margaret and Benny as anyone.

"But I recall a few years later, we had been watching Carol Lynn with Scott, and there was just something funny about it, about how she acted with him. I said to Jane later, 'I think there's more to Scott's background than we realize, or that they are telling.' "

By the time Scott was born, his adoptive parents were clearly wealthy, and wanted for nothing. Consequently, neither did he. His toys and his clothes were simply the best, says Carol Lynn, "far better than what my children had." But it wasn't the material excesses that bothered her. "My mother used to treat him like a little emperor. This was when he was a little older, but it was typical: he would get up in the morning and come down and lie on the couch and watch television, and then my mother would dress him! He wouldn't even move to help her or do anything but watch television. She would raise his leg or his arm, and if she blocked his view he would scream at her. He was like royalty. My kids would watch in amazement—and so would I."

By the time Scott was going on six years old, Carol Lynn's brief marriage to Tom Kendall had ended, and she had two babies, only eleven months apart in age, to raise. She had moved back to Lancaster in 1969, where her parents bought her a house around the corner from theirs, and for a number of years she made it a practice to include Scott in outings. It was not an unusual sight around Lancaster to see Carol Lynn Benson Kendall with three little boys in tow, one twice the size of the others.

Carol Lynn says that despite what her parents had told her when she finished college and asked to have Scott, she hung onto the hope that they would change their minds and let her raise her first child along with his stepbrothers. If she had a chance, it was not apparent to outside observers, who saw Margaret as an increasingly devoted, even doting, mother. According to Mary Miller Glose, Margaret would regale their bridge club with young Scotty's exploits, to the point that certain members complained in private.

One family friend still shakes his head when he recounts an incident he witnessed himself. "Benny had this beautiful cherry inlaid desk, with leather on the top, in his office at home. And one day when Scott was small, I was there and I heard this pounding. I opened the door, and there was little Scott. He had a carpenter's hammer and he was pounding on the desk. I went and got Margaret, and said, 'Margaret, did you know that Scott has a hammer and he's pounding on Benny's desk?'

"She said, 'Oh my,' so I walked in the den with her, and she says"—at this point he affects a plaintive, almost simpering tone of voice—" 'Oh honey, please give Mommy the hammer, I don't want you to do that.' And I thought, 'Oh, my God.'

"I can remember that from years ago, because I would have pounded the kid's ass."

In 1971, an incident took place that indicates how strong the bond between Margaret and Benny and their adopted son had become.

Carol Lynn has a vivid recollection of the time when she and her mother were shopping in Lancaster and Margaret Benson suddenly realized she could not get home by the time eight-year-old Scott returned from school. "My mother burst into tears, and started talking about 'poor little Scotty.' It was amazing. After all, there was a housekeeper at home. But my mother actually started *crying!* She was just so obsessed with him."

According to Carol Lynn, her marriage to Kendall had been, almost from the beginning, a marriage in name only. Shortly after the wedding, they moved to California, where, he assured her, he had a job waiting for him. When that did not pan out, she was forced to conclude that he had expected her to support him.

Once again, it was Daddy to the rescue. Benny flew out to California and brought his daughter and her husband back home to Lancaster and the family fold.

The marriage fell apart, a divorce came through, and for the next decade not only did Carol Lynn do very little dating, but she had very little social life. Lancaster, Pennsylvania, then as now, is not the kind of town that makes a place for women no longer married, whether divorced or widowed. (In fact, its attitudes still seem rooted in the 1950s: a divorced male attorney recently told a visitor, "If your wife and I were to have lunch together in a restaurant, it would automatically be assumed that we were having an affair.")

On a Canadian trip in the early 1970s, she met Don, a businessman from Montreal. They got on famously, and before too long they were in the middle of a long-distance romance.

What attracted Carol Lynn to Don were much the same qualities that have attracted her to all the "significant" men in her life. Not too surprisingly, they were much the same qualities that she so greatly admired in her own father. "There was, first of all, a sense of presence, a quality that you could see immediately. When my father walked into a room, whether he said anything or not, you knew he was there. He made an impact. All the important men in my life have had that quality, starting with my first true love, [Charlie] from Texas. With all of them, I know that if it became necessary, they would take care of me."

Eventually, Don moved to Lancaster and lived with Carol Lynn and her two young boys. After some months, Don asked her why she always included Scott when she took her children on outings. "I told him Scott was my son. After all, Don and I were not just living together—we were talking about getting married."

Don was very upset at this news initially, but he came to accept it. What concerned him, however, was the indulgent way that Margaret and Benny were raising the boy. He was hardly alone in making that observation. Everyone from Harry Hitchcock to Benson family friends recall either seeing or saying that Scott was being allowed to do almost anything he wanted. Carol Lynn's sons were not very old before they began asking their mother why "Uncle Scott" could do things their grandmother would yell at them for doing.

At a party, Don made the mistake of mentioning to a friend of Margaret and Benny's that he thought they were spoiling the child. The friend then made the mistake of reporting the criticism to Margaret. Don was summoned to the Benson home and told, in no uncertain terms, to mind his own business. Incensed, not just at being treated as if *he* were a child, but also over the fact that the Bensons were ignoring what he felt responsible parents would have taken as constructive criticism, he packed up and moved out of Lancaster and, as it happened, out of Carol Lynn's life. (In 1985, when mutual friends heard of the bombing and Carol Lynn's near death, they informed Don, but he never contacted her.)

Carol Lynn recalls, "When Don left me, my life hit rock bottom. It took me several *years* to get over it, but it did have a positive effect, because it forced me to sit down and evaluate my life. I was able to work out, for myself, not just why I did the things I was doing then, but why I had made the major decisions I'd made throughout my life. And I've been a much stronger person since then. But losing Don was a devastating blow at the time, and, to a great extent, I have my parents to blame for that loss."

Oblivious to the storm around him, Scott grew up a sunny and thoroughly pampered child. He spent most of his summer days at the house on the Jersey shore, and later at the Lancaster Country Club, around the pool with the other kids, one of whose fathers remembers seeing the boy at the snack bar one afternoon with a hundred-dollar bill in his hand. Asked where he got that kind of money, young Scott Benson replied equably, "My father's a millionaire."

He did as well as he needed to in school, and his great-grandfather remembers him as a sunny, affectionate child. "He used to say to me," says Harry Hitchcock, " 'Boppa, when I grow up I want to be just like you.' "

Janet Lee Murphy also recalls Scott's open affection. "He was the kind of boy who would say, 'I love you, Aunt Jan,' with no embarrassment."

One side of his personality may have developed too early for Scott's own good. According to one family member, the boy was sexually active as early as the age of twelve. Steven became, by default, the person with whom Scott would discuss the birds and the bees, which was somewhat ironic, in view of Steven's less than wide experience. But Nancy recalls that Steven was understanding with Scott and sincerely tried to help the boy. She says she felt then that Steven would be a good father, and that the many times she and Steven babysat for Scott turned out to be good practice, at least for Steven.

By the time Scott got to high school—at James McCaskey, a public school, rather than Country Day—he was quite receptive to whatever recreational drugs were available. Never having been given much reason to curb his behavior at home, he showed little tendency to do so away from home.

Nancy Ferguson Benson, then still married to Steven, started to become worried about Scott. "I remember sitting down and talking with Scott, and saying, 'Don't you know what the studies say about marijuana . . .?' I had no motherly experience, but I was trying to warn him, and to get a feel for why he was doing it. I knew he was into marijuana then, and I knew he was driving cars before he had a license, and I knew the girls he was involved with, so I just saw a disaster coming down."

She also recalls how manipulative Scott was, even as a small child. People who knew Scott in Florida, when he was older, also remarked on what had become by that time an obvious character trait, Scott's public displays of affection for Margaret, which, according to those closest to him, were absolutely genuine.

"One thing all of the children knew," says Nancy Ferguson in reference to Steven, Carol Lynn, and Scott, "was that their parents would never follow through on their threats to cut them off financially. And Scott probably took the greatest advantage of this. Later, when Scott was older, Margaret just wasn't strong enough to put up with that."

Nancy's final impression of Scott Benson is by no means all negative. "There *was* a lot of good in Scott. But there was too much offered to him for nothing, and he grew up to learn how to get what he wanted. Unfortunately, he became a master manipulator."

Even though he finished high school in three years, played on McCaskey's tennis team, and had a private coach and training regimen, Scott could not say no to his favorite temptations. He preferred to run with a fast crowd that smoked a lot of marijuana and had parties whenever they could find an empty house—not always the easiest thing to do in conservative, family-conscious Lancaster.

He was in a variety of minor scrapes and a few that were not so minor.

Early on, Scott indicated that he wanted to become a professional athlete; first a tennis player, then a skier, and then again, until the end of his brief life, a tennis pro. He had learned the game from a series of young pros at the Olde Hickory Racquet Club in Lancaster. One, Fred Frazier, recommended that Scott attend a summer camp run by Anna Kuykendall, the well-known coach of the tennis team at the University of Miami in Florida as well as of Virginia Wade and her own daughter, Kathy, once ranked twelfth in the world. She came to know Scott Benson very well and retains a deep affection and love for him and for his family. But she has few illusions about his behavior, his character, or his tennis ability.

Mrs. Kuykendall is effusive in her praise of Scott's friendly nature. "He was," she says, "a big teddy bear." Although he was a teddy bear who, time and again, had to be removed from her tennis lair.

"I knew Scott from the time he was thirteen to about nineteen, and a lot of that period he lived in my home. He was always a loving and a lovable child and young man, but there is no mistaking the fact that he could drive you crazy. And he would never follow the rules. That was why, eventually, we had to tell Margaret and Benny, and then just Margaret, that he couldn't stay here any longer."

Mrs. Kuykendall has coached, run camps, and had players in her home (mostly in Miami) for more than three decades. And when players come to stay and "study" with her—at a considerable price, though one that families like the Bensons could certainly afford—they were expected to live by her rules. "Scott," she says, "always found that difficult. When he was younger, it had to do with use of the telephone, getting long-distance calls from his friends or calling them. When he was older it involved cars and girls."

She met Scott through Fred Frazier, then Scott's coach, when he attended a tennis camp she ran one summer outside of Washington, D.C. Frazier told her that he couldn't do anything with him, in large part because he ran with such a "rowdy bunch" but also because his family indulged him too much.

They also indulged themselves. They refused to hear anything negative about Scott's ability and promise as a tennis player. Two of the Bensons' closest friends found this out the hard way, and it almost cost them the friendship. Judge and Mrs. Newcomer have a son-in-law who is a professional tennis instructor, and for a while he was Scott's coach. After working with Scott for several months, the coach gave the Bensons an appraisal of Scott's future in tennis. He was asked, could he make it as a pro on the circuit and support himself as a tennis player?

"Not likely, unless he learned some discipline," is what he said. Not only was he immediately fired as Scott's coach, but Margaret and Benny stopped seeing his in-laws, the Newcomers, socially. In addition, says Jane Newcomer, Margaret went out of her way to try to hurt the coach, maligning his teaching ability and speaking against him to people who might hire him. This strain in the two-decade friendship lasted about a year. Finally, the Newcomers made overtures to the Bensons, and the rupture was healed. Jane Newcomer explains, "We had been friends for too many years, and, after all, you accept your friends for what they are, faults included."

Anna Kuykendall says much the same thing. "People have asked why, with all the problems that Scott and Margaret caused me, I kept him on as a student for so long. I tell them that you had to know them to understand. They were more like family than anything else. They were such *human* people."

One of Anna Kuykendall's most vivid memories of the Bensons involves a phone call in the autumn of 1980. It was from Edward Benson, and once again he was asking that they bend the rules and give Scott another chance. Scott, who was sixteen at the time, had been sent home to Lancaster for breaking any number of rules.

"A few weeks before he died [of cancer], Benny called me, and after we had talked a while he told me he was dying. Then he said, 'Anna, I know how good you and Kirk have been for Scotty, and so I want you to promise me that after I die you'll let him come back and live with you again, and you be his coach.'

"And then he said, 'Anna, I'm setting up a trust fund for Scott's tennis; would you be interested in being its trustee? There's enough money for you to give Scott lessons for as long as you live.'

"I was about to weaken and say 'yes,' but Kirk, my husband, was there, and he figured out what was happening. He got on the line and he told Benny 'no.' He said, 'Benny, you're doing the same thing you always do with that boy. You're giving him another present. What you have to do is discipline him.' Well, Benny took it, but he didn't like it. I felt kind of bad, but of course Kirk was exactly right. And Kirk loved Scott too. We both did. You couldn't help it."

Shortly before the phone call, Scott had told Anna that his father, sick as he was, would go out on their home tennis court in Lancaster and throw balls for him to hit. When she suggested that perhaps his father was too sick for that kind of physical exertion, Scott insisted, "But, Anna, they love to do things for me."

Death of the Father

When his son Steven went to work for Lancaster Leaf, it marked both the beginning and the end of Edward Benson's dream.

A proud and a private man, Edward Benson had been fighting a number of corporate opponents for years. Not only did he have to compete with the various tobacco families and their companies in and around Lancaster, but he also had to fight with his own parent corporation, Universal Leaf. Unfortunately, certain people in the home office of Universal Leaf in Richmond, Virginia envied the success of both Harry Hitchcock and Edward Benson and apparently looked forward to the end of their "era."

According to people who knew the industry, both Benson and Hitchcock felt that Universal was no longer in the hands of "tobacco people," but had been taken over by green eyeshade types, short-sighted accountants who knew little and cared less about the proud history of tobacco as a cash crop in America.

Unlike Edward Benson and, to an extent, Harry Hitchcock, they did not think in terms of a family dynasty. It mattered little to them that under the leadership of Hitchcock and Benson, Lancaster Leaf had grown to a full and healthy adulthood. As long as profits held up, they were satisfied.

Some outside observers say that in the late seventies, Lancaster Leaf's sales had slipped a bit, but Harry Hitchcock disagrees firmly. "There was no setback in Lancaster Leaf. There was just a different way of looking at it on the part of the home office of Universal Leaf."

While the home office may not have been dynasty-minded, Edward Benson was justifiably proud of what he had wrought, especially his role in having internationalized the company and set up profitable operations in the Philippines and Europe. Not the least source of his pride was the fact that the Universal people had doubted Lancaster Leaf's chances from the very beginning, and these days they had to admit to his and his father-in-law's success.

Now he attempted to carry on the tradition by bringing in Steven. Whether the idea was Steven's or his father's is now academic. Regardless, the folly of that move was apparent to almost everyone from the very beginning.

Manny Murray, a very successful Lancaster builder who had known the Benson family well for years, says, "Since he was a little boy [Steven] always talked big, always walked with his head up. He was bright, there was no question about that, but he didn't have common sense; he might have had brains, but he definitely lacked common sense." According to Murray, it was clearly a mistake to bring Steven into the family business.

Harry Hitchcock also feels that way. "It was Benny's dream that Steven would one day succeed him as president of Lancaster Leaf. He used to take Steven around with him on calls, so he could build up his customer contacts, just as I had done with him when I first hired him."

"But Steven wanted to start at the top," says Murray. He wanted to follow in his father's footsteps the way Benny had followed in his father-in-law's, but without working his way up. "So eventually Benny was very disappointed with the way that Universal, in his opinion, had treated Steven. But one day, after his father had died, Steven came into the office and found his desk was gone."

Another close observer was Nancy Ferguson Benson, who was still part of the family when he gave up on his landscaping business and went to work for Lancaster Leaf. To her great dismay, Steven would not, or could not, keep regular business hours. "There was a good bit of goofing off. Steven just didn't live by a time clock. He wouldn't be at work at eight o'clock in the morning. He'd wander in when he felt like wandering in." Nancy recalls ruefully the number of mornings she took calls from people at Lancaster Leaf who were trying to find Steven. "You feel terrible," she said recently, "saying your husband has already left for work, when it's ten-thirty and he's still sitting across the room from you, and you have to lie to cover for him."

Nancy remembers something else that could be meaningful. Apparently, in all the time that Steven worked for Lancaster Leaf while they were married, the only people from the company he ever brought home for dinner, or with whom they ever socialized, were "the carpenters and the plumbers, and people like that. Never any of the other executives, the people on his level."

It should be kept in mind that at the time he went to work for his father, Steven had a long history of successfully manipulating both of his parents, and at times also his grandparents, in order to get what he wanted. As Nancy says, "He had learned his lessons very well."

And it should also be kept in mind that his parents had an equally long history of giving in to, and covering up for, their son Steven. Once, Harry Hitchcock handed Steven two thousand dollars in cash to buy Mr. Hitchcock's annual supply of tulip bulbs. Steven ordered them on credit and spent the money on something else. When the bill came, his parents paid it, fearing, Carol Lynn says, Hitchcock would be disappointed if he learned the truth.

Another incident had to do with a Lancaster hardware store that was going out of business. At the sale, Steven evidently had a kid-in-a-candy-store reaction. "He bought out the whole place," said Carol Lynn, "But when it came time to pay for it, he had no money, and my parents had to pay for everything. Today, you can go up to the third floor of the family warehouse in Lancaster and there it all is, bins of nails and boxes of hardware supplies, even bags of fertilizer. It looks like the hardware store was simply moved from one spot to the other."

In spite of such experiences, both Margaret and Edward Benson held out high hopes for Steven when he came into the family business. "I never could understand," says Nancy Ferguson, "how his parents could be so blind to what he was doing—or to what Steven wasn't doing—at Lancaster Leaf when he began to work there. There was a lot of resentment, and I could understand it. Part of it was because he was the boss's son, but the other part of it was that Steven just had a lot of grand ideas, but couldn't follow them through. For example, he would approach the plant manager with this wonderful idea, go out and purchase all the equipment and all the materials he needed to do it, and then it would never be completed."

It was a classic example of what Steven's sister calls "his *modus operandi*—plan, spend big, then fail to follow through. He did that throughout his life. Steven was a great planner—that's the business he should have been in—but he could not manage or follow up. He simply got bored."

The former Mrs. Benson feels that Steven's experience at Lancaster Leaf was what really destroyed their marriage, not his adultery, or her "careerism," or their inability to have children, all reasons given by her in-laws. "A couple of times—no, *many* times—when Steven would come home frustrated and say that the people at Lancaster Leaf didn't like him, I would say, 'Look, you don't *have* to work for your father.' He was skilled in carpentry, electrical work, plumbing—there were just lots of things that he could do. I'd say, 'We don't need to live in this house. I can work. We can go *anywhere*, and start anew.' "

But they never did. "It was," she says, "too comfortable. Things had been handed to Steven all his life and it was *much too comfortable*. But along with the comfort was all that tension and stress. . . ."

As Willem van Huystee remembers: "Steven, who was never a sunny child, suddenly showed up at Lancaster Leaf after he'd shipwrecked at Franklin and Marshall. He was twenty-one. He was the responsibility of two other executives, not me, thank God, because if you leaned on him too hard he would run to his father. I remember that he drove a big yellow Ford as a company car, and within no time at all [he] became a general aggravation."

Van Huystee's father, an important businessman in Europe, had started his son off at the bottom. One day van Huystee suggested to Benny that he do the same with Steven. Benny ignored the suggestion; it suited him, for some reason, not to give Steven a title or a job description. That, says van Huystee, did not help Steven at all. "I remember that he sent him to Manila once, and when Steven got there I received a cable from one of my men." It read, "The little shit has arrived—and on first class!"

While van Huystee has a negative opinion of Steven's worth as a businessman, he still believes that whatever judgment is passed on Steven, a share of the good and bad should go to Benny. "[His father's] influence made him what he was. He saw that his father commanded people, so that's what he wanted to do."

Manny Murray points out that for all his softness in dealing with his children, Edward Benson was a tough guy in the business world.

And it was a tough world in which he operated, especially as a newcomer to the Lancaster area. One longtime businessman who is not in tobacco nonetheless observed it with fascination over the years. "Two or three tobacco firms would control the whole county. They'd have lunch, and say, 'What are we going to pay this year? Tell you what, we'll have only two buys or maybe three. I'll go out at seventy-five cents, and if a farmer holds out on me for more, then I won't go out any more, and I'll tell all of them I'm not interested in any more tobacco.' But then that owner would tell the others to go out at, say, sixty-five cents, or sixty cents. For what's left they would give the farmers two cents more per pound so they wouldn't keep it until spring in hope of a better price. Then the tobacco companies would divvy it all up, based on the average price. Now that's antitrust. But they've pulled that for *years* and *years* and *years* around here.''

If the farmers, or some of them, got bold, held out, and did not sell their tobacco until spring, the prices would be considerably lower. "Or," says this observer, "sometimes the companies would say that they weren't going to buy *any* tobacco that season, and the farmers would panic, and the price would drop to something like thirty-five cents a pound."

Now, he says, the farmers have finally gotten smart. They hold an auction for their tobacco, which has created interest on the part of out-of-town buyers, and that gives the farmers some protection.

Harry Hitchcock was a genius at competing with the established tobacco powers. "And," says a man who knew them both quite well, "Benny was a workhorse. He was always on a plane for somewhere, and in those days, going to Manila, for example, wasn't as easy as it is today. You had to change planes several times; it took forever, but Benny would go, go, go."

After a while, Edward Benson sent Steven out to check on the various tobacco factories that Lancaster Leaf owned in the United States. Steven started out by driving each day to Mount Joy, ten miles from Lancaster, where the company had a factory and a warehouse. There, he met the woman with whom he had an affair while still married to Nancy.

Later, when he and Nancy were separated, Steven was sent to Virocqua, Wisconsin, to check on another factory. According to Carol Lynn, on one of his first days there he met Debra Larson, a young married factory worker who eventually became the second Mrs. Steven Wayne Benson, the mother of his three children, and the wife who was nowhere in sight when he stood trial.

After a few years, even Edward Benson had to admit that Steven was not—to put it charitably—making much of a mark in the family business. Those years, the last of his life, were hard for Benny. His sister-in-law, Janet Murphy, recalls that he would come home and seclude himself in his small "office" on the first floor of the house on Ridge Road. "I can recall many nights that he'd be sitting alone in that room and meditating."

The "office" was the power center of the house, and the house was the focus of the Benson clan's universe. Originally, it had been the dining room, but after one of the many remodelings it became Mr. Benson's own special room. Each night after work he would come in, go directly to the den, mix himself a Chivas Regal and water from the decanter on the sideboard, and sit at the desk. His family would gather in their respective chairs before him.

"The whole family would talk," Carol Lynn recalls. "My mother would take the first chair, because it had a footstool, and then Steven and I would 'fight' to see who got the other comfortable chair. It wasn't that my father would summon us, or we'd come in like we'd been ordered to, but Daddy liked to use his den, and his chair there was better for his back.

"We'd talk about whatever family business needed to be talked about. I can remember once, years ago, we were in there, and Scott was in the kitchen screaming at my mother. Steven was amazed and said, 'Gee, Father, if Carol Lynn or I did anything like that you'd have knocked us across the room.' "

"Father" was the favored term of address. Carol Lynn called him "Daddy," as did Scott when he was a young boy, but Steven generally called him "Father." While she was Steven's wife, so did Nancy Ferguson.

Edward Benson was a relatively formal man. As Manny Murray, a friend for almost three decades, recalls, "Benny was not the kind of guy who would say to another man, 'Hey, let's go fishing' or 'let's go hunting.' " If it wasn't work, it was a formal social affair.

"Take bridge. When you went to their house for bridge," says

Manny, "it was very, very formal. Everything had to be gourmet, and you had to be really proper. You didn't take your coat off to play bridge, even if it was hot as hell, which it always was because Margaret always needed a lot of heat. It was that type of life."

Willem van Huystee remembers not only the formality, but also the increasingly expensive entertaining. "After a while," in the mid-sixties, "when they got their big money, they became a hard couple to keep up with. It wasn't that they were any less friendly, but they could afford to go out and spend a hundred dollars on dinner and think nothing of it."

And spending was a favorite pastime. One friend and business acquaintance of Edward Benson said that both the Bensons liked to go to auctions and estate sales, and that Benny seemed to get the most pleasure out of finding a bargain. "He would never buy, say, a table, simply because he liked it. He would buy a table for fifteen dollars and then later sell it for a hundred and that's what he would talk about. It was always that kind of table."

Another man who knew Edward Benson well (but who asked that his name not be used) said, "I doubt if Benny ever paid full price for anything. I did one job for them, but there was always something wrong with it, and they didn't want to pay all of the bill. Margaret would drive you nuts with changing her mind about the way she wanted things done, and with him it was always, 'Things cost too much, it can't be this expensive, this is what I'm going to give you.' So I agreed to take less, and after that one job I always managed to have an excuse when they called me again. But we stayed friends, and it was better that way."

Van Huystee says something that has a similar ring. "Benny was not comfortable with wealth. He wanted very much to be natural with it, but he couldn't manage. He found his money very hard to part with."

In contrast to this, Carol Lynn says there was a side to her father that no one, even his family, knew about until his final illness. He received numerous cards and letters of thanks from factory employees to whom he had made loans and gifts without telling anyone.

Yet another acquaintance believes that Edward Benson spent as much and as openly as he did because he knew that it pleased his wife, and above all he enjoyed pleasing his wife. "Ben didn't need these toys," says this person. "Margaret was the one who needed them, first the boat, the cabin cruiser, the house in Ventnor, the house up in Canada. This was all Margaret's doing. Whatever Margaret wanted, Ben wanted to give her." In Edward Benson's life there was work and family, and little else.

One Lancaster businessman who had been in on a number of deals with Edward Benson said, "No one ever got close to Benny. He wasn't the type of guy who would say, 'Hey, come over and we'll watch a football game.' Never. If anything was done, it was done with Margaret. It was always a couples situation."

And a lot of what was done was for show. "As soon as they got something new, they wanted to throw a party and show you. Like when they put a new swimming pool in, then the whole gang was invited for a Sunday afternoon swim. Or the tennis court, the same thing. That house was added to and added to."

At one point, Edward Benson decided to become a contractor himself, and he added to their colonial house what one friend called, "a stupid looking contemporary carport made out of cement blocks. It was really a hodgepodge. But they put a *lot* of money into the house, a lot of money. And the furniture was very gaudy, not in real good taste. There were a lot of wood carvings, and trinkets that he may have picked up in Manila or Malaysia or some place like that, a lot of that flavor around the house. A lot of what you call conspicuous consumption. Oh, yeah. And whatever Benny bought was always 'the best,' at least in his opinion."

Carol Lynn also takes issue with any suggestion that her parents' home was decorated in poor taste.

Manny Murray was the builder, and he remembers with affection the whole group of friends that included Margaret and Edward Benson. He has a vivid recollection of the latter's personality: "Benny never joked. Benny didn't laugh. Or if he did, it was a nervous laugh. Margaret was more fun all around."

Willem van Huystee makes a similar point, in somewhat less delicate language: "I never saw Benny laugh a full pee-in-your-pants laugh. Margaret could cut loose on occasion, but not Benny. And Margaret could laugh at herself, but not Benny; he wouldn't tolerate that. Benny's laugh and Steven's laugh were the same, dry."

If van Huystee exhibited a grudge or hard feelings against Edward Benson it would be understandable in light of the fact that the two had a falling out that caused van Huystee to leave Lancaster Leaf after more than a decade with the company. The parting was so bitter that Edward Benson went out of his way to make things tough for van Huystee—now in a tobacco importing business of his own—even to the point of telling bankers in town not to lend him any money. But several years before Edward Benson died, he sought a reconciliation, which clearly pleased the younger man.

Willem van Huystee speaks easily now of his onetime boss and friend, and with what seems an excellent memory. "I can still see Benny, wearing his Hickey-Freeman suits and chain smoking those Viceroys. But he'd always put a pack of our customer's cigars in his coat pocket before he went out on a call. He used to drink Chivas Regal, on the rocks mostly, and he'd have wine and brandy, but I never saw him drunk. He could relax when he was overseas on business—though he never fooled around; he was totally loyal to Margaret. He liked the Philippines and he liked getting his picture in the paper. Our Chinese partners always made sure of that.

"He always wore his hair combed straight back, and dressed very conservatively. Benny had a tremendous amount of self-control. He'd had polio as a child, and it left him with a certain oddness to his walk, his gait. He kind of rolled a bit. Toward the end of his life there were times when he would sit down and say, 'heart attack,' but he never actually had one. I think it was probably anxiety.

"Benny is a good memory for me, not a bad memory for me, on balance. But Margaret is a happy memory."

Manny Murray laughs at one particularly vivid recollection. "If you were having bridge, they were always late. They were never there on time. And if they said, 'Bridge at our house tonight. Cocktails at 6:00 and dinner at 7:00,' forget it. Dinner would be at *ten*. They always ran late. And sometimes it would get so late that it was too late to play cards. Never on time, never." Those who knew the family agree that it was Margaret's tardiness. Edward Benson was a model of punctuality.

"But I must admit that they were very generous with their holdings and belongings. They would invite us down to the shore and were very good hosts."

Another friend from the group recalls that Margaret and her "projects" were a favorite topic of discussion. "She was always going to tear something out or put something in, and spend a big pile of money. Change all the furniture or tear the back wall out. Always something."

Like other couples of the time, the Bensons and their friends took candid camera shots on vacations and business trips. In so many of these pictures, while the others may be smiling, even mugging for the camera, Edward Benson stands back, only the hint of a smile on his lips.

Willem van Huystee, who appears in many of these pictures because he and his wife made many trips with the Bensons, has a theory about why his friend smiled the way he did, why he lived the way he did. "In Dutch we have a term for it, 'tiny heart,' and we use it to describe someone who is afraid to show their heart, how they really feel. Now Harry Hitchcock, he has a very large heart and shows it. But Benny, I'm afraid, just could not show his."

Steven Benson's involvement with Debby, the Wisconsin woman who in the late 1970s became his second wife, was a watershed of sorts. The relationship did not thrill his parents—though Carol Lynn swears they tried hard to make Debby feel welcome—and it may have been the occasion for his father's final loss of faith in Steven's future with Lancaster Leaf. If it wasn't, then the timing was unusually coincidental, for Edward Benson's friends and colleagues all pinpoint this time as the period when he became more and more, to use the word a surprising number of them used, "somber."

The Virocqua Leaf Tobacco Company in Virocqua, Wisconsin, a small town in the southwestern portion of the state, is a subsidiary of Lancaster Leaf. Its "plant" is little more than one medium-sized building where the company buys and receives Wisconsin tobacco. The basic sorting or picking, the process by which foreign objects such as chicken feathers and bottle caps are removed from the tobacco, also takes place there. This menial task is performed by a handful of minimum-wage employees, and the rest of the operation is also relatively simple.

In 1978, Steven Benson, the boss's son, arrived from Lancaster on a routine inspection tour. When he walked into the plant to check things out, he himself was being checked out by one of the pickers and sorters, a young married woman in her early twenties by the name of Debra Franks Larson. There amongst the tobacco leaves she saw what she wanted.

Later she told Carol Lynn, " 'I saw Steven come into the factory and I knew he was the boss's son and that he was either separated or divorced, and I made up my mind right then to get him. Of course I didn't want to be too obvious about it, so I brought a girlfriend along, later that day, when Steven took us out for drinks."

Steven's attraction to Debra was instantaneous. According to Carol Lynn, the trip to Wisconsin turned out to be much more than an inspection tour. Before Steven got back to Lancaster with

Debby he had taken her and several members of her family to a dude ranch in Montana. They lived together for about a year, right across the street from his parents and next door to Carol Lynn. Sometime that year there was a quick trip to the Dominican Republic for a divorce. Carol Lynn says, "Steven and Debby were married on June 7, 1980, and, as far as I'm concerned, there's been nothing but trouble since then."

Carol Lynn has never attempted to hide her dislike for her sister-in-law. As she told the police from her hospital bed in Boston, less than three weeks after the bombings, in reference to her mother's will, "Not only was there concern that Steven would go through his money in twenty-four hours with some big scheme, there was also the problem of Debby. Because she under no circumstances wanted Debby to get a grain of sand that might have belonged to my mother——" and then, as if what she had just said might not have been sufficiently clear: "of any kind."

She continues, "We were trying to think of all sorts of different ways a will could be worded so that even if Debby divorced Steven she couldn't get any of it."

But if Debby introduced discord into the Benson household, it was only part of what made Edward Benson so somber toward the end of his life. Various people who knew him well suggest various reasons, including Scott's increasingly troublesome friends and their behavior. No one knows for certain, but it is likely that Edward was affected by all of these things. And, of course, there was Edward Benson's cancer.

Willem van Huystee put the problem in an interesting perspective: "Who knows if Benny's being so somber was caused by the cancer—or vice versa?" The only thing that was certain was the speed with which it took him.

Carol Lynn recalls, "Steven and my mother accepted that my father was dying. My father and I—oh, we both knew he was dying—but we took the approach that he wasn't dying *tomorrow*. My mother refused to ask the doctors in New York any questions at all, which made me *so* angry. So I had to do it. I can still picture myself cornering the doctor out in the hall; my mother wouldn't do it. She had no hope at all, even though at that point the doctor said the prognosis was about a year."

Illness and aggravation were taking a heavy toll on Edward Benson during this time. Margaret confided to a close friend that she and her husband had not made love for a year. Later, she told another friend that it was more like several years. She said she had no doubt that her husband loved her—no doubt at all—but she regretted the fact that he found it so hard to express that love.

In the autumn of 1980, it had all begun to come apart. For more than a year, Edward Benson had been on the verge of calling it quits and retiring from Lancaster Leaf. He announced he would retire on January 1, 1981. Between what he had earned and what his wife had inherited, they would not have to worry about living comfortably, as long as spending was kept under reasonable control. He was tired of fighting with Universal, and—if he would ever admit it—disappointed in the way his children's lives were turning out.

Carol Lynn had not remarried, and had made scant progress on her often discussed career plans. As a businessman, Steven was a disaster, pure and simple. Young Scott, then a sixteen-year-old high school junior with dreams of becoming a tennis pro, was a loving and affectionate son with an almost total lack of self-discipline—and an increasingly dangerous social life.

So Edward and Margaret Benson decided that he would retire and they would move to Florida. Perhaps there, they would get more enjoyment out of life in a new and warmer Paradise.

In 1979 Fred Merrill was working for the Mueller Company selling real estate at the downtown office on Fifth Avenue South in Naples, Florida. The Bensons walked in one morning and wanted to take a look at some real estate. He showed them a number of houses then available in Port Royal, the premier residential section of town, but they found nothing of particular interest and went back home to Lancaster. Eventually Merrill sold them a beautiful, large residence on Galleon Drive, one of Port Royal's most desirable streets. Behind the house were ample docking facilities for the boat the Bensons said they planned to buy. Fred Merrill recalls that a five-thousand-dollar difference almost scotched the sale of this property, which went for just under half a million dollars. He also recalls that in the end it was the Bensons, not the seller, who gave in.

Shortly after the sale, by which time the Bensons and the Merrills had become better acquainted, Edward Benson brought some household belongings down to Naples in a car that he planned to leave there, and he went to the new house to begin getting things in order. Late that afternoon, Fred and Bette Merrill drove over to lend a hand and to invite him to dinner that night.

"He begged off, saying he was tired and did not feel well. He said he was going to leave the next day to go back to Lancaster because he was scheduled for an operation on his hip." While Fred Merrill recalls Edward Benson looking tired on that occasion, Bette Merrill says she noticed a marked difference.

"He didn't act himself," she says, in her native Mobile, Alabama, drawl; "he didn't talk like himself, and he didn't have his usual energy. I said, 'Benny, why don't you come over to the house for dinner tonight?' and he said, 'Oh, I am *exhausted*'—I didn't think he'd done *that* much—'and I'm going to go back to the motel and just go right to bed.' Later I said to Freddie, 'Gee, he didn't look good to me.' His face just looked really——"

Fred Merrill interrupts, "I met him the next morning for breakfast at the Clock Restaurant and we had breakfast and I think I drove him to the airport. I guess his operation was scheduled for a day or two after he got back. I didn't hear anything for a while, and then I called, and the sequence of events, as I recall it, is that they opened him up and found him all full of cancer, and immediately shipped him up to New York to Sloan-Kettering.

"I tried to call up there and ask about his condition and maybe talk to him, but I couldn't get through. Margaret was up there spending most of the time right with him. Within a month he was dead.

"Margaret was upset because here they'd bought the house, and he really had no chance to come down and enjoy it. She wanted him to be able to come down and *enjoy* sitting out on that patio, enjoy the weather and the sunsets. Margaret was just very disappointed."

There had been two trips from Lancaster to Sloan-Kettering in New York City, the first one to see if the doctors at the famed cancer institute would accept Benny, and then another trip only weeks later when the next bed opened up. On both trips, Edward Benson had his own nurse, his and Margaret's longtime friend, Mary Miller Glose, who had been a registered nurse before taking over her first husband's home improvement business after his death.

She recalls both trips well, in part because she was bothered by a clear impression that none of the family was taking Benny's illness seriously enough. Contrary to Carol Lynn's recollection that her mother and Steven had accepted the imminent death sooner than she and her father had, Mrs. Glose feels that they were all denying the reality.

On the first trip, Steven did the driving; Benny, Margaret, and Mary Glose rode. On the second trip they used a chauffeur, and Scott came along. "I remember," says Glose, "because he sat next to me in the back seat and complained under his breath that he was missing a tennis tournament."

Another reason she feels that Margaret was denying the severity of her husband's illness was that during the time he was in bed at home, one of the private-duty nurses, recognizing that his condition was terminal, suggested that he would be happier and more comfortable with hospice care given in the home. That nurse was summarily fired.

"In the afternoon of the day Benny died, Steven's wife Debby asked me, 'What's happening?' " It was obvious to Mary Glose that she didn't know how serious his condition was.

After his chemotherapy treatment, the doctors at Sloan-Kettering let Edward Benson go back home to Lancaster, under the agreement that a Lancaster doctor would check his condition daily. An instant hospital room was set up on the first floor of the house.

He checked on Benny once, soon after he came home, according to Carol Lynn, but they never saw him after that. Still angry more than six years later, Carol Lynn says, "Every day my father got progressively worse. And *seriously* worse. One day my father was walking with a cane, the next day he had to be in a wheelchair, and the next day he couldn't even get up to get in the wheelchair.

"I was getting ready to leave for Florida, but Mary [Glose] kept saying to me, 'Carol Lynn, I don't think you ought to go.' But I had no reason to believe he was dying. The doctors had told me he was going to live a year. He was supposed to go back up to New York to be checked over again in two weeks, before we went to Florida for Thanksgiving.

"One morning, suddenly, he couldn't breathe. We wanted to get him into the hospital, but we couldn't even *find* the doctor. So I called Daddy's doctor at Sloan-Kettering, and he said, 'Don't you worry, I'll get your father into the hospital. There's no reason why he should be in this conditon; I don't understand why he's in this condition. But get him stabilized and we'll get him right to New York.' "

Several hours later and, according to Carol Lynn, noticeably past her father's medication time, her father's internist finally showed up at the hospital. "He checked on my father, and my father's condition was getting worse and worse and worse. This was on a Friday or a Saturday, and the doctor said, 'Okay, we'll see him on Monday morning for tests.' and he *leaves*!

"Well, we were getting just frantic. Mary was getting upset. My father's breathing is more labored, and he is comatose. And this sister comes in, the head of the hospital, who knows my father, and asks if there was anything more they could do for him. And I say we really wanted him to have another CAT scan but we'd been told the machine had been turned off for the week-end. So she goes and gets them to turn on the machine again."

Mary Glose recalls this scene, but she also remembers the family's inability to see how very near death Edward Benson was. "The idea of a midnight X-ray was ridiculous, but Margaret was determined to keep him alive until the next morning so they could get him up to Sloan-Kettering. I took one of the nurses aside and said, 'At least give him a shot for pain, if he's going to be put on a gurney and taken up in the elevator and bounced around in his condition.' "

Carol Lynn describes what happened next. "They took my father down there, and by this time all his veins had collapsed, but they were able at least to take an X-ray. And we *still* don't know where our doctor is. Steven keeps calling and calling and calling, from the nurses' station, but no doctor. Here my father is *dying* in the hospital, and he can't be reached. Finally his partner calls back and says he really doesn't know anything about it and will 'try' to reach him. So they don't really give a shit!

"After a while even the partner won't return our calls. And it really isn't a big deal for the doctor to come in, because we all only live two minutes from the hospital. Eight blocks."

At around 10:00 P.M., Carol Lynn sent for a priest. Margaret was in and out. Mary Glose was still there, doing what she could to help. Steven and Carol Lynn had never left since their father had been brought in.

"Around 11:00," says Carol Lynn, "I was out in the hall, and I still didn't know what was going on. My father's veins had collapsed, he could no longer breathe, he was gasping for breath, unconscious, and we couldn't get hold of the damn doctor.

"So once again Steven and I were standing at the nurses' station, trying to get the doctor, and we decided that if we didn't reach him that time, Steven was going to drive over and drag the son-of-a-bitch bodily back to the hospital.

"At this point one of the nurses came over and said"—here Carol Lynn lowers her voice in imitation—" 'I really shouldn't tell you this, because I could get into trouble, but I've been sitting here listening to you trying to get hold of your doctor, and I think there's something that you really need to know. I don't think your father is going to live until my shift is finished—and I get off at 11:30. I've seen your father's X-rays, and he has no lungs left. Your father is drowning.'

"And that was the first I heard of it!" says Carol Lynn. She asked the nurse, "Can't you do *something*? We just need to get him stabilized, to get him to New York. The doctor said——"

The nurse interrupted her, "We can drain his lungs, but it isn't going to do any good. There just isn't anything left of them. They're just going to fill right back up again."

"She was very serious," Carol Lynn remembers.

"At this point Steven was on the phone with the answering service, and he really gave them hell: 'My father is *dying*. You get a hold of him right now or I'm going to come over and get him myself.' Well, the doctor was there in two minutes.

"He walks in. Walks into my father's room. Walks out, and says, 'Your father just died.'

"At that point I became hysterical. Absolutely totally screaming hysterical. There are two things that I can remember, absolutely vividly, people saying to me at that moment. One was, 'Dear, you have to be quiet. You're disturbing other people.' Well, at that point, I didn't give a . . . whatever . . . about anybody else. And two, somebody saying, 'Dear, you'll just have to get hold of yourself because your mother needs you now.' I didn't need that either.

"Nobody had any sympathy for me, nobody cared how I felt, nobody cared how I was reacting. The only thing anybody could say was that I wasn't allowed to grieve because I had to be there for my mother.

"But if anybody needed comforting it was me, because my mother had resigned herself to my father's death, as had Steven, a month before. My mother had told me that she had cried for my father then—not that she didn't cry after his death, and not that it wasn't a terrible moment for her—but she and Steven had comforted each other. They had sat with their arms around each other and they had cried and cried and cried for a couple of hours.

"But, for me, it was a horrendous blow. Because the doctors had told me that my father wasn't supposed to die; I had had the doctor on the phone that day tell me that this shouldn't be happening. I managed to live with it only because I thought that God does things for a reason."

Edward Benson, aged sixty, was buried in November 1980. The funeral service was held at St. James Episcopal, Lancaster's finest and most socially acceptable church. There were eight active pallbearers and fifty honorary pallbearers, and guests came from all over the United States, from Europe, and from as far away as the Philippines. They also came from the best families of Lancaster, including the tobacco families.

Noting this, one businessman who was aware of the feuding that had gone on between some of these families and the Bensons, said to his wife, quietly, during the service, "I guess there's honor among tobacco men after all."

Two

The Florida Bensons

The Widow Margaret

The people who knew Margaret Benson well as a widow have repeated one statement of hers, one comment she made to each of them, that characterized her life before the death of her husband. They recall her saying, "Until Benny died, I had never written a check in my life."

Whether she meant this literally or not, Margaret Benson clearly had not been the one who paid the family's bills, and she certainly had never balanced a checkbook.

All of that changed, however, when she moved to Florida and found herself, for the first time in her life, in charge of the money that was now all hers—by birthright and by dint of Edward Benson's hard work.

And for those who wonder about such things, the amount of money that she had access to hovered in the neighborhood of ten million dollars—which is, as they say, a very pleasant neighborhood.

One should be cautious, however, about picturing Margaret Hitchcock Benson as the stereotypical widow who is made to handle the family finances for the first time in her life. In contrast to the comments of people who knew her as a widow are those of people who knew her and her husband during the years of their marriage. Jane Newcomer and her husband, Federal Judge Clarence Newcomer, Mary Miller Glose, and the van Huystees, for example, paint a somewhat different picture.

These friends recall a Margaret Benson who, while clearly devoted to her husband, was very much accustomed to getting her own way. Both Judge Newcomer and his wife agree that if there were a difference of opinion as to social plans or some project regarding their homes, Margaret would always say she'd do whatever Benny wanted to do. "But then, somehow," said the judge, "they'd end up doing what Margaret wanted."

He says, unequivocally, "Margaret called the shots in the family. Both *would* do what the other wanted, but Margaret usually got her way."

Jane Newcomer recalls that when Margaret would talk about one of their homes she would refer to it as "*my* home in Ventnor" or "*my* house in Canada," not "our" beach house or "our" lodge. "And," says Mrs. Newcomer, "Benny accepted this."

Janet Lee Murphy, Margaret's sister, remembers something similar. "It was some years ago, and Margaret wanted to buy something, a big purchase. One of the houses, I believe. And Benny didn't want to. They argued and argued about it, and then finally Margaret said, 'Well, it's my money, and I want to buy it, and I'm going to.' Benny gave in, and she bought it, whatever it was. Later Margaret told me that was the last time he ever said anything about her spending. She said he never mentioned it again after that."

Carol Lynn affirms this. She says her mother explained that many of the major purchases were made with *her* money, and so her husband was "not going to tell her that she could *not* spend it the way she wanted to spend it."

Willem van Huystee feels that while Margaret was "smart, she was also simple," in the good sense of the word, and that she may have been overwhelmed, at least initially, by her new "freedom." He also feels that she had done a good many things just to please her husband and to live up to what she perceived as her place both in her family and in society; and then when her situation changed, she was set adrift, at least emotionally.

"Maybe," he muses, "that quiet Margaret we usually saw was not the real model. When I heard that she was breezing around Florida in a Lotus and a Porsche 928, I got the impression that she might have been having a second childhood down there. I'd always had the feeling that she didn't get a chance to blossom under Benny."

Scott's tennis mentor, Anna Kuykendall, agrees. "When Benny and Margaret were married, I always felt much younger than Margaret. Margaret was kind of quiet, and she dressed in earth tones, very sedate. And she used very little makeup, usually none. . . . She always reminded me of someone much older than I. And she always needed help. I felt *protective* of her. But after Benny was dead," she said in 1987, "Margaret just bloomed out. You wouldn't believe it. She lost weight. She started wearing shorts. Put blonde in her hair. I even accused her of having a minilift, and she said, 'You'll never know.' But she never denied it. 'Oh, Anna,' she'd say, 'you're always trying to find out things. I'm just real young and pretty.' Her personality came out. That's all you can say."

Gerald (Jerry) Hester, who lived next door to Margaret's first house on Galleon Drive in Naples, says Margaret was "almost demure" when he first met her. Others noticed this too, commenting, as did Anna Kuykendall, on the fact that after moving to Florida Margaret began to dress far more colorfully. But Jane Newcomer cautions that some of this change was simply a reaction to her no longer having to "dress Lancaster."

As for the question of Margaret's handling money, Fred Merrill says that Margaret may never have written a check while Benny was alive, "but I'll tell you, did she learn fast!"

The house that she and Benny had bought, but in which only she and the children got to live, was a beautiful example of Naples at its best. Made of stucco and stone with a handsome gray tile roof, the house sits at the apex of a horseshoe drive and is separated from the street by lush plantings, a wide lawn, and a six-foot hedge. Two lighted pillars grace each end of the curved driveway. Set on a lot and a half, the house is on a canal that leads directly to Runaway Bay, which in turn leads fairly directly to the Gulf of Mexico. There is docking room for four boats. The outside of the house, in short, is classy. Inside, much the same is true, certainly in regard to the architecture and the room design. Margaret Benson had a great fondness for all that she owned, and there were those who felt her house was too crowded with furniture and "things." Those same people liked it when Carol Lynn occasionally prevailed on her mother to thin things out a bit. Several have vivid memories of Margaret's huge papier maché animals. "They were art works by Bustamante, the Mexican artist," laughs Carol Lynn, "an alligator and a baby hippo."

The monster living room, thirty-nine feet by twenty-four feet, was filled with furniture, as was the more often used lanai (what people in other states had called a "Florida room," and much of the furniture, even that of the casual variety, was large and bulky, if not heavy.

For those who wanted to be a little closer to nature, a thirty-five-foot-deep screened "yard" ran the full length of the house. Within it was the swimming pool. Anyone wanting privacy could retire to the roomy library at the eastern end of the house.

Although she did not do a lot of cooking—nor, as a matter of fact, had she done that much herself back in Lancaster—Margaret had the equipment for it. There were two wall ovens and two refrigerators to start with. A central island was used for food preparation. The kitchen was actually small, though, in comparison to the rest of the house.

Adjacent to the kitchen, on the west wing, was a large family room, at one end of which was a beautiful stone fireplace. This room had hidden pull-out doors that could close it off if another bedroom were needed—in addition to the huge master bedroom suite and the smaller second bedroom. It must be said that in Naples, even the finest homes seldom have more than two or three bedrooms. These homes are owned by people who have raised their families; their children are not apt to need to return to the nest.

All in all, a spectacular house in an equally spectacular neighborhood. And it should be no surprise that Margaret soon found some interesting and accomplished neighbors.

The Hesters soon became close friends. Jerry Hester, a very successful import-export businessman, speaks warmly of all the Bensons—except for Steven. "Ours was a normal neighbors-to-neighbors relationship. We exchanged pleasantries, and that sort of thing. We met Margaret and Carol Lynn and her children, Travis and Kurt, first. They were delighted to have us as neighbors and we were delighted to have them."

Jerry Hester, knowing that there was no husband in the house, often did small household repairs for Margaret, and says he was in her house probably as often as once a week. She would ask his advice on a variety of matters, usually how and where to find someone to take care of some larger problem around the house and grounds. He recalls, "I found Margaret to be a delightful person. She was a very sensitive person, a very caring person, and there was no indication of any excess of any kind, whether it be money or bad habits or morals, anything of that sort. We felt that she was inclined toward establishing a good, neighborly relationship. We also made her grandchildren welcome at our house. They fished with us off the dock, and we thought they were nice kids. That's Carol Lynn's kids. I never met Steven's children."

Hester observed Carol Lynn's boys closely. "They were thirsty and hungry for a father image, and when they were here [in Florida] they spent a lot of their time at my house because I had a lot of things going on—in the workshop and with boats—and they could talk and relate. Kurt was interested in aerospace activities and I'd been in that industry and could talk to him about that. Travis was getting interested in girls, and I used to kid him about that.

"Carol Lynn was just as nice a person as you would ever expect to see. So was Margaret. We extended many invitations to them to come and have dinner with us. Sometimes they would bring the boys and sometimes they wouldn't. Gradually we began to realize that there were few places that women could go into alone and feel comfortable, so we always felt that if we went to the Port Royal Club it would be nice to have them go with us, and often they did.

"On important holiday occasions we made sure we knew where they were and we'd invite them to our house. We had them over several times at Thanksgiving, and on New Year's Eve we would all go to the club together and dance and have a good time. Margaret, who loved to dance, was a fun-loving person."

Another new Port Royal friend was Olga Hirshhorn, the widow of Joseph H. Hirshhorn, financier and art collector, whose collection of modern sculpture and paintings is now the Hirshhorn Museum in Washington, D.C. She and Margaret became friends somewhat by accident; it stemmed from Margaret's rather surprising decision that her house on Galleon Drive was not big enough.

"We met when Margaret Benson was interested in building this *huge* house in Port Royal, and the neighbors and the neighborhood association decided it was too big. Most people felt it was too big for her lot. I had a lot that was larger than hers, so I called her and invited her to tea to discuss the possible purchase of my lot. She didn't buy my lot, but we became good friends."

Exactly why Margaret wanted a much larger house is not clear. Apparently she never told anyone just why she felt the magnificent Galleon Drive property was inadequate. Perhaps she did not know herself, considering the frequent turmoil of her life following her husband's death. And certainly Steven may have had a hand in the matter, for after a brief but spectacular failure in the tobacco business immediately after his father's death, he turned to his mother for financial support for various entrepreneurial ventures. But Steven's involvement could not explain why she wanted such a *big* house. Carol Lynn may be closest to the truth when she says that her mother simply wanted a house big enough for all her things. "Remember," says Margaret Benson's only daughter, "my mother had a warehouseful of furniture back in Lancaster, and the house on Ridge Road that had not yet been sold was filled with furniture."

Her plans varied. At first she was only going to add onto the house, then build a new one, then build onto the house she bought in Quail Creek (the house she lived in at the time of her death), and then finally a whole new property on several lots. And the square-footage figures continued to grow—from 18,000 to 21,000 to a maximum of 28,000 square feet. Olga Hirshhorn believes that Margaret did not fully comprehend how large the planned residence would be: "I told her one day that her architect should drive her down the Tamiami Trail and show her a *bank*, to give her some concept of what 28,000 square feet would look like."

Mrs. Hirshhorn agrees with Carol Lynn's suggestion that Margaret wanted such a big house because she had more furniture, and other objects, than would fit in a conventionally sized house. "She wanted a place big enough for all her possessions. Margaret loved to buy, loved to go to auctions. She was a compulsive buyer. I once told her that I had six antique chandeliers in storage, and she bought them all, sight unseen."

Judge and Jane Newcomer, who visited Margaret several times in Florida after she'd moved there, recall the time they went to an estate auction in Naples. Margaret bought some very fine jewelry. "By the time she was done she had spent about $65,000. Toward the end, when the auctioneer put up a mixed lot—watches and other jewelry—Margaret called out, 'What *else* will you throw in?' He said, 'You can pick an oriental rug out from upstairs.' So Margaret went up and picked out this *beautiful* Persian."

The two widows, Benson and Hirshhorn, hit it off. Says Olga

Hirshhorn, "We became good friends. We went to movies together. Because we were both widows, both living in the same
neighborhood, she could call me at the last minute, and say, 'Let's
do something, let's go to a movie,' and we did that a lot. I'm a
boat person and I operate my boat, a twenty-four-foot Boston
Whaler, myself, and Margaret wanted to learn how to do that.
We had a lot of fun. We even went to the swamp buggy races
once. I had hoped to continue this very comfortable friendship. . . ."

In addition to liking Margaret Benson, Olga Hirshhorn worried
about her. She was concerned that Margaret was too much of a
neophyte in the business and financial worlds. "Margaret was the
kind of person who was easily influenced. I knew that she was
providing the funds for Steven's businesses, and I knew she'd
had problems with Steven and Debby. And with Scott who, she
felt, was too dependent on her. She used to say, 'All he ever does
is play tennis.' But she always spoke well of Carol Lynn, with
whom she'd not had the problems she'd had with the other children."

That same failing, being too easily influenced, also bothered
Margaret's neighbor, Jerry Hester. "She was the kind of person
you could browbeat into something," he says. Margaret always
asked him for advice. "She didn't always take it," but she always
asked. Hester did not like, on principle, the idea of Margaret's
being in business with her own son. "The only advice I ever gave
her was, 'When you've got family involved in your business, you've
got trouble.' " He urged Margaret to get control over her money
and to find a competent and experienced financial adviser. There
is no evidence that she ever heeded this advice.

There is no question that in 1980, when her husband died, she
was unprepared to take control of the strings of such a large purse.

But Margaret was intrigued by the idea of being a businesswoman. And, having backed Steven in various (unprofitable) ventures over the years, she was receptive to his proposals, especially
after he joined her in Florida and began to use her Port Royal

house as his base of operations. Following her new friend Olga Hirshhorn's example, Margaret used part of her garage as an office, moving in a big wooden desk and several large metal filing cabinets. By 1983, she was involved in any number of small- to medium-sized companies set up by Steven.

Mr. Hester, her next-door neighbor for most of that time, continued to worry. "I was concerned. She told me about meetings she'd had with her [new] attorney [Wayne Kerr] in Pennsylvania, and said, 'Isn't an attorney supposed to do what you want him to do, not what he wants you to do?' And I said, 'Absolutely.' "

"She said, 'They're suggesting I do things I don't agree with. There are certain business relations and dealings that they want me to engage in and run my business in a direction in which I don't want it to go,' and I said, 'Well, you better get yourself another attorney. Or at least get a second opinion.' That was within a year of when I met her, say 1981."

"When I asked Margaret who this attorney was, she indicated he was a friend of her son's. . . . I didn't know the exact relationship, but it seemed there was a very close relationship with some member of her family, and I assumed that to be Steven, with this attorney."

When Hester heard this he said, " 'Uh-oh, we got problems right now.' I told my wife, 'When you get two, quote, experts, unquote, together, you've got double trouble.' We wanted a relationship with Margaret that would fulfill something in her life that wasn't there—and that was a good friend and a good neighbor, to Margaret and Carol Lynn both. And that was the way we tried to maintain our relationship with them."

That decision, however, did not keep the Hesters from worrying, because it was all too obvious that this was not exactly your model American family. "On many occasions, Margaret would be distraught and frustrated and bewildered as to why her son and his wife would treat her the way they treated her. With disrespect. With animosity. With outright rudeness.

"We couldn't understand this either, until she began to tell us, in confidence, that she had allowed Steven to become in effect her business manager. We began to observe this [business equipment] in her home, and we said, 'Margaret, get this kind of activity out of your house because your home is your home. You don't want a business . . . you've got a three-ring circus coming in here every day. You've got [Steven] coming down here every morning from Fort Myers, this secretary coming in, this housekeeper coming in, you've got this pool maintenance guy coming in, and you've got this boat maintenance guy coming in. . . . You've got *turmoil* here."

The Hesters were not the only friends who worried about Margaret. Fred and Bette Merrill were also becoming increasingly concerned. Not long after her husband's death, Margaret had told them that she was "just trying to figure out what I have." Fred had advised her to get a good estate attorney, as Jerry Hester had, but she ignored his advice as she had ingored Hester's.

It would be wrong to picture Margaret Benson as a weak person who could never say no to her children. While she clearly did not use that word as often as she should have, it *was* in her vocabulary, and she would definitely use it, but almost always after she had given in and said yes for far too long, and at too great an expense.

Her children had a pretty good track record when it came to asking for money. Steven led the pack, followed closely by Scott, with Carol Lynn considerably behind them, in part because Margaret definitely employed a double standard as far as the "needs" of men versus those of women were concerned. For instance, Anna Kuykendall once told Margaret that she saw no reason for Scott to have such expensive automobiles, and Margaret told her, " 'Oh, Anna, Benny always had fast cars. I wouldn't want to see Scotty in one of those cheap little things.' " One family observer said, "After Benny's death those kids drove Margaret crazy asking for money, demanding money, and from Harry [Hitchcock] too. They always had their hands out."

But when Margaret agreed to give it to them, she ran into some unexpected trouble. The fund she wanted to tap was the money their father had left, his estate, and while it was approximately one-tenth of what his wife owned, it still came to about $900,000. Edward Benson, however, had not watched his children grow up without noting their habits, especially their spending habits. Even though Carol Lynn was in her mid-thirties and Steven almost thirty at the time their father died in 1980, at that time only Margaret received any money. Carol Lynn explains: "Our estate lawyer convinced my father to leave the money in trust to the children for their 'old age,' because we stood to inherit from our grandparents, with mother receiving all the interest until her death."

Later, when Margaret called the old-line Lancaster attorney who had handled Benny's estate and told him who wanted how much and why, he startled her by saying that was impossible under the terms of the trust. That marked the beginning of a battle that ended with Wayne Kerr, the neophyte young lawyer from Philadelphia by way of a middle-class Lancaster background, as the sole legal representative of Margaret Hitchcock Benson.

Kerr had been recommended to Margaret by a rather unusual young stockbroker—at least he seems unusual for a stockbroker in Lancaster. Harry Glah, a broker for Dean Witter in Lancaster, is a local product whose father, a medical doctor, was in an investment club with Edward Benson and others for several years. What sets Glah apart as much as his shoulder-length hair is his iconoclastic attitude. Although his clients include Lancaster's elite, he does not aspire to those heights. And he felt Margaret needed a lawyer with that same point of view.

"Wayne Kerr is real smart," says Glah, who has the habit of talking to people very intensely from inches away (if you back up, he comes closer). "He has a C.P.A. degree, but he got bored with that kind of work so he went to Penn Law School and did real well. The main reason I introduced him to Margaret Benson was because he knows a lot about taxes, and she was having tax problems, but another important reason was that Wayne doesn't really give a shit about 'Old Lancaster.' He doesn't know any of those people, and he doesn't get or expect to get any business from them, so if he feels that the bank is screwing one of his clients, he can tell them to go fuck themselves. Which he did, on several occasions on behalf of Margaret Benson, and she loved it. He once got the bank to refund a *penny* in interest that they had overcharged Margaret, and she thought that was fantastic."

This new lawyer was looked on with great favor by Steven Benson. He may have figured that as the Benson estate lawyer lost influence over his mother, he himself would play a more prominent role. And he and Wayne Kerr *together*—well, that might make a most influential team. This is not to suggest that Steven had any illegal schemes in mind in those days, but only to point out that Steven welcomed Kerr's arrival on the scene with pleasure. That the two became friends was an added bonus; when Kerr got married, he chose Steven Benson as his best man.

At about that same time, Anna Kuykendall and her husband came up with an idea that would have given Scott something quite respectable to do, in light of the fact that he seemed to be the only one left who thought he had a chance at a career as a tennis professional on the circuit. They suggested that the Bensons fund a tennis camp in Naples. They would oversee it as directors, and Scott could be the teaching pro. By all accounts Scott *was* good with younger players; whether he would have had the self-discipline and requisite authority to handle the business and interpersonal ends of such an undertaking is another question.

Everyone liked the idea—until Steven got wind of it and tried to carve out a role for himself. Finally, Kirk Kuykendall shut the whole thing down, telling Steven bluntly, "I'm not dealing with you or with Wayne Kerr."

The question of Scott's tennis was to become a central one in Margaret's life. But few people had a fix on just how central. While one friend said Margaret lived for Scott and his tennis (a view Margaret herself expressed to Carol Lynn), another says she worried that he was too preoccupied with it and with his girlfriends. She wanted something more substantial for him to do.

Yet another says that she looked on it as the only way she could save him from his own nature.

As she adjusted to widowhood, Margaret Benson was at least *trying* to simplify her life, to make it somehow more manageable and therefore more enjoyable. But that was a huge task, in view of her history and her temperament. As Carol Lynn points out, "This is a woman who would get up at three o'clock in the morning to do her accounts."

Her relationships with her children remained tempestuous. For all their fighting and all their periods of estrangement, Margaret and Carol Lynn were close at the end. "My mother had become my best friend," says Carol Lynn. "If we didn't see each other as often as we would have liked, we talked on the phone daily. While my mother and Scott were in Europe that spring, we ran up an eight-hundred-dollar phone bill just chatting."

A rather large amount of give-and-take had been required for them to reach that point. Carol Lynn's life could hardly have been called a mother's dream. She had dropped out after completing a year of law school to marry, divorced soon after, and raised two sons, mostly in Lancaster, living either around the corner or across the street from her parents in houses they owned. She'd made several attempts at supporting herself, but was not able to do so, in part because she felt she was neglecting her children and in part because Lancaster is not exactly a hotbed of opportunity for single working mothers. After the death of her father, which she admits she took "very badly," Carol Lynn and her mother had a series of increasingly bitter arguments, which culminated in Carol Lynn's leaving town, unannounced, for Texas. "Only my grandfather knew where I was, in case of an emergency, and I'd sworn him to silence. After six months, I made up with my mother and went back to Florida." In 1982, she moved to Boston to begin work at Boston University on a master's degree in communications, and while her mother helped her find housing, there were moments of great strain. Margaret reminded her that *she* had passed up a graduate scholarship to marry her father. According to her daughter, Margaret felt that Carol Lynn should have been seeking a Mrs., not a master's. (Carol Lynn has a favorite anecdote: "I called my mother to tell her about the new position I had at the television station—head of production. I was *so* excited and proud. When I'd finished, she said, 'That's nice, dear. Now tell me about the important things. How's your love life?' ") By 1985, however, Margaret had apparently accepted her daughter's situation, and while she had not condoned it, the two of them ironed out their differences.

Margaret's relationship with Steven was equally intriguing and troubled, but in a very different way. While he was taking advantage of her—at first opportunistically and then, at the end, systematically—she seemed to be depending on him for any number of things, from buying boats to playing host at dinner parties. At the same time, her relations with Steven's wife resembled open warfare.

Steven's second wife, Debby, had been married when Steven noticed her among the sorters in the tobacco plant. Almost immediately, she had left her husband to live with Steven. While there was never any question that Edward and Margaret Benson did not approve of the marriage, Carol Lynn says that her mother was always polite and cordial to Debby, an observation also made by both Ruby Caston, Margaret's housekeeper, and Scott's girlfriend, Kim Beegle. True or not, the relations between mother and new daughter-in-law went downhill at top speed, and by 1984, and perhaps even earlier, Steven, because of his wife's ultimatum, no longer brought her and the children to his mother's house even though he was there almost every day. And Margaret was clearly not welcome at Debby's. "My mother could not go to Steven's house," says Carol Lynn, "without an appointment."

As for Scott, Margaret doted on him. Toward the end, she feared him. From the time he was about thirteen, he had been off at one tennis camp or another, living away from home for months at a time, sometimes in the homes of his coaches (as with the Kuykendalls) or in apartments of his own. Often, he was evicted from apartments because neighbors complained about loud music and wild behavior. Even as a young teenager, Scott had used nitrous oxide, or "laughing gas," and eventually this use became abuse. In 1983, while he was living in Florida with his mother, and on a day in which witnesses say he had been using the gas heavily, he got into such an angry and violent argument with his mother that the police had to be called to come and take him away. Under a Florida law that covers potentially violent juveniles, he was hospitalized for five days, during which time he was examined by a psychiatrist and finally deemed fit to return home. But his problems were not only drug related. In that same year, a former girlfriend filed a paternity suit naming him as the father of her daughter. By 1985, however, he seemed to have quieted down considerably, and while he had hardly given up laughing gas, marijuana, and cocaine, he was again living with Margaret and talking, if not playing, a good tennis game.

Her children's problems, while serious, did not occupy every hour of every day, and thus, little by little, Margaret Benson was able to carve out a new, and decidedly comfortable, life on her own. All by herself, she joined a tour group that went to China. In fact, she *met* the group in Japan. The next year she made a trip to the Holy Land with the Hesters, took boating lessons, and overcame a fear of water to take scuba diving lessons with her new friend Olga Hirshhorn; she even joined a singles club where she could dance, as Anna Kuykendall put it, "with an actual man."

Olga Hirshhorn remembers how brave Margaret was in her new pursuits. "It really bothered her that she couldn't drive a stick shift, and she was determined to learn so she could drive the Lotus. [Her Porsche 928 had an automatic transmission.] It seemed to me that, just before the end, she was much less uptight, much more relaxed. I think she was finally on the verge of becoming her own person."

Steven and Debby

When Steven's lawn business—and his landscaping business and his fencing business—did not work out, he had gone to work for his father and grandfather at Lancaster Leaf. It was part of a pattern that at one time or another absorbed many of the males in and around the Hitchcock and Benson families. And his fate was no better than theirs, for, with the single exception of Edward Benson, no one brought into the business because of his ties to a Hitchcock or a Benson female succeeded—not Janet Lee's former husband, Martin Murphy; not Carol Lynn's boyfriend, Scott's natural father; not her husband, Tom Kendall; nor any number of other boyfriends over the years.

Of course, in Steven's case the failure was sadder than in that of the others, at least to the Bensons and to grandfather Hitchcock, because he was a blood member of this fiercely clannish family. It should be kept in mind that this was a clan that had come out of nowhere, had begun with nothing, and had ended up owning about one-quarter of a very successful local, national, and international tobacco company.

Although Steven was not given a specific title or a specific job when he was brought in, it was clear from the beginning that he was the boss's son and the founder's grandson, and was being groomed for the top spot. His father took him on trips not just around the country but around the world. At first, he sent him out to factories not far from the home base of Lancaster. Then, for the better part of two years, Steven was made manager of Virocqua Leaf, in Wisconsin though he commuted from Pennsylvania.

People who worked with him at the time speak with warmth and admiration of Harry Hitchcock and Edward Benson, but not of Steven Benson. It is not that they dislike him, only that he was clearly not the man his grandfather and father were. As Lincoln Johnson—now seventy-five and formerly president of Virocqua before Lancaster Leaf bought a controlling interest—says with characteristic Midwestern directness, "He was a nice enough fella, but he was in the wrong business."

Kenneth Olson, foreman of the company and in charge of the warehouse when Steven held the top job, says that he was a good boss. His reason is that Steven would approve anything Olson wanted for the warehouse. "He spent hundreds of thousands of dollars on security devices and other modernizing equipment, which was great. The company could afford it, but he also put in a whole lot of stuff that we really did not need. He brought his own plumber and electrician from Pennsylvania, and they all stayed at motels and had rental cars, and Steven drove a big Cadillac or a Continental. None of it was what you'd call cost-effective."

Again, as in Lancaster, Steven was apparently more at home with the blue-collar work force than with fellow executives. One of the coworkers with him during that whole period said, "He should have been in production. That kind of stuff he was good at."

Steven did not work the kind of hours or schedule the other men did. If he came in at nine o'clock, he was apt to be gone by

Harry Hitchcock, approximately age
five, when he began his career
in vaudeville.

Margaret Hitchcock, also about five,
student of the dance. Years later, she
was to name her child after her
dance teacher.

Margaret Virginia Hitchcock Benson
in her twenties.

Harry and Charlotte Hitchcock and their girls.

Hughlett, as young Edward Benson was called by his family and friends.

Captain Edward Hughlett Benson,
U.S. Air Force.

Edward and Margaret Benson on their
wedding day, December 11, 1942.

"To my darling wife, Benny." During World War II, Captain Benson was a flight instructor for the Air Force.

Margaret and Carol Lynn, July 1944.

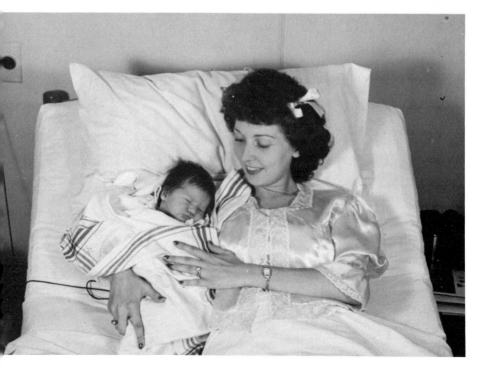

The Quadrille Dance Club. Margaret is third
from left in the first row. Benny is fourth from
left, standing. Fourth from left in the first row
is Mary Miller (Glose).

Margaret in a Lancaster fashion show in her
early thirties.

Benny in charge of the backyard barbecue.

Above: 1515 Ridge Road, Lancaster, Pennsylvania.

Right: The Hitchcock home on Hillen Road in Baltimore, where Margaret grew up.

Carol Lynn's house on Wilson Drive. Travis and Kurt, her sons, are in the yard.

The Benson Canadian ski lodge in Ste. Adèle, Quebec.

The summer home in Ventnor, New Jersey.

Carol Lynn with baby brother
Steven, 1951.

On the beach at Ocean City, Maryland. Margaret restraining Steven.

Steven on his own.

Carol Lynn and Steven.

Mother and son, backyard pool, Lancaster, Pennsylvania, 1955.

A happy Steven at two.   In grade school.

Steven Wayne Benson, obviously the youngest, as a member of the student government at Lancaster Country Day School.

Growing up.

High school. To this day, Harry Hitchcock keeps this photo of his grandson Steven in his home.

CAROL LYNN BENSON
Entered L. C. D. S. 1955

J. V. Hockey, 1, 2; J. V. Basketball, 1, 2, 3; Hospital Work, 1, 2, 3, 4; Art Club, 1, 2, 3; Chorus, 1, 2, 3, 4; President of Chorus, 4; Bazaar, 1, 2, 3, 4; Class Treasurer, 4; Yearbook, 1, 2, 3, 4; Chairman of Typists for Yearbook, 4; Drama, 1, 2, 3, 4.

Page of the Lancaster Country Day yearbook.

Carol Lynn, beauty queen, and her family. Left to right: Steven, Margaret, Carol Lynn, and Benny.

"BENNY"

From a 14 to a 7 with self control . . . blonde or brunette? . . . boys, boys, men . . . long, long eyelashes . . . homework? . . . just advanced math . . . I just can't express myself in writing . . . why no French this year? . . . summers in the Southwest, and Mexican signors . . . Ford Sunliner convertibles do mix with Jaguars . . . June's the month . . . girls or coed, I can't decide . . . saddle shoes . . . rings, jackets, sweatshirts, O. K., I've got everything . . . slumber party debates . . . I don't care, that's what I believe . . . no more F. and M. . . . nope!

. . . And a modeling session in New York.

Margaret with Carol Lynn's baby, Scott, whom she and Edward Benson adopted.

Carol Lynn and Scotty, who never knew Carol Lynn was his mother, summer 1966.

Steven, Carol Lynn, and Scott.

The Benson clan: Steven, Margaret, Scott,
Benny, and Carol Lynn.

Scott, Carol Lynn, and Steven.

"How do I look as a blonde?" Carol Lynn and Steven
horsing around with a wig.

Mother and daughter.

Carol Lynn's wedding day. Scotty is the ringbearer.

Margaret and Benny, dancing at their daughter's wedding.

Carol Lynn.

Benny and his Stutz roadster.

two-thirty. He also traveled to other tobacco facilities around the state, and when he did that he would be gone for several days. He was not the kind of manager the employees knew well.

"He must have spent," says Ken Olson, "half a million dollars remodeling the warehouse, alarm systems, new wiring. Some of it was necessary, but not all of it. Yet he was tight with his own money. He used to come in and ask me if I had any money in the cashbox. That got to be a regular thing. But he kept forgetting to pay it back. So one time his father came in from Pennsylvania, and I happened to leave the cashbox open, with all of Steven's I.O.U.s showing, which probably totaled a hundred dollars or more, and Mr. Benson saw it. He called Steven on it right away. He said, 'Go out to your car and get your checkbook and make this good, right now.'

"Steven was just kind of different. He was smart, but he had no horse sense. He was born with a silver spoon in his mouth, but he didn't know about tobacco. I have to say, though, he was a *genius* with electronics."

Olson says that on occasion Steven would join the rest of the workers for a beer at the American Legion Post on paydays, yet he says most of them remained kind of "leery" of him. "He didn't have any *enemies*, but I wouldn't say he was well liked."

When he returned from Wisconsin in 1979, he brought Debby with him, and, much to the displeasure of his parents, the couple lived together for almost a year before marrying. Steven went back to work at the main office of Lancaster Leaf, but he was no more successful there than he had been earlier.

Willem van Huystee recalls that it was a bad situation that soon got worse. Van Huystee himself had left Lancaster Leaf at this point—"It had become clear to me that I was no longer the heir apparent, and I got out." But with Edward Benson's death, the handwriting appeared on the tobacco plant wall for Steven, whether he knew it or not. He was quickly eased out. Steven retaliated by starting a business in direct competition with Lancaster Leaf. If his attitude toward expenses had been cavalier as an employee, once he was in business for himself they became downright grandiose.

A successful Lancaster businessman, who had known the family well, had a visit from Steven not long after Edward Benson's death. He recalls, "Steven came into my office, which is good-sized, and told me that he was going into the tobacco business for himself, and that he wanted my advice on decorating and outfitting his office. He said he had been downtown and looked at a floor, a whole floor, of the building that used to house one of the newspapers, but he said that was too small. 'Well, how much do you need?' I asked him, and he looked around my office and said, 'Oh, maybe about ten times this much space.' I asked him if he was planning to hire a large staff, and he said, no, just himself and a secretary, at first, 'But it's important to look successful.'

"Then he said, 'I can't use any of the office designers around Lancaster, but you must know some in Philadelphia and New York you could put me in touch with.' I said I did, and then I asked how much he had budgeted for decorating his offices, and he said, 'About a half a million.' I allowed as how he could get a pretty nice-looking office for that amount of money."

Steven did end up renting an entire floor from a Lancaster real estate broker. The man later reported to friends his amazement over the set-up: there were signs on each of the doors indicating "Marketing Division," "Electronics Division," and, of course, "Tobacco Division," but the rooms behind the signs were empty.

Not long after that, Steven rented space from Willem van Huystee, and though his office was only a room and a phone line, that did not stop Steven from naming the new operation with characteristic exaggeration.

"I think it was," says van Huystee, "something like, 'United International Industries, Incorporated.' " If it was a flamboyant name, it was also an unclear one. "No one could pin it down," says van Huystee. "Steven was hardly ever in the office, but he did get a lot of phone calls, which my secretary had to answer. So she began to shorten the name, just saying, 'United Industries,' or whatever, but he told her no, he wanted her to give the full name of his company each time she answered the phone.

"She gave him a long look, and then said, 'Go fuck yourself.' She thought he was a windbag."

According to van Huystee, Steven had been in his office only a few months when he managed, somehow, to get himself appointed United States agent for a Spanish tobacco importing company, and, in furtherance of that connection, Steven went to the Far East. He had been there but a few days when van Huystee got a call from a friend who claimed that Steven Benson was trying to take over his business. When Steven got back, he was told to find different office space. "My attempt at kindness," says van Huystee, "had fallen on infertile ground."

It was during this same period that Steven managed a feat that still causes van Huystee to shake his head in amazement when he thinks of it. "It really should be in the Guinness book of *business* records. Steven went to the Swisher Company, a huge tobacco company that was responsible for a great deal of the business of Lancaster Leaf, and a company with which both Harry Hitchcock and Edward Benson had had excellent relations. Indeed, you could say that Lancaster Leaf greatly depends on Swisher's business.

"Steven told the tobacco buyer, 'I'm going to put Lancaster Leaf out of business.' The buyer later told me, 'The kid made such an ass of himself that I almost threw him out of my office. I told him never to come back.' You know, that really takes talent, to be able to fuck up fifty years of a solid business relationship in one hour."

According to van Huystee, it all happened within a year and a half of his father's death. Not long after, Steven left the tobacco business and went south.

"He was obsessed with her to the point of idiocy." That is Carol Lynn's blunt assessment of the way her brother Steven felt about

Debby, his second wife. While others in the family are somewhat more polite, their opinions are not much different. Ruby Caston says, "He was crazy in love with her."

Carol Lynn's antipathy toward her sister-in-law has nothing to do with whether Debby or her family had money, but rather with the fact that she believed Debby never cared for Steven. "She admitted to my face that she didn't love him. I can remember it very vividly. I was getting ready to move to Florida, and we were standing in the parking lot—Debby had come over for something. It was either two or three days before they were to get married. And it was late afternoon, the sun was about to go down. I can see this *so* clearly. I'd walked out to the car with her, and we were standing behind it. And she said, 'I just don't know if I should get married or not.'

"I said, 'Why, Debby?'

" 'Well, I really don't love Steven.'

"And I said, 'If you don't love him, then I really don't think it's a good idea that you get married.'

This exchange took place, according to Carol Lynn, well over a year after Steven and Debby had met and begun to live together. But it was not eye-opening news. She'd felt from the beginning that Debby had spotted Steven, marked her target, and moved in for the kill. Steven was in the bag before he knew what had hit him.

"The first we"—meaning the family—"knew about her was when she showed up at Steven's house in Lancaster, bag and baggage." She had simply packed her bags, moved out on her husband, and come from Wisconsin with Steven.

"She moved into Steven's house. But right from the beginning, she never acted like somebody who cared about him. I have to admit that right from the start, I did not like her. My mother and father, while they didn't like her, didn't feel as strongly as I did. My mother did not approve of the fact that Debby was living with Steven without being married, but then my mother didn't *say* anything to Steven.

"My mother's position was, if that makes Steven happy, fine. I'll support anything that makes Steven happy. That was her position with Debby to the very end. She constantly went out of her way to be nice to Debby, even though Debby could not have been more vicious or more cruel.

"Debby was certainly not keeping Steven's house. The place was a complete disaster. She wasn't doing any laundry. She wasn't doing any cooking. She slept late, she was living the life of Riley."

In 1981, Debby Benson gave birth, by cesarean section, to twins, a boy and a girl, at Hershey Medical Center in Hershey, Pennsylvania, under the care of a special premature birth pediatrics team. One quiet night in quiet Naples, the following summer, when the family was all in Florida, Debby took the babies, and—without a word to Steven, who was on an overnight business trip—went back to Wisconsin.

According to his sister's interview with the police after the bombing, Steven almost went crazy:

Steven just absolutely adored the children, besides being crazy, crazy about Debby. And for months on end he would call, for hours, spend hours on the phone pleading with her to come back, and she wasn't interested. And a couple of times when she did allow him to come out, every time after he had been out there, he would be sicker. Steven's health had not been real great before, but during the time he had been married to Debby his health had continued to deteriorate, little bit by little bit, and then when the divorce thing was going through, every time Steven would go out there, he would have very serious attacks, almost like heart attacks.

In December 1986, in the comparatively relaxed and comfortable surroundings of her lawyer's office, Carol Lynn Benson Kendall elaborated on what she and her mother had watched Steven go through.

"Steven had to go out of town overnight for something—which he rarely ever did at that point, and which she didn't approve of because by then she ruled everything he did—and when he gets home the house is unlocked, the cars are there, and Debby is not there and neither are the children. Steven was just frantic. And the clothes are there; apparently she didn't take very many of the clothes with her or anything. She had just absconded with the children in the middle of the night.

"He thought they had been kidnapped. He was just panic-stricken. He was calling everybody. He came over to us to see if they were there. I don't know whether he contacted the police at that point, or what, but he was just terrified when he came over to mother's. He thought that they had been *abducted*, because that was what all the indications were: the clothes were there, the cars were there, and they were missing.

"It wasn't until a day or two later that he even found out where they were. I think he called [Debby's] mother to see if she had heard anything or if Debby had said she was going anywhere, and learned they were all in Wisconsin.

He had, according to Carol Lynn, "no inkling" that something of this magnitude was even in the offing. "He would call her from my mother's, hour after hour after hour, crying and begging and pleading with her to come back. But she wouldn't.

"An example of how she loved to torture him is what she did to Steven when he wanted to come out and be with the children on their first birthday, which fell in the week after Christmas. She kept refusing to allow him to come. Then, the day before Christmas Eve he was talking to her on the phone long distance from my mother's. It must have been about ten-thirty at night, and he had been on the phone with her for hours, begging and pleading with her.

"You could tell how she was speaking to him from the way he was reacting. You could hear him crying. It was just a heart-rending situation.

"So it got to be about eleven-thirty at night, very late, and she finally says to him, 'All right, I will let you come, if you get here tomorrow.'

" 'Tomorrow' is Christmas Eve! And to get to this place in Wisconsin from Florida is about an eight-hour trip, because you have to fly to Chicago, and you have to change planes and fly to somewhere else, Milwaukee, maybe, then you have to change planes *again*, and go to God knows where, and then you have to rent a car and *drive* for a couple of hours. So it is a *long* haul; it's not like flying to New York, or something, nonstop.

"It's eleven-thirty at night, and not only does he have to get a reservation for Christmas Eve, but he has to *be there* on that same day. So Steven was on the phone until about three o'clock in the morning, calling every airline, and finally he figures out a way he can get there.

"He hadn't planned to stay at my mother's house that night, but he was so depressed and so distraught that he did. The next morning we learned that he had finally gotten a [flight]—and it wasn't anything simple, like a direct flight to Chicago, but something crazy, like New Orleans to Tennessee to Kansas City to Chicago; it was going to take him all day. He was all ready, and he was about to race home and throw something in a suitcase, and he calls Debby. He wasn't allowed to call her until a certain time.

"You could hear her laughing on the phone. Then she hung up.

"He just sat there and cried . . . like someone had died."

Steven remained at his mother's house that day and again that night. "Mother said, 'Honey'—that's what she called him, 'honey'—'why don't you just stay here with us?' So he stayed there, and he was horribly depressed. I guess Debby wouldn't talk to him on Christmas Eve, but on Christmas Day he talked to her, and he begged and pleaded with her to let him come, and finally she said that he could. But he had to get there immediately!

"He had like twelve hours. So, again, he was on the phone and on the phone, and this time he managed to get there within the time limit that she had set. If he got there too late, she said she'd simply shut the door and not let him see the children."

About a year after she took the children, and during which time a petition for divorce was filed and then withdrawn, Debby Benson returned to Steven with the children. But she did so—according to a variety of Benson relatives and friends—with a clear-cut and, on Steven's part, clearly understood, set of conditions.

This was at the point when his mother's control of the Benson estate became increasingly central to Steven's business plans. Debby made it clear that Steven's contact with his family was to be minimal. Originally, says Carol Lynn, she wanted him to agree that he would have no contact with any of them again, but, seeing that Steven's mother was bankrolling the several businesses he had just started, so severe a stricture would have been unrealistic. She settled for his pledge that they would never live in the same city as Margaret, that Steven would talk to his mother only during business hours, and that none of his family would be allowed to visit Steven or Debby at their home. This last condition was enforced gradually, but by 1985, and perhaps even earlier, it was an absolute rule.

Carol Lynn says that Steven told both her and their mother, on several occasions, that "he lived in constant fear that he would come home one day and the house would be empty again."

Carol Lynn has her own opinion as to why Debby agreed to come back at all. As she told the police investigators in July 1985, Steven and Debby's divorce was pending, but in the interim Harry Hitchcock became ill, and all were very concerned that he would die. "When the news trickles down to Debby that my grandfather was so ill, suddenly she changes her tune and is more amenable to not having the divorce. Of course she had her whole list of conditions."

Carol Lynn's speculations aside, Debby did return, and she

and Steven did reestablish their household in Florida and even had a third child, a baby girl. Their home was not in the same town as that of Margaret Benson. There seems little doubt on the part of Margaret's friends that she and her daughter-in-law did not get along very well.

Jerry Hester recalls that on many occasions, Margaret would express frustration about the way her son and his wife treated her. She found Debby domineering. If Margaret wanted to see her grandchildren, Hester confirms, she had to make an appointment. Debby would go into a tirade if Margaret dropped in. In general, according to Hester, Margaret was very disturbed when they got back together.

Hester says, "Though we tried to stay away from all this stuff, we spent a lot of time in neighborly chats." During the course of the conversations, the talk would eventually get around to Steve, whom they had met at her house one evening, wearing a dinner jacket, pouring drinks, and playing host.

"And she would say, 'He lives in Fort Myers and drives down every day.'

"Margaret told us she never understood the marriage, but she went along with it because it was what her son wanted.

"I remember something she said when we were on the Holy Land trip with her. We were buying things, and she said, 'I don't have anybody to buy for, except my grandchildren,' and I thought that was strange, and I said, 'Margaret, for heaven's sake,' and she said, 'Well, Scott doesn't need anything,' so she got a few things for herself and for Carol Lynn. I bought a cross for my granddaughter, and Margaret said, 'That would be nice for my two granddaughters,' and she bought two of them. Later on when we asked her about the crosses she said that Debby threw them back in her face. It hurt Margaret tremendously."

Hester offers his assessment of Debby and Steven Benson, their personalities and their characters, and the effect they had on Steven's mother. "I could never understand why, under these circumstances, this thing developed the way it did, and the only answer I can come up with goes back to this relationship between Steven and his wife. From what Margaret had told me it is clear that this woman was a true rival of Steven's, and he had no control over her. I think she threatened to take their children and leave if he didn't do what she told him.''

Fred and Bette Merrill, Margaret's first Naples friends, came to hold much the same view. "Although Margaret was an optimistic person, and was very protective of her family to the point that we never *saw* any of these conflicts, we did come to understand the situation.'' It was hard to miss seeing the way Steven did things. As far as the Merrills were concerned, Steven had no real job, "But when he and his wife reconciled, she came down here and they rented a house. I remember being told that the house had three bedrooms, a pool, and all of that. *Still* I had no idea what Steven did.''

They were to find out. After picking Fred Merrill's brain for several months regarding real estate matters, Steven went into that same business. He worked for a Naples broker long enough to get his license, and then apparently went into business for himself.

Suddenly—and right after Steven got his real estate license— Margaret's beautiful home on Galleon Drive in Port Royal went on the market. The broker was *not* Fred Merrill, who had found the house for Margaret and Benny, it was Steven Benson. Merrill says that Margaret never said anything to him about it. "Perhaps she was too embarrassed.''

One of Fred and Bette Merrill's most vivid memories of the Bensons involves Steven and Debby. "We invited 'em for dinner—Carol Lynn, Margaret, Steven, and Debby. We had it all set up as a formal dinner party and everyone came. Steven and Debby came and brought the twins,'' says Merrill, his voice rising as if in amazement.

"So, Steven sat down there on the floor with the twins, and Debby was over there,'' he says, gesturing across the room, "and

Margaret and Carol Lynn and my wife and I were over here, and we chit-chatted for a while, and then I said to Bette, 'I think you ought to get started setting the table.'

"Then Steven or Debby, one of them, said, 'Oh, we can't stay for dinner.' And they didn't stay for dinner. They'd been *invited* for dinner, and hadn't said they could only come for a short period of time. But they got up and left."

Mrs. Merrill adds, "I had bought presents for the babies, only because I was such a close friend of Margaret's and they were her grandchildren. So I bought, as a matter of fact, silver wineglasses. I thought it would be a nice thing to store for the kids; somebody had done that for my children. Well, they're still in my closet. I never gave them to them. I mean I didn't want to after *that!*"

Later she told Margaret about the gifts and asked if she should give them to Steven and Debby, "And Margaret said, 'No, don't do it.' She told me many times she'd go and try and give the kids presents, and Debby would refuse them."

After the pipe-bomb deaths of her son Scott and her mother, Carol Lynn Benson Kendall still could not shake her belief that the pressures of Steven's marriage were a factor in this monstrous crime—a possibility that was also being considered by the police.

Among the things she said about Debby in recorded sessions with the police were these:

So [Steven and Debby] come back [from Wisconsin] and she has the other baby. And my mother, meantime, has been completely shut out of everything. Debby hated my mother. And she *told* my mother that she hated her. She told my mother that she was jealous of her money, and that she wanted everything that belonged to my mother.

. . . there were incidents where she exhibited violence toward my mother. I mean, you never knew my mother, but my mother was about five-foot-four, weighed about 110 pounds and [was] Little Miss Milquetoast if you ever met one. Always diplomatic, always said the right thing, because she never wanted to hurt anybody's feelings.

To illustrate the difference between the two personalities, Carol Lynn recounted an event that took place in Naples, before Steven and Debby were separated. Carol Lynn and her mother drove over to Steven's house to pick up the keys to one of Margaret's cars, which now were all at Steven's. While her mother waited in the car, Carol Lynn went to the front door and rang the bell.

I could see Debby sitting in there by the pool [but] she didn't come and answer the door, so I went around to the back and just stood at the screen door, and Debby still doesn't come so I finally said, 'Well, are you going to let me in?' Then she gets up and comes over, she unlocks the door and then just about slams it in my face. I said, 'Is Steven here? I'd like to speak to Steven,' because all I wanted to do was pick up a set of keys so my mother could have one of her cars. . . .

By this time my mother was getting a little concerned about what had happened to me, so my mother came to the front door and rang the bell, and Steven by this time had come in, and he answered the door, and I told Steven what we had come for, and Debby comes over and starts screaming at my mother, that how dare she show up at their house, and that she was never permitted ever to show her face at their house without having called for an appointment first, and started swearing at her and raised her hand. It seemed to me she was about to strike my mother.

. . . I stepped in between them and pulled my mother back. And Steven didn't say a word to Debby. If it had been my wife I would have given her a piece of my mind for having done that to my mother, but Steven was just so under her influence that he didn't. . . . I could see he felt bad for my mother, but he didn't come to her aid or anything.

After Steven and Debby's reconcilation, things still did not improve. Indeed, it could be said that they went from bad to worse.

Margaret, says Carol Lynn, was not allowed to see the grandchildren at all. She couldn't give them any gifts, and she wasn't to call Steven on the phone, even though Steven was her employee. If Margaret or Carol Lynn would call, Debby would slam the phone down and then take it off the hook.

Steven made no attempt to reconcile the women. Once Carol Lynn complained that he didn't bring his children to see their grandmother. "Steven wouldn't bring them down. That made me mad. . . . I didn't see why Steven couldn't stand up to Debby. I even said something to Steven about it, that I thought he should bring them down, and he got really, really nasty at me, and he told me to shut up.

"Steven was six-foot-two. He was big enough to pick up his three little kids and bring them in the car and say, 'I'm taking my children to see my mother whether you like it or not.'

"But Steven would never do anything at all to cross Debby. . . . Debby used the children as a manipulative tool . . . she knew she could run off with the children at any time with impunity, because she could run back to her little sanctuary in Wisconsin."

In 1985, not long before her death, Margaret Benson told Mary Miller Glose, one of her closest friends from the early days in Lancaster, that she was worried about Steven. "She said," recalls Mrs. Glose, "that he had 'too many things on him,' too much pressure, too much responsibility. . . ."

Mother and Daughter

An outside observer given access to the complete history of the relationship between Margaret Hitchcock Benson and her daughter Carol Lynn might well wonder if the two were in fact as close as Carol Lynn swears they were. Certainly they had, as Carol Lynn readily admits, their "off" periods. And they also had a very rough six-month separation following the death of Edward Benson. But long before the summer of 1985, all major differences seemed to have been resolved, and they were "fast friends" in the way that only a mother and her only daughter can be.

Carol Lynn firmly believes that it was preordained that they were allowed to make their peace before violence ripped their family apart.

"God didn't want me to die. I really believe that there was something there, some spirit that saved me. I have no doubt in my mind at all. It was necessary that I survive because I had to take care of my sons. My mother couldn't have done it, and certainly Scott could not have, and Steven and Debby *would* not

121

have. So I had to be saved. But God let me and my mother make up and become close again before the tragedy occurred."

Her mother's friends confirm that Margaret Benson and Carol Lynn were "good together." As mentioned earlier, Olga Hirshhorn says that Margaret always spoke well of Carol Lynn because her daughter had not given her the same kind—and *size*—of problems that her sons had. And both the Merrills and the Hesters link Margaret and Carol Lynn together when they speak, as if the two women constituted a couple or a family unit.

The friends also mention that whatever Margaret may have given Carol Lynn from time to time in the way of financial aid, Carol Lynn "earned" it, in the sense that whenever she visited her mother she did a lot of work for her. Both the Merrills and Olga Hirshhorn mention the elaborate dinner party that Margaret gave in early 1985, and they point out that while Carol Lynn prepared and served an excellent dinner, which consisted of several courses, she did not join the party. She ate in the kitchen, after which she cleaned up and did the dishes.

Apparently, this fitted a pattern. Carol Lynn says that for years, when she and her two young boys lived in Lancaster ("on very little money"), her mother would invite them to the beach each summer. But Carol Lynn would be expected to do everyone's laundry and cook all the meals.

And Jerry Hester recalls Carol Lynn telling him that Margaret had two sets of rules—one set for her and her children, and an entirely different, and very relaxed, set for Scott.

These relatively minor differences aside, Carol Lynn and her mother did a lot together and for each other. Carol Lynn was her mother's official, unpaid home furnishings and design expert, the one who did most of the driving to pick up this and that, the one who drew the rough sketches and saw that the various workmen followed them to her satisfaction.

As Carol Lynn told the police in July 1985, "my mother and I were very close, and we didn't have anybody else except each other. . . . But the way I think about families, families are the things of the world. You know, you stick by your family."

For Carol Lynn, it was not always thus. There were years at a time, when she was much younger, that she stuck by her family only in spirit. Physically she was far away. Carol Lynn always had "plans," grand designs, career and professional hopes, all of which were to be somehow sandwiched into that early dream of marrying an executive and giving him six little boys and six little girls. Chasing those dreams, and having at least part of that family—although she never married a successful business executive—was to lead her from Lancaster to Washington, D.C., to Texas and California, back to Lancaster, down to Florida, and then to Boston.

During all of that travel, and through all those seminars in the graduate school of diminished dreams, there was one constant: her belief in the importance of family, her single-minded insistence on the importance of being a Benson, being part of the Benson *clan*.

In 1965, Carol Lynn left Goucher College before her graduation and moved to Washington, D.C., where she already had a job on Capitol Hill, an apartment in Georgetown, and a place in the Fall 1966 freshman classes at American University's law school. She was able to "leave early" because her college was on a trimester system and she needed only a few courses for her degree. But by the time she finished those academic requirements by taking summer courses at George Washington University, it was too late for her to graduate with her own class, that of 1966, and she had to accept her undergraduate degree along with the class of 1967. She had been one credit short, she says, of meeting the requirements and graduating with her own class. "I was so mad at Goucher that the only reason I went to the graduation ceremonies in 1967 was to please my mother."

Her reason for choosing American University was that its law school offered a degree in international law, which she says intrigued her. "I might have been thinking I could use that to get a job with Lancaster Leaf and work on the overseas business end of the company." But then a voice from her past led in a different direction. Charlie, the young man from her junior year in high school, reappeared on the scene. A telephone call inviting her to come down to Texas for the weekend turned out to be portentous.

"I went, we had a long talk, and the result was that by the end of my visit, I had a new apartment, a new job, and I was enrolled in St. Mary's University Law School, and we had decided, after years of separation, to get married."

It was in San Antonio that Carol Lynn met Joella Smith, a spirited, dark-eyed brunette who became not just a friend, but, as Carol Lynn says, "like a sister." Like most good friends, they had a good deal in common, and some differences. Joella's father was a doctor, and her family had the same kind of social cachet the Bensons had become accustomed to in Lancaster. Unlike Carol Lynn, she *had* made her debut, but she definitely did not have the means to live as comfortably as did Carol Lynn.

All the fictions associated with Texas to the contrary, not many first-year law students at St. Mary's drove brand new Chevrolet Corvettes. Nor did they live in large, well-furnished and decorated one-bedroom apartments in the Alamo Heights section of the city, an area favored by established professionals, not by students of those professions. "Carol Lynn used to complain," says Joella Smith, "then and throughout the later years, about the 'strings' that were attached to her parents' generosity, and I'm sure what she said was true, but in 1968 in San Antonio, she lived very well. She was also, I must hasten to add, very generous, and when she left to go home for the holidays she would leave me her car. And [I] didn't mind one little bit tooling around town in that beautiful, dark green Corvette."

Carol Lynn's law-school career lasted just over a year. She did well academically her first year, but her marriage plans with Charlie never materialized. Enter Tom Kendall, a handsome, fit, and devil-may-care young athlete, a water skier from Florida who was performing at Hemisphere. Kendall was not just your average water skier: he once had held the title of world's champion, and was so good he could ski across the water *without skis*—a handy skill, metaphorically speaking, considering the shoals he was about to enter. Kendall was to be Carol Lynn's first and only husband.

Carol Lynn's marriage to Kendall was a disaster from the outset. Indeed, on New Year's Eve, after they'd been married all of six weeks, she sat at a party and looked up to see her husband, across the room, "necking with some girl!"

They had moved to San Francisco, where he told her he had a job waiting, but as it turned out, he only had friends there. Back in San Antonio, when they'd been dating, Carol Lynn would light a Benson and Hedges cigarette and tell people, "My family makes these.' " Most of her friends knew she was kidding; Tom Kendall did not. She says that when they got to California she learned how firmly he believed in the idea of her being rich—"He thought he was going to live off me and my family and not have to work."

The money that Harry Hitchcock had given her as a wedding gift soon ran out, and her father had to come out and rescue them. He brought them back, talked a friend into giving Kendall a construction job, and put them in the house at the New Jersey shore, while Carol Lynn was in the last months of her pregnancy with Kurt.

Carol Lynn says that on the way to the hospital Kendall told her, " 'Be sure you don't have an anaesthetic. I'm told they delay things, and I don't want to have to wait any longer than necessary.' "

After the baby was born, Benny moved the young family into the house on Wilson Drive where Carol Lynn and her sons would live for a decade and gave Kendall a menial job at Lancaster Leaf. One weekend Carol Lynn and her mother returned from the shore with the baby—Carol was pregnant again—to find that Kendall had cleared out without a word. It was the last she would ever see of him.

"Thirteen months and two weeks after I'd been married, I was served with divorce papers," she says, in a tone that indicates continuing amazement after a decade and a half, "and read that he was suing me for divorce—and asking for support! I countersued, and the judge granted me total permanent custody, with no visitation rights. My parents had hired a private investigator to find my 'husband,' and the investigator learned that he'd been married before."

Kendall had not been in the picture for very long—indeed, today Carol Lynn says, "It wasn't really a marriage at all"—and as the new decade of the 1970s began, she was very much on her own with not one but two baby boys to raise.

For the entire decade, Carol Lynn lived in Lancaster, for the most part on Wilson Drive, and then during the last year or so directly across the street from her parents. In a sense, she was proving that you *can* go home again, though it was hardly an ideal existence. Although she made a few attempts at supporting herself and her boys by working, she says that the necessary arrangements turned into a series of impracticalities. Basically she was being taken care of by her parents and by the fairly regular generosity of her grandparents. The situation made her feel like a second-class citizen, if not quite the poor relation.

"My life was not easy during that period," says Carol Lynn today. "In fact, it was very, very difficult."

One of the toughest parts was having to put up with the way her parents treated her small children, at the same time that they were spoiling Scott outrageously. "One of my sons recently wrote something as part of his college application, and I found the way he described growing up very interesting. He said, 'while my brother and I lived in a nice middle-class neighborhood in a nice middle-class house, once we came home and got inside everything was quite different. My brother and I used to laugh at the television shows that depicted loving and caring grandparents and showed all the things they would do with and for their grandchildren, because our life wasn't anything like that.' "

She first realized her sons' attitudes years ago when she was driving a car filled with seven- and eight-year-olds, one of them hers. One of the other kids had just told a story about all the wonderful places his grandparents had taken him, and all the things they'd bought him over the weekend, when Carol Lynn's son reacted by saying, in a tone of wonder, "Oh, so that's what grandparents are supposed to do."

Things eventually got so bad that when the Kendall boys saw their grandmother drive into their driveway, they would run upstairs and hide or crawl out an upstairs window and "escape." According to Carol Lynn, her parents frequently criticized her children for such things as leaving their toys outside—especially toys they had bought—and criticized her for her generally sloppy housekeeping.

Carol Lynn's housekeeping, or the lack thereof, is legendary. A man who worked for her grandfather said bluntly, "Carol Lynn lives like a pig. When you walk into her house you have to kick her fur coats out of the way." And one of her mother's friends recounted a story that holds a special place in the Benson family annals. While Carol Lynn was living on Wilson Drive in Lancaster, her house was robbed. When the police came to take the report, one of the cops looked around and then said, earnestly, "I see you've been ransacked, too."

"No," replied Carol Lynn, "that's the way it always looks."

Carol Lynn defends herself by explaining that, unlike other people, she has her closets and her drawers *perfectly* organized. She says that she has always arranged her sons' closets both by color and by type of garment, making certain that all the short-sleeved shirts, for example, are hanging neatly by themselves and not mixed in with the long-sleeved. As for her own room, she says it displays "creative chaos," and she can always find what she is looking for as long as it's in a closet or drawer. As for the piles of clothing scattered about, now that's a different story. "My problem," she says, laughing, "is that I never hang anything up or put anything away."

Carol Lynn had no voice in the decisions as to which house she and her children would occupy. "I was dependent on them for certain things. I was using my own money to live, as much as I possibly could, but they owned the house. My kids used to say, 'Mom, why do you let them treat you like that?' I would tell them that I had to make a choice about how I wanted to provide for them. Certainly it was not a pleasant situation for me, and in certain respects it was not pleasant for the children. But what the children could get, by my putting up with it, was greater and more important for them than my pride. It was the neighborhood all their friends were in, it was the kind of socioeconomic situation they were used to. They were in a good school district. They had a yard and nice surroundings, and they could be on the swim team at the Y and the soccer team, in the basketball league and the cub scouts—the whole suburban scene that families have. We had a three-bedroom house, and each boy had a room. These were things I couldn't otherwise have provided them with, so I was willing to make the sacrifice for them because they are my main responsibility in life. And they are the most important thing in my life.

"It was a matter of choice: do I do it for them (and a little bit for me; it was nice living in a pretty house and not a little teeny apartment) or do I make some other arrangement that would have been chiefly for me, and not nearly so beneficial to them?"

One of the worst parts of the arrangement, according to Carol Lynn, was that she could never anticipate when something she felt was minor would escalate into a full-blown domestic crisis. Like pets, for example.

"The music teacher gave the kids a pair of kittens that some stray had had in her studio, and we just loved them. But my mother said we couldn't have the kittens because Scott was allergic to cats. And then she decided that *she* was allergic to cats, which was such shit. So it had become, 'I can't come to your house, either, 'cause I'm allergic to cats too.' Well, my mother wasn't allergic to cats, but she had made up her mind that she was allergic to cats because I wouldn't get rid of the cats because of Scott.

"I said, 'If Scott really wants to see me that badly, I can [travel] the block and come over and see him. I'm not preventing that child from seeing us because we have pets in the house.'

"Then I said we'd keep the kittens outside, because they'd insisted we get rid of them. When we knew they were coming, we'd hurry and put the kittens outside, so they thought we just kept them outside. I still have one of them, but we lost the other because one day my mother and Scott chased it away."

Vacations were another problem. "I never had any money to go away for vacations; in all those years I went away twice on a ski trip with the Lancaster Ski Club. Any other vacation was always to a place that was owned by my mother, and then I was the cooking-and-cleaning lady, because my mother always said she wasn't going to spend any of her time waiting on us. It was never a situation where I could go out for dinner, on a date, and my mother would feed the children. If I wanted to go out, I had to feed them and get them ready for bed first, before I could go out. I was responsible for *always* doing for them; my mother would never say, 'Well, honey, why don't you go ahead and go and I'll put my grandchildren to bed.' It was never that.

"My mother wanted me to get married. It wasn't that she would keep me from a date, if we were in Canada, or something, where I was dating Don. But I had to have fed them and gotten them ready for bed before I could go. I'm not saying my mother never, ever took care of them when I had a date, but 99.99 percent of the time she would not.

"And even if she were home, if the kids would come back from the ski slopes at lunch, then I had to come back too, and feed them. And they couldn't buy lunch over there, because my mother said that was too expensive.

"She was just *weird* when it came to my kids. Once when we were down in Florida where Scott was taking tennis lessons that ran into the thousands and thousands of dollars, Travis went over to the club and took a tennis lesson and charged it to my mother. She made him pay her back for that tennis lesson. I'm not certain if he had to pay her back in cash or if she took it off as his birthday present."

One year Margaret Benson invited Carol Lynn's elder son, Kurt, to come visit her in Florida to see Disney World during his spring break. When he got back to Naples, she told her grandson that she would like him to program her personal computer, to which she wanted to transfer all of her financial and business records, a task that would take him days to finish.

When he said he thought it would be fair if she paid him a nominal fee of $5.00 an hour (he knew she'd been about to pay an outsider at least $7.00 or $8.00 an hour) she told him she was offering the minimum wage of $3.35—and that he really should do it for nothing because she'd taken him to Disney World. Then, the next morning, she woke him and told him to pack right away. As soon as he was ready, she drove him to the airport and put him on a plane for Boston.

Even now, Carol Lynn says, "I never really understood completely my mother's attitude toward my kids. Her attitude toward me probably was a part of it, and then of course the whole thing with Scott. . . ."

While Carol Lynn had clearly been Daddy's little girl, as she grew older—and obviously after his death—it was Mother who helped her when she got too far out on a limb. "My mother was always there for me," she recalls, "she was always supportive. If I *really* needed help, I mean. If I were completely overwhelmed and so far in debt that I couldn't get my head above water, she'd be there. Like those times of the year when I needed new clothes for my kids, I was always robbing Peter to pay Paul, and figuring out which bill I'd put off that month and which ones I could pay."

Carol Lynn says that she only went to her mother when she was "absolutely desperate. For one thing I really didn't want to have to ask for help. But once or twice a year I would just get so far in debt I had to."

Margaret Benson would react by giving Carol Lynn a little lecture about not budgeting properly. If she really needed it, Margaret would help her out. But Carol Lynn says she never went to her mother until after she had to deplete whatever resources she had—a little bit of stock, the van her father had left her, whatever.

Her father's death did not improve Carol Lynn's financial position, or Steven's either, for that matter. Benny left virtually all the money to Margaret, and she proved quite intractable about relinquishing any control over it. According to Carol Lynn, when her father suggested during his final illness that he leave his modest non-tobacco stock portfolio to their children, Margaret said no.

In 1982, when she decided to return to graduate school, Carol Lynn tried to make it on her own in Boston. Her mother did not favor the idea. She thought Carol Lynn should be looking for a husband.

"I had a little bit of income from my grandmother's trust, and I was able to get a loan at the bank, an educational loan, to pay for my tuition, and I was just going to try to live off what I had. I was also going to try and get myself a job. As it turned out, because of the constant involvement with this condominium my mother was involved in, I didn't even have time to do my schoolwork, much less get a job."

When Carol Lynn would tell her that she had a paper or a project to do, Margaret would respond that schoolwork had to take second place to her property. And she would claim that if Carol Lynn hadn't been up there, she wouldn't have bought the property in the first place.

The experience was paradigmatic of Carol Lynn's entire history with her parents. "I was going to rent something," she explains, "and mother came up with me to help look for things to rent, and that's when we found things were so expensive. And while we were looking, Wayne [Kerr, Margaret Benson's young lawyer] suggested to my mother that she should buy something and rent it to me, rather than my renting from someone else." It was an attractive proposition from the point of view of income taxes.

"So then we started looking for something to buy, and we weren't able to find anything that we liked that had what we needed. At that point, she had a certain amount of money that she was looking to spend. Unfortunately, she was not familiar with the market. She was trying to find something for $150,000, which was ridiculous for Boston. We needed to spend something like $235,000."

They ended up buying a less expensive condo apartment which, inevitably, turned into something like the plot of a Neil Simon movie, and eventually cost more than a three-story condo Margaret had vetoed. "They told us in August that the place would be ready to live in by the end of September, and by the following March it still was *nearly* ready."

The plan was that Carol Lynn would live there with her two boys until she finished her graduate degree, and then the place could be rented to someone else or sold. "And," she points out, "I was to pay market rent. I wasn't going to get any break on the rent."

Because the apartment wasn't ready when Carol Lynn showed up to start school at the beginning of September, the realtor promised to find them someplace else in the neighborhood, an apartment, until the end of the month. He found what she describes as a minuscule, unfurnished one-bedroom apartment that was really a "divided efficiency," and it was too small.

In addition to the fact that it would never hold all the furniture

that she was having shipped up, there was another serious flaw—
the apartment was a fifth-floor walk-up. The good news was that
there was no lease and the rent was "only" six hundred dollars a
month.

"Well," says Carol Lynn with a shudder at the memory, "we
had our sleeping bags. September turned into October, and October into November, and November into December, and the
situation with the condo kept getting worse and worse, and we're
still in the same place, and still without furniture. And I have no
savings left, 'cause I'd spent all that, and I have no money left to
bring up furniture, and my mother wasn't going to help me move
it twice. My mother was even upset about having to help me with
the six hundred a month, because that wasn't part of the original
plan, but there wasn't anything I could do about it. At this point,
I couldn't go out and get a job because every free moment I had,
and even every *un*free moment, which should have been spent
doing my schoolwork, was being spent on this condominium. It
was my responsibility to do *every*thing with it.

"To find the different tiles, and appliances, and carpets, and
paint, and go over every day to supervise, and sometimes during
the day to check on them, because they were constantly doing
things wrong. The guy who owned it and his contractor had a
deal going that the more the contractor could skimp on the specs,
the more money he could make. So they were doing all the work
incompetently, and I kept catching them on things that they were
doing wrong.

"One day the guy tried to punch me out. It was a Saturday,
and the people had come to put in the tile. I had to be there to
tell them how the pattern was to go." But the tile man discovered
he didn't have the proper tool, and before he left, he told her it
couldn't be tiled properly without using that specific tool. Later
that day, she returned to find the job finished, badly.

"I asked the contractor, and he said he told the men to go
ahead and finish it because he wasn't going to pay to have the tile

man come back. I told him the tile man had told me it couldn't be patched properly, and he got so mad he tried to take a swing at me. But I was able to duck."

It may come as no surprise that the matter ended in a lawsuit. But it never progressed beyond the deposition stage because Margaret Benson's doctors told her it was getting her too upset. "They were harassing her so badly—they were doing things that were just on the verge of being illegal—that they were causing her to have heart problems," says Carol Lynn. "So the doctor said she just couldn't be involved any more."

While the matter pretty much ended there for Margaret, it continued for her daughter. "Even though I didn't own the place, the guy had put the electric bills in my name, and he kept charging all the bills to me, and I'd call and say 'These aren't my bills,' and he would say, 'Oh, yes they are.' And even after the suit had been settled out of court, and he was showing the place to other people, he still kept charging all the electric bills to me. And it still causes problems for me because the Credit Bureau has on file that I didn't pay a two-thousand-dollar electric bill, an electric bill that was never mine in the first place."

Carol Lynn was "saved" by a man she was going out with at the time. He became so angered at the whole living situation that he "packed us all up and moved us in with him for about a month and a half until school was over." When she came back to school in the autumn, after a difficult search she found "a small three-bedroom brick house which rented for $1,400 a month. Boston rents are very high.

"As long as I could, I was paying the rent out of my money from my grandmother's trust, which was eventually raised to $2,600 a month. I admit that's a tidy sum, but $1,400 was a pretty big bite out of it. In any event the whole process of trying to find a decent place to live in turned out to be almost more trouble than it was worth. Eventually, at my suggestion, mother and I bought it, so that my $1,400 a month could go to building up equity instead of merely paying rent."

The relationship of Carol Lynn and her mother had its curious aspects, right up to the end. While her daughter was the one to whom she turned for all sorts of help, from traditionally "female" tasks such as picking out fabrics to supposedly tougher jobs like dealing with workmen, Margaret continued to defer to Steven on any number of matters. And she all but looked the other way as far as his financial manipulations were concerned. Carol Lynn also continued to observe a double standard between Margaret's strict treatment of Kurt and Travis and her overindulgence of Scott.

"When Steven and I were growing up," she said recently, "the rule was that you didn't have to eat all of something you didn't like, but you had to at least *try* it. When my kids would eat at my parents' home—and, granted, we did that a lot through those years—she would heap piles of things on their plates and insist they eat all of it. But if Scott, who'd be at the same table, didn't like something, he'd whine—and my mother would get up without a word and fix him an entirely different dinner!"

Carol Lynn Benson Kendall now says, "People who knew me when I was growing up will probably say two things about me: that I was spoiled, but that they remember me fondly." With almost no exceptions, she is right.

Manny Murray, the Lancaster builder who knew her parents well and saw her grow up in Lancaster, has an interesting appraisal. "Carol Lynn could be a lovely girl, but then she'd get these cocky streaks. She was a real fifty-fifty combination of her mother and her father. Her dad could be cocky, tough; and her mother was a sweet, kind, loving type of person. Naïve, though. God, was Margaret naïve.

"Carol Lynn is really a good, All-American gal. But *spoiled!* It's going to take a very wealthy man to really satisfy her. And that would be the serious problem: whether she could be satisfied."

Another Lancaster businessman, only slightly older than Carol Lynn, who also watched her grow (and who for obvious reasons asked not to be identified), has a particularly vivid memory of

Carol Lynn. "I must admit, I always had a great interest in her. I always thought—Jeez, what an ideal, beautiful, lovely, and *built* young woman! And she could handle herself *so* well. She knew how to come into a room, the smile and so forth. There were a lot of guys who felt like I did, local guys who were very much interested in her, but, unfortunately for Carol Lynn, they just didn't want to get tangled up with the hierarchy of the Benson-Hitchcock situation."

What is considered, in the mind of a typical Lancaster male, a "cocky streak" on the part of an intelligent and beautiful young woman? Could it be something as commonplace—in other areas of the country—as going to law school? Or seeking a job in broadcasting? Or going for a master's degree at the age of thirty-eight? Perhaps so.

Brett, Scott's natural father, who was interviewed in the autumn of 1986, a year after the bombing and more than twenty years after he had fathered Carol Lynn's first child, said to his interviewer, "Let me ask you a question. What has Carol Lynn been doing all these years?"

When told, he responded by saying, "Huh. Then none of her grand plans worked out, did they?"

Scott Benson:
Teddy Bear or Holy Terror?

"The first day I met the kid, in one of my tennis lessons, he told me he had just almost been killed racing his speedboat, and he'd decided that tennis would be a much safer sport. I didn't know whether to laugh, or what. But I have to tell you, I liked the kid. He was no great tennis player, and he could practice until Doomsday and he'd never be a great player, but I still liked him."

The tennis coach is Bill Bowden, one of at least half a dozen tennis instructors with whom Scott studied, in Florida or Pennsylvania or Maryland, all of whom ended up saying much the same thing about him: that he was a sweet kid who was starved for affection, especially from a father figure, a sweet kid with a big forehand and not much else (especially not a winning mental attitude), who fully believed that one day he would be a professional tennis player.

Anna Kuykendall, the best known of his coaches and certainly the one who knew Scott best, says, "He was a teddy bear and I loved him, but he was almost completely irresponsible and perhaps even emotionally disturbed. As far as his tennis prospects were concerned, he lived in a fantasy world."

And Stephen Vaughan, the tennis professional at the Quail Creek Country Club and the coach with whom Scott studied for eight months at the end, says much the same thing. In December 1985, in a deposition taken by Steven's defense lawyers, he was asked how accomplished a tennis player twenty-one-year-old Scott had been. He answered by saying, "Scott was not physically capable of being in the top ten like he wanted to be. He was improving all the time, and getting to be a better player; but he wasn't going to, you know, knock down the world or anything."

In an interview one year later, he was read that answer and asked to expand on it, to explain why he had given it. "He worked very hard at it and did his best. A lot of it was for his mother, who really wanted him to be a good tennis player, so he did a lot of it for her. But he did work hard. I'd have him out there a lot of times for two-a-day sessions for a couple of hours each."

How does that relate to the amount of practice put in by those who *are* professional tennis players? "That's about the norm, four hours. If you go out and *play*, you can play six hours, but for good work, four is plenty. I would feed him balls, I'd have him hit serves for forty-five minutes, I'd have him do all kinds of drills, and I'd invite other players in and he'd work out with them, under supervision, two-on-one drills—anything that would make Scott hit the ball eight million times."

Vaughan says that any developing player, despite his or her chronological age, goes through a stage that he calls the "fourteen- to sixteen-year-old stage." That stage is characterized by: "temper, going for winners, trying to overhit the ball, things like that. Well, Scott was just *ending* this stage, even though he was twenty or twenty-one years old. So he was really just beginning to understand what the game was about. His strokes were solid, he was beginning to hit the ball and understand what he was doing, and I was just beginning to get into his head."

According to his coach, the strengths of Scott's game were that he had "a huge forehand, topspin, and a big serve. He was a strong kid. He could have been a serve-and-volley player."

Asked to compare Scott Benson to a known tennis professional, Stephen Vaughan hesitates, and then says, "He wanted to be like Johan Kriek, who lives here in Naples."

Johan Kriek is the one professional tennis player whose name Carol Lynn Benson Kendall mentions in connection with Scott. She says Scott once beat Kriek. On hearing this, Stephen Vaughan laughs, and shakes his head. "No. I was just beginning to get him a little exposure. This trip to Europe that Scott and his mother took in the spring of 1985 right before he was killed was something that we had planned. I wanted to get him a little exposure, but also to get him some A.T.P. [Association of Tennis Professionals] points and get him on the computer. So we were selecting small satellite events that he might be able to qualify for, win a couple of matches, get some points, and get on the computer. Once you're on the computer you can get into qualifiers and then you can start to do something.

"He had a good opportunity in Denmark. He hit a qualifier that only had five entrants, and there were four spots in the main draw. Well, he didn't get in. He had a *great* chance. I was really mad at him about that, and I let him know it. He had tried hard enough [but] Margaret went with him, and she had walking pneumonia at the time. I don't know if that influenced what he was doing, how much he was practicing; I didn't have any control with him gone. I'm not so sure that he put forth the kind of effort he would have if I'd been in control of him."

Vaughan provided a quick overview of how the competitive tennis world is structured. "The A.T.P. and U.S.T.A. [United States Tennis Association] print schedules of tournaments and satellites all the way from $350,000 grand prize events all the way down to these $25,000 satellites. Anybody can go and try to get into a qualifier. What they do is, once you get to a qualifier, they take all the players that are on the computer first: any players who are available—ready to play at nine o'clock Saturday morning—

they let into the qualifier until they have the required thirty-two players for the tournament. If not enough players who have rankings show up, then anybody can get in. But in the small, satellite tournaments there aren't enough people with computer rankings who show up and try to play. Because if it's a $25,000 tournament, and you win it, you may [only] get $7,500, which is not great, especially if you have to travel to Europe."

For someone in Scott Benson's situation, that was a great place to start. "It's easier to go over there," says Vaughan; "not that many players over there are going to get into the small tournaments. But if you try to play a satellite tournament here in Florida, there are people who are ranked thirteenth or fifteenth in the world who will stop by—because it's close to their house or they want some practice, or just to pick up a few bucks. The U.S. is just so much tougher.

"So it made sense to send Scott over to Europe. Plus, he had the financial means to do it, and when you've got that, you can, basically, write your own ticket. You can travel to some of these smaller tournaments and you can earn some points.

"My plan was to get him in some of the smaller satellites over there, and see how he did, and then let him see what it was like to be out there, what the competition was like, and what he was going to have to do to meet it, how much harder and how much farther he was going to have to go to meet the competition. You have to be exposed to it even to *understand* what the quality of play is. Some guy ranked one-thousandth in the world would still *drub* Scott. But he had no conception of that."

Physically, Scott was a good size for tennis. He was almost six feet tall, about 175 pounds, and, according to Stephen Vaughan, quite strong. "He was a strong kid, and getting stronger. When he first came to me he was kinda flabby. And he had a problem with his legs, in that his thighs, for some reason, just wouldn't develop the way athletes' normally do. I never did get a fix on why that was. He was strong, he could run—though he was never really fast—but his legs just didn't develop like they were supposed to. His thighs kind of rubbed together, that kind of thing. This may have limited his speed. He was a strong player, not quick, not agile—but getting better."

The coach had a much higher opinion of Scott Benson as a person than as a player. "In July 1985, I really thought that Scott was coming along as an individual. He was polite, extremely polite. I don't know what he was like with the family at home, but in public he was very, ah, *adoring* of his mother. Always kissed her, always told her he loved her. Never ever slandered her in my presence. Was always very nice.

"Then again, I had something to do with that, because if he did start to get off base I'd let him know. But that was so rare that I can't ever remember that happening. He was such a nice person. Anything I needed done, he'd help me with it."

Scott's coach said he was well respected by everybody at the club and looked up to by the younger players, who were impressed by all the hard work he put in.

"There was no way," says Vaughan, "that Scott could have been a touring pro, no way. But he could have been a pro at a small club, or an assistant pro at a larger one, because he was polite to adults and the kids loved him. He was real good with kids."

He was also good at having fun, and the tennis regimen did not put much of a crimp in that activity. Vaughan witnessed the end result of one night of fun on the part of Scott and his girl-friend, Kim Beegle.

"I arrived at the club one morning about eight, and the parking lot was filled with police cars, all of them surrounding Scott's Lotus. Apparently he was coming back from somewhere, and he'd been doing 160 miles an hour, or some incredible speed, on Interstate 75," a beautiful new highway that leads to Tampa, "and of course the police car—which could only do 110—fell behind. Scott told me later that the only reason he got caught was that he slowed down to a crawl at the entrance to the Quail Creek development because the automatic sprinklers had left a puddle and if he went through any faster he'd splash his clean car. So he slowed down—just long enough for the squad car to catch a glimpse of him."

Vaughan also had to say something to Scott about his attractive and curvaceous girlfriend, Kim, whom Scott occasionally brought with him while he worked out. "She would always wear these real brief outfits, and then she'd go to the exercise room and work out while Scott was on the tennis court. Apparently she made some of the members a little nervous. I had to tell Scott not to bring her with him any more. He laughed, but he did what I said. It was like the deal with the police car. Scott just loved to have fun. And he had the money, so why not? That was his attitude. But I could never stay mad at him."

Anna Kuykendall was another person who couldn't stay mad at Scott Benson. And she'd had a lot more experience with him than Stephen Vaughan. "He absolutely loved to be babied, and was forever asking me to rub his back or, especially, his feet. If you wouldn't do it he would moan and carry on and tell you how his mother would do it for him at home and how hard he was working. Years later, he'd use the same technique when he'd ask me if his girlfriend could come and stay with him at our house where he was working out and practicing.

"I'd say no, and he would carry on, saying, 'Oh, Anna, look how hard I'm working. She makes me feel so good and makes me so relaxed. You don't want me to be all nervous when I'm working this hard, do you?' I'd say no, and then a few minutes later he'd start in all over again. That was the way he'd always been. He wasn't used to people saying no to him, so he would keep at you until you gave in. Or at least that's what he'd try and get you to do. But I had other children, other tennis players in my home, and I wasn't going to allow two unmarried young people to stay together. It was ridiculous, what he was asking, but he would try and try and try."

Mrs. Kuykendall was one of the few people to guess, many years after the fact had been covered up, that Carol Lynn was

Scott's real mother. "I'm sure, or at least pretty sure, that Scott did not know it. But I remember when he first moved in with us, Scott was about sixteen, and it was Carol Lynn, not Margaret, who came down with him and made sure everything was all right, and settled him in, telling him where to put things, and helping him arrange everything. I just always had a feeling after that time that maybe she really was his mother. It just seemed to us, and my husband felt much the same way that I did, that Carol Lynn took on a lot of responsibility for Scott."

While he stayed in their home off and on for years, Scott put the Kuykendalls through the wringer with his constant demands for special privileges. And if Scott wasn't causing a problem, his mother was. Mrs. Kuykendall relates a story that she considers all too typical. "Scott was about nineteen years old, and I thought it would be a good idea for him to get some experience working at a tennis club in Naples. I mentioned a couple of the local clubs, and I told Margaret, 'Even if the guy won't pay Scott, let's see if he'll use him anyway, and let him be around the tennis. He'll learn a lot, and he'll get to hit with the old men and the young kids.'

"So Margaret asked me if I would call Bill Bowden and ask him if he would hire Scott. I said, 'Margaret, I'm not going to call Bill Bowden and ask him if he'll hire Scott. We're trying to get Scott to show a little initiative. You have Scott put on his nicest tennis outfit, take a couple of racquets, and go out there. He knows Bill. Maybe Scott can take a lesson from Bill, or something, and hit with him, and then see. Have Scott say I'd like to come out here and work for you, and right now you don't even have to pay me.'

"Instead of doing that, Margaret goes out there and talks to Bill about her taking tennis lessons, or that they will become members out there, and, naturally, no sign-on-the-dotted-line unless you hire Scott. So Bill called me and said, 'What's this about you wanting Scott out here?' And I told Bill what was going on.

"That was the way Margaret started operating as soon as Benny died. Before that, Benny would kind of handle things, and Scott was pretty independent, kind of his own man. But when Margaret took over the purse strings, well she dominated practically the whole thing. Scott was really just on the leash, and bored.

"But that was a complete change of personality for Margaret. She was using the money to control him. I know that's the way it was with Scott because I was usually there and saw it with my own eyes."

Anna Kuykendall also noticed a trait mentioned by others, that the Bensons seldom paid full price for what they bought. "That's right—but Benny never did that. Even when I would suggest charging less during times when Scott was on the road, Benny would say, 'Look Anna, he'll be calling in, and you all'll be talking, and taking up your time. Just forget it.' And that's the way it was with Benny."

While things may have changed when Margaret took control, that did not alter how Anna felt about the Benson family. "A lot of people have asked me why I liked Margaret so well, and why I liked Scott so well with all the problems they threw at me; but for some reason they were more like family. I guess because I had made so many promises to Benny I felt guilty that I wasn't able to fulfill them. I did the best I could, but I felt like Scott *and* Margaret kept me from fulfilling some of them. I would say to Margaret, 'Margaret, I don't want him to have the car,' and Margaret would say, 'But Benny always had fast cars, and Scotty he just has to have a car. . . . .' And I couldn't take Scott's car away from him if Margaret wouldn't do it.

"Or he would want to go up to the shore, or go here or go there, and I would say to her, 'He's just getting in shape, and we've got a tournament coming up,' and she would say, 'Oh, he's worked so hard. Come on, Anna, let's let him do it.' Okay, so there I am. It was just like on the telephone, with the long-distance calls. She thought it was good for him to keep in touch. I said, 'Margaret, he's keeping in touch with the wrong people' But she'd say, 'Oh, he might feel like he can't call me. You'll let him call now, won't you?'

"She was kind of tying my hands, and undermining my authority, but the way she did it was always real sweet."

Anna Kuykendall had her task complicated by her personal relationship with the Benson clan. Others who did not have that complication were able to be stricter with Scott. She arranged for him to live with the Damian family, Carol and Vincent (a Miami lawyer) and their two children, for about six to eight months in 1980 and 1981. Their daughter Melissa was also working with Anna, and it was convenient for them to have Scott, because he could drive, thus freeing Mrs. Damian, a college professor, from chauffeuring the young athletes. Mrs. Kuykendall says she remained the one who was responsible for Scott.

There was an initial meeting with Scott and Mrs. Benson, and the Damians were impressed. The arrangement began well, but Mr. Damian recalls being worried about Scott's obvious affluence and his equally obvious lack of direction. "He was looking for something to tie onto. I got the impression that he was rather disoriented, had no firm plans, no business plans, or any idea where he wanted to go to college, if he did."

One of the first things that bothered Vince Damian was that shortly after Scott moved in with the family, he totaled his 280Z, and within seven days he had a brand new car. That concerned Damian and his wife. "Our kids were very well off, but we were always very careful about *not* giving them everything they wanted, but teaching them they had to work for it."

Scott had not been with the Damians too long when Mr. Damian noticed Scott's dedication was not what it had originally been. He sat down and talked about it with Scott, who told Damian that he'd never before had anybody who'd given him any direction, that he felt he could get anything he wanted from his mother at almost any time, and that she would believe anything he said, and that life had been, really, too easy for him.

"Those were his words," says Vince Damian. "He also told

me that he'd had no relationship with his father to speak of, that [Edward Benson] was a very distant type of person. But he told me many, many things about his father, and that he admired him a great deal."

Not long after that, Mr. Damian noticed that the level in the whiskey bottle behind the bar in the family room was dropping suspiciously. He asked Scott if he had been drinking liquor, and the youth readily admitted it, said he had been drinking for several years, and that it relaxed him. "He listened politely, argued with me a little, and then politely disagreed with my conclusions. He also asked me if it was the money that I worried about, because he would be glad to pay for the booze himself."

The final straw came after Scott and a neighborhood boy got drunk one night on the local golf course. That, and Mrs. Damian's suspicion that Scott was involved with drugs, caused them to call a halt to the experiment. "We sat down with him," says Mr. Damian, "and told him how much we liked him, but that the arrangement was not working out. We didn't set a hard date for him to leave, but several days later he said he had talked with his mother, and he was moving out. And just like that he was gone."

Carol Damian says, "Oddly, Scott never argued the dismissal. And after that when I would see him at the club or at some tournament, he was always very polite to me; in fact he was almost docile. Scott had always been incredibly polite, extremely so, and always very respectful of adults. I don't believe he had a mean bone in his body. I really liked him.

"I think Scott was a lonely boy who never had anybody who gave a damn about him. I think that's one of the reasons he took up tennis. He had nothing else, and he needed it. I never knew him to have friends, except for his girls, and they were real showpieces—skintight pants, high heels, and big busts. I never saw him make the acquaintance of anybody his own age."

Mrs. Damian says she tried to impress on Scott the value of an education, in case his "unrealistic" tennis plans did not work out. "But I got nowhere. Since he had no monetary concerns, the idea of having a goal and working toward it did not concern him. Certainly, betterment wasn't his goal."

After Scott left her home, Carol Damian continued to run into him—and to worry about him. "I think he had wrecked two or maybe even three cars and a Bronco. I worried about him living in the fast lane. He could buy whatever he wanted, like an elaborate stereo system for his car, and he flaunted all these toys. I had to tell my kids that this was not the real world.

"After we'd kicked him out, I told him he could come back any time and get the rest of his clothes. And he said he would, but he never did. He left a *roomful* of expensive clothes—suits, tennis things, leather jackets, great sweaters. I finally had to box it all up and give it to the Goodwill."

Bill Bowden, one of the pros from Naples, was another observer who felt Scott lacked both direction and discipline, not to mention tennis talent. "I've probably seen eight to ten thousand people on the court in my lifetime, and a good pro can watch someone hit ten balls and know if they're any good. Scott looked good swinging the racquet, but that was about it. He was a typical rich kid who would pull up in his 280Z and walk in with six to eight racquets under his arm, all of them nothing but the best. But he didn't have much discipline, and he hung around with a real rowdy crowd. We'd all heard about his cracking up the cars and eluding the police.

"I had met his mother, of course, and thought she was real nice. But it was obvious that she couldn't control him.

"Scott had an odd habit. When he was sincere he would put his head down and look at the ground. He couldn't look you in the eye. I'd been raised to believe you had to look someone in the eye when you were serious. It was the damndest thing. But, like everyone else, I liked Scott."

Many people who knew Scott Benson talk about his rowdy friends, or say he traveled with a fast crowd of irresponsible young people. But no one can remember any names. It seems Scott much preferred the regular company of his girlfriends to that of any males. Stephen Vaughan recalls wondering why Scott didn't run with a crowd from someplace like Fort Lauderdale, which was much more of a party town and filled with kids near his age whose backgrounds were similar to his. Vaughan once asked Scott why he didn't date girls from that group instead of his current girl. "He just laughed, and said, 'Because [she's] so good in bed!' "

An interesting split-screen picture of Scott Benson emerges from his Florida years. One half shows the playboy of the southwestern world, flashing by in a fast car, the blonde hair of his "showpiece" girlfriend trailing in the wind. On the other side is a portrait of an overgrown kid, an emotionally starved loner reaching out blindly in several directions at the same time, trying desperately to figure out who he is and exactly where he belongs in this very unusual family.

There is truth in both images.

When Scott was not living with a tennis family, Margaret often set him up in apartments of his own and furnished them completely. It was not long before neighbors complained about the noise, or the antics of some of his guests. Anna Kuykendall says Scott seldom had any cash on him, and she had to give him money for groceries; but others say he had little need for cash because he always carried one or more of his mother's credit cards.

While in Port Royal, Scott often used nitrous oxide, and there were many times that the telltale high-pitched laughter could be heard from behind his locked bedroom door. That he smoked marijuana most weekends and also used cocaine on occasion were accepted as facts by family members who chose to think about it. The demolished boats and automobiles are matters of private record.

One of Scott's last escapades was successfully covered up by—of all people—his brother Steven. Just weeks before his death a tired Scott allowed a friend to drive his truck on the way back to Naples from the east coast of Florida. The friend lost control on a curve, and the truck ran for hundreds of yards across a golf course, before it plunged into a lake. Scott awakened, kicked out a window and pulled his friend from the vehicle. The next day, it was big brother Steven who arranged for a wrecker to get the car out of the lake and saw to it that Margaret learned nothing about the adventure. Her secretaries did, however, and after that took to calling Scott's friend "Aquaman."

And then of course there was the very ugly incident that caused Scott to be hospitalized for five days in 1983. An argument over the behavior of his beloved guard dog, Buck, got more than a little out of hand. Scott, who apparently had been taking some pretty good hits from the laughing gas cannister that morning, lost control and began screaming at his mother.

He told her, loudly and with some profanity, that Buck was a fully trained attack dog (a point that, thankfully, was never actually proved). All he needed to do, screamed Scott, was to give Buck the command and the good-sized dog would "rip you to pieces." His continued abuse so frightened Margaret that the police were called in, and he was held until a psychiatrist declared him fit for release.

Opinion as to whether Scott *himself* would rip anyone or anything to pieces is divided along rather interesting lines. Tennis coaches Anna Kuykendall and Stephen Vaughan say no, unequivocally. Yet Carol Lynn told the police in July 1985 that *both* she and her mother were "afraid of Scott," and, she says, "for good cause." Ruby Caston, Margaret Benson's housekeeper for several years in Naples, when told that the tennis coaches did not consider Scott to be violent, blurted out, "Huh! That's not the way I saw it."

Then there's the still pending lawsuit to determine whether the four-year-old daughter of Tracy Mullins, once Scott's premier showpiece, is also the child of Scott Benson. At the time she filed suit in 1983, Scott denied paternity. In a statement given to his lawyer at the time, he said, sounding suddenly like a remorseful Sunday school teacher: "My mother, who had thirty-eight years of marriage to my father, a greatly respected man of the highest character both in business and his personal life, is herself a religious person of high integrity and moral values. She, not being blinded by the forces of sexuality, very quickly perceived the true character of Tracy Mullins and was very much opposed to my seeing her. My relationship with Tracy was always a very turbulent one. I had never known anyone like this before. I suppose I have a strong sex desire, and Tracy's voluptuous figure, plus her vast sexual knowledge, I think from the beginning just overwhelmed me."

That is one side of Scott Benson's personality. The other side is a genuinely likable but very troubled youth, driven to excesses in large part because he simply could not figure out who the hell he was.

Yet Scott's cousin, Brenda Murphy—a twenty-six-year-old young woman whose picture could be placed alongside the dictionary definition of the word "level-headed"—loved Scott so much that she asked him to be in her wedding. One of the things she now remembers most vividly is that her grandmother Hitchcock—"Boppa's" wife—would always refer to Scott as "poor Scotty." Says Brenda, "It wasn't until after the tragedy when everything came out about his real parents, that I realized just what she meant."

Anna Kuykendall remembers, "He was so affectionate it was embarrassing. He used to kiss my husband Kirk on the lips, even in public, and think nothing of it! I remember one time it was Kirk's birthday, and Scott was still with Tracy then, and they missed us at home so they chased us down on the highway so Scotty could give Kirk his birthday present and a bottle of champagne he'd gotten for him. We got out of the car, and Scott ran around and gave Kirk a kiss on the lips, right out on the highway! And Kirk got so mad. He said, 'Damn it, Scott, you're a man now and you should be shaking my hand!' But Scott just laughed. He was so happy he'd found Kirk and not missed his birthday."

In late November 1980, Anna Kuykendall happened to call the Benson home in Lancaster and Steven answered. He told her his father was too ill to come to the phone, but that he didn't want her to send Scott home. As soon as she hung up, she made arrangements to get him on the next plane. "Scott told me later that, thanks to me, he was able to hold his father's hand before he died."

Mrs. Kuykendall also remembers a particular night when Scott was very upset. For some reason Steven had picked him up at the airport, and Scott was "high as a kite on something." She says he was crying and rambling on incoherently, and she remembers him saying, " 'soldier in San Antonio who's my real father.' He also said, several times, 'Damn you, Carol Lynn.' "

"He was so upset. I can remember how he would just stand up and rock back and forth on the balls of his feet, and he would hit his thighs with his fists. That night is the main reason I feel he could not have been violent to anyone other than himself."

Brenda Murphy, Scott's youngest female cousin, says a very sad thing: "We all loved Scotty so much, but in a sense we pitied him." The last time she saw Scott was the winter before the bombing. "We went out to breakfast with Boppa [Harry Hitchcock] and my mom, and [a woman from Mr. Hitchcock's church who works for him part-time]. We went to Dempsey's in Lancaster.

"It was about ten in the morning, and Scotty seemed like he was on drugs." She thinks he might also have had "a bottle of whiskey" the night before, and was still showing the effects. "He was really out of it. I don't know really what it was," says Brenda, "but he wasn't normal for ten o'clock in the morning.

"So we were all sitting there eating breakfast, and he was in a daze, and [the woman] says, 'Scotty, what do you want to *do?*'

" 'What do you mean?' he says, 'I'm going to be a professional tennis player.'

"And she says, 'You know, after you can't play tennis any more, when you get older?'

"And he says, 'Well, I'm going to be an entrepreneur, just like my brother.' Of course. He always wanted to copy his big brother."

Family Business

In February 1984, when Evelyn Goldsmith and her husband, old friends from the days at the Jersey shore, visited Margaret Benson in Naples, Margaret was, as Evelyn puts it, "all excited" about Meridian Security, the new business of Steven's for which she had provided the funding. Two years later, Margaret visited the Goldsmiths in Lake George, New York, and confided in Evelyn. It was shortly before she and Scott were to leave for his European tennis trip and five weeks before she was killed.

Margaret's attitude had undergone a complete about-face. Instead of being Steven's chief backer, financially and emotionally, she had come to the point, she told her friend, of accepting the fact that she must deal realistically with Steven. She hoped that it was still possible to get him to mend his ways, to be a responsible businessman; but she worried that it was already too late for that.

As evidence, she told Evelyn Goldsmith that in the four years since his father's death, Steven had gone through somewhere between two and a half and three million dollars of her money.

Evelyn Goldsmith was startled by the amount, but not by the news. She and her husband had known Margaret and "Ed," as she called him, since the mid-sixties, and she'd been hearing about Steven's commercial misadventures for years. She was well aware of how much money Margaret had lost when Steven had talked her into backing his purchase of an "estate" in Columbia, Pennsylvania, among other things. This figure, however, was something else, even for the young man Evelyn Goldsmith still called "Stevie."

"What are you going to do?" she asked.

"I don't know yet," said Margaret, "but when I get back from this trip with Scott, I'm having Wayne Kerr, my lawyer, come down from Philadelphia, and we'll get to the bottom of the whole thing."

In November 1984, Margaret Benson, the widow who until 1980 had never written a check, the same woman who confided to a friend six months after her husband's death that her biggest chore was trying to determine just how much money she was worth, finally had her lawyer draw up a personal statement of her finances. The total came to $9.4 million. (That kind of money, even if invested poorly, still grows at a very nice rate.)

The breakdown showed that her major assets were in stock and real estate, with cash and real possessions (cars, boats, jewelry) fighting it out for a healthy third place. The single biggest asset was her stock portfolio, and that was a truly lopsided affair. She held stock in eleven different companies. In ten of them, the amount held did not exceed a thousand shares. There was, however, one company in which Margaret Benson owned a great deal of stock. That was, of course, Universal Leaf, the parent corporation of Lancaster Leaf, the company her father had started and her husband had served so well. She owned 224,500 shares of stock in Universal Leaf, which at the time had a market value of $21 a share, making her Universal Leaf holdings worth $4,714,500.

The other stock accounted for an additional $162,150, bringing her total common stock holdings to $4,876,650.

In addition to these assets there was more than $1.7 million in four tax-free fund accounts with brokerage houses (Sears, Calvert, Jeffries, and Voizard).

The real estate was detailed as follows:

13002 White Violet Drive	$ 310,000
Admiralty lot	400,000
112 S. Baltimore	350,000
1515 Ridge Road	400,000
3739 Domestic Avenue	180,000
Warehouse	60,000
336 Russett Road	158,000
Total Real Estate	$1,858,000

There were "Other Assets" listed: half a million in furniture and fixtures; $210,000 worth of boats; another $200,000 in automobiles; plus a $71,000 mortgage she held on a friend's condominium. These assets represented an additional $981,000. Even with the deduction of $1,225,094 in liabilities (all but about $200,000 of which appears to be debits for stock pledged as collateral or stock she had ordered but not yet paid for) that still left Margaret Benson more than $8 million to the good.

One would think that with all of this money and property, Margaret Benson would have been able, more than four years after the death of her husband, to relax and enjoy her future with no worries about money. Unfortunately, that was not the case.

As Carol Lynn told the police in late July 1985:

One thing my mother had a terrible fear of, was ending up in a nursing home, and so she thought that she had enough that she always would have, at least, a nurse in the house. And I told her it didn't matter anyway because she could always come and live with me. . . .

And she said that she knew she could come stay with me, that she knew she couldn't go stay with Steven because Steven had already told her that if she ever got sick or anything not to call on him—he wouldn't take her in.

Earlier, Carol Lynn had given her explanation of how her mother had come to be in this highly undesirable situation:

The family always came first, and she was always doing things for Steven. But Steven was, well, he took advantage of my mother. He would get involved in these really big deals, and then at the last minute, without telling my mother he had already committed himself to it, he'd tell her and he'd get money from my mother, money like fifty thousand dollars.

This had been going on for a while. . . . Then there was the Meridian Company that my brother had started, and there were all sorts of funny things going on about that. When Wayne [Kerr] had come down last year they had found "irregularities," so to speak, that were probably . . . embezzlement. But my mother wasn't about to do anything about it at that point.

[But] it kept getting worse. Steven was moving things to Fort Myers, and he never wanted my mother to know anything. So what finally happened was that Steven had gone through about two million, two and a half million dollars of Mother's money. And since my father had died, my mother was really upset because she was afraid that she didn't have enough money left now to even build herself a house.

She was at my house, and she was crying because she didn't know how she was going to come up with the money. She said, "I don't even have a house to live in any more." . . .

She was really upset about that, and then while we were there we talked about a lot of things, about how she felt and everything. And then we found out that Steven had bought himself a house. And that really, really upset my mother. As mother put it, "It was the straw that broke the camel's back." She finally was going to do something.

Margaret was not a woman who learned from her mistakes, at least not from her (and her husband's) mistakes about Steven's business acumen and ability. One would think that after two full decades of backing economic ventures that never showed any profit she might have reached the point of saying "No!" to her eldest son. One would be wrong.

From what she told friends, it appears that Margaret believed—or "chose to believe"—that Steven's notable lack of success in the tobacco business was caused by the jealousy of others, by bad blood. That is, because her father and her husband had been so very successful, other, smaller men took it out on her son. Evelyn Goldsmith, in particular, recalls Margaret telling her that Steven was "pushed out" of Lancaster Leaf after the death of his father.

Certainly the difficulty she'd had with some bankers and lawyers in Lancaster over access to her husband's estate could have fed that attitude. And obviously, Steven did nothing to disabuse her of that notion. Indeed, one has to wonder about Steven's connection with reality from that time on (if not also before). As Manny Murray and others have pointed out, Steven's plans were *clearly* unrealistic.

There is a possibility that Steven did make an effort to earn his own way after he reached Florida. In fact, he did get a real estate license and did work, at least temporarily, for an established broker. Unfortunately, there's little evidence to suggest that he stuck with it for very long—or that he ever sold a house.

Fred Merrill, who *was* in the real estate business, recalls that for a while Steven was intensely interested in that field. Merrill says that when they first met, "I never knew what he did or what his background had been, but during some of this period of time, he'd talk real estate with me. And when we were finding the lots [for a possible joint business venture], he wanted to know how I would do it, how I would find property, and so forth.

"Several times he mentioned, and wanted to know if I had, my broker's license. And I said, no, I was not interested in becoming a broker. I explained that I didn't want the trouble and responsibility of opening my own office. Steven told me he had been in real estate in Pennsylvania, and that he'd had his real estate license up there—in fact, I think he told me he'd had his broker's license—and he wanted to know how we did things down here. He was pretty knowledgeable in regard to real estate.

"We sat up in my office one night, for three or four hours, and just talked, nobody else around. But he was talking about development, and he wanted to know if I could get him some land for a large development. I tried to pick his brain to find out what kind of development he was talking about—industrial, commercial, shopping center, residential? And he said, 'The whole thing.'

"I said, 'Where's the money coming from?' and he said, 'I've got access to lots of money, European money.' "

Later on, using his contacts and experience, Fred Merrill found a large tract, eight thousand acres near several major highways and with waterfront exposure. It could have been used for any purpose, or a combination of purposes. When he asked Steven just what use he planned for the tract, and did not get the kind of answer he expected, Fred Merrill realized he had better rely on his experience and instincts and deal at arm's length with his friend's son.

"I don't like to reveal location to sources until I know who's serious and how serious they are. But I had called the owner of the property, and he was willing to go any way we wanted, so I went back to Steven and said, 'Now it's really in your court. I need some money if you want to tie some property up, we got to be more serious.' Well, nothing ever came of it."

Not long after that, the Merrills realized that Steven was actively studying, on his own, for a real estate license. "He bought all our source books," says Fred Merrill, "which are on the open market, but are quite expensive, and he made all sorts of trips up to the courthouse in Fort Myers to study documents. He was working at it."

This was after Margaret Benson had bought her lots in Port Royal, but before she had sold the house on Galleon Drive that Merrill had found for her. Finally a light went on in Merrill's head. "I got to thinking, later, that they [Margaret and Steven] may have wanted me to go to work for them as a broker, so that I could deal in real estate for them. But when I appeared not to be interested in going for my broker's license, then *he* went and got his broker's license. That may have been the plan, but of course they would never tell me that."

True or not, there was no denying the fact that as soon as he got his own real estate license, Steven Benson listed his mother's house himself. Fred Merrill, friend and real estate adviser, had suddenly become Fred Merrill, friend and *former* real estate adviser.

But isn't that the kind of situation where *Margaret*, friend to both Mr. and Mrs. Merrill, should have said something, something like, "I'm sorry to take the listing of my house away from you, but after all it's my son, and he's in the business now"? Wouldn't that be the proper thing to do?

Fred Merrill smiles uneasily. "You'd think that, wouldn't you? My feeling was," about the fact that Margaret said nothing, "there was a little embarrassment there."

Bette Merrill, however, adds an important point: "You must remember that Margaret not only would be embarrassed, but she would go to any length to avoid a *confrontation*."

Steven got involved in a few real estate deals in Florida, in particular a fairly large one, on the Isle of Capri, a small community near Marco Island. But, according to his sister, it was the kind of project that was too small for the big developers and too big and complicated for the small ones like Steven. As a result, he got burned again, and before he could extricate himself from the situation, he was stuck paying ten thousand dollars a month interest rates and mortgage costs. "And of course," says Carol Lynn, "you know whose money that was. In fact, Steven once told me that for three or four months after he'd told Mother that he was out of the deal, he was actually still paying that money."

Carol Lynn says that while she does not recall the details of all the "entrepreneurial ventures" Steven was involved in after his father's death, she does remember her mother mentioning two or three occasions when she had to give Steven fifty thousand dollars. Carol Lynn feels that her brother was simply repeating his earlier pattern of getting in over his head, without "permission," and then coming to his mother to bail him out—and Margaret was repeating *her* earlier pattern of cooperating in this eventually self-destructive course.

There was another element involved. Margaret viewed herself as far more than just a financial backer—an angel—of Steven's ventures; she seemed to like her new role as businesswoman. Several of her Florida friends remarked that she often asked them, "Did you see my ad?" referring to yellow pages or small newspaper ads for the businesses Steven had started—with her money. Like Steven, she had business cards printed, and she professed a growing interest in things commercial.

Steven's symbiotic relationship with his mother intensified after Debby returned from Wisconsin with their children. That relationship became even more noticeable, especially in retrospect, when his career as a real estate developer died aborning.

Steven made his mother's house his base of operations, and it was clear that at that time he had no intention of setting up one of his own. The arrangement seemed to suit Margaret because—at least to all appearances—she allowed him to do any number of things for her that involved money.

Neighbor Jerry Hester has a less-than-fond memory of the boat that Steven purchased for his mother. "Margaret had said that they used to have a boat up in Pennsylvania, or somewhere, and she comes down here and says she wants a boat. Well, that's all Steven has to hear, and it's 'Okay, Mom, that's another project for me.' So he goes out and buys a boat in Fort Myers, a thirty-five-footer. He buys this radar and everything, and three months later he's got it all fixed up. A hundred-thousand-dollar boat with another hundred-thousand worth of electronics on it. And then I noticed that it was powered by gasoline! You don't buy a boat that size and have it gasoline-powered; it should be diesel-fueled. And it had 255 gallons of gasoline on that boat. It was the most dangerous boat I'd ever seen—a floating time bomb! I swore after one trip I'd never get on it again.

"That showed Steven's inexperience again. . . . If it wasn't the boat, then it was something else. Everything was a little project that he could do to—in his own mind—earn his keep."

Hester thinks things *might* have been different if Carol Lynn had been around, because she was clearly, in his opinion, so much more level-headed than Steven. "But Carol Lynn wasn't here on a day-to-day basis. Margaret let Steven in there to do his thing, and poor Carol Lynn would come back and here's all this money spent again. I'm sure she was incredulous over it. Because she had made up her own mind that she was going to do things on her own; she had backbone, and I give her every bit of credit in the world for doing it. She didn't want to live with her mother; she had her own family to raise. And she was trying to get her own career going in Boston."

Yet Mr. Hester sensed that, somehow, "Margaret sorta felt sorry for Carol Lynn, living alone up there. And maybe it's natural that a mother would feel that way. But Steven was different. We met him at a couple of parties where he was acting as host for his mother—his wife was not there, by the way—and he acted more like the hired help."

Hester adds a sad comment, "The person Margaret trusted most was Steven."

He also believes, however, that had Margaret Benson lived, in a few years she would have "just washed her hands of Steven and his wife, because nobody could put up with that kind of situation."

For the record, it would be helpful to know just what caused the "situation" between Margaret and her daughter-in-law. Unfortunately, Debby Benson, who returned to her parents' home in Wisconsin late in 1985, while Steven was in jail, and who did not return to attend the trial in summer 1986, is not talking to anyone, at least not for publication. It is necessary then to rely on the comments of people who knew both women.

Carol Lynn, of course, feels that her mother did nothing to antagonize Steven's second wife, that she made friendly overtures to Debby at all times, and especially after the couple had reconciled. Then, as Carol Lynn tells it, relations just broke down and her mother had no contact with Debby. She told the police in July 1985 that Debby had told Margaret that she hated her and was jealous of her.

Evelyn Goldsmith, the friend whom Margaret had visited five weeks before her death, said Margaret told her that "Debby had admitted to her face that she was jealous of her and that she wanted what Margaret had. As far as I could figure, from what Margaret had told me, nothing seemed to please Debby."

Another friend has a different view. "I think that Margaret, in the usual Benson manner, would assert her influence and her will right into their private lives. And this was unacceptable to Debby. And I can certainly understand; it would have been unacceptable to me. When Debby put her foot down and said to Margaret, 'That's the end of it, I don't want any more,' the iron curtain dropped. Margaret couldn't accept that. So Debby then had to prohibit her from seeing the kids. At that point it was open warfare. And there was Steven in the middle."

Carol Lynn makes no bones about her own negative attitude toward Debby. "No one could see what he saw in her. Not some knockout figure, and certainly nothing particular to look at—not that she was unattractive, but you wouldn't turn around to look at her twice.

"She really didn't associate with the family. She wasn't interested in the family." Debby had committed what Carol Lynn considered the unforgivable sin.

Were there never any "normal" periods—days, weeks, and months in which everyone got along with one another? "No, never," says Carol Lynn. "First of all, in the beginning I didn't like her [because] I didn't trust her. But my mother convinced me that I should try to be nice to her, so I did.

"I would not have felt the same way about her if I had met her in different circumstances. But I didn't think she was good for Steven. And then when she started mistreating my *mother*, that was it!"

Wherever the blame lay, and in whatever proportions, Margaret Benson's relationship with Debby over the last few years was openly hostile, at least on Debby's part. If Debby's phone rang, says Carol Lynn, and Debby even suspected it was a member of Steven's family calling, she'd simply hang up—or slam down the receiver.

Carol Lynn says further, "In the three years since Debby came back from Wisconsin, my mother may have seen Steven and Debby's children five or six times. And in the last year of her life, my mother saw the children exactly twice. Once, at Christmas, when Steven *finally* brought them down to the house, but not until eight o'clock at night. Imagine, bringing little babies out at eight o'clock at night. And they were allowed to stay for twenty minutes. *Maybe* half an hour. Long enough to give the children their presents. Even at that point my mother still bought a Christmas present for Debby.

"I can remember that Christmas so vividly—and it sticks out in my children's minds, too—because my mother was so devoted to those babies, and loved them so much. I can still see her allowing Christopher [Steven's son] to stand on the piano bench and jump up and down, and she wouldn't even allow my grown children to *sit* on the piano bench. And Victoria was *banging* on the piano.

"The only other time she saw them was when my grandfather came to Naples. He and Janet Lee were there for a week, and my grandfather kept saying to Steven, 'I want to see your children. Bring the children down,' but Debby wouldn't allow it. No children, no children, no children. So it's the day before he's to leave, and Boppa says to Steven, 'Either you bring the children down, or I'm going up there' [to Fort Myers, where Steven and Debby lived, a half-hour's drive from Quail Creek]. I guess Debby didn't want that, so she agreed to bring the children down, but she wouldn't bring them to my mother's house. She would only bring them over to the Meridian trailer [out of which Steven's companies conducted business in Naples]. So my grandfather and my aunt have to go over there, have to sit outside in the heat on the little picnic bench my mother had gotten for the trailer. So, Debby arrives with the children, with her full-time housekeeper, and they were allowed to stay for a grand total of fifteen minutes. At one point, four-year-old Christopher went up to my mother, stared at her, and said, 'Who are you?' "

In 1984, having finished, so to speak, with both tobacco and real estate, Steven Benson went into the business business. He founded not one, not two, and not three new service businesses in the Naples – Fort Myers area, but, over the next few months, well over a dozen brand new businesses, most of which were nothing but ideas.

And of course, being Steven Wayne Benson, he gave them grandiose names. Meridian Security, which installed burglar alarms in homes and businesses, at least had a shot at becoming a profitable, self-supporting company. The others either never had a chance, or were never *given* a chance by their founder. Steven's pattern in operating these businesses was exactly the same as it had been back home in Lancaster: great initial enthusiasm and even some hard work, and then decelerating interest, followed, predictably, by diminishing returns. Or none at all.

There was, however, one difference this time. Steven did start one company that he was still trying to hold onto, still trying to improve and expand, up until his conviction. That company was called Meridian Marketing, and it was designed to serve all the other Meridian companies by functioning as their marketing arm. On paper, and even in practice during its short life, Meridian Marketing seemed to be a good idea, one that might even have worked. But there was one fundamental problem with the company—Steven had kept its existence secret from his mother.

Dishonest (and dangerous) as that action may have been, it was but the latest in a long series of business transactions and inactions that characterized Steven Benson's business career. Two months after the killings, Margaret's attorney, Wayne Kerr, gave a statement to the prosecutors. A preview of what was to be his testimony at Steven's trial, it was the kind of statement that could have been made about *any* of the companies that Steven Benson was ostensibly running.

Kerr said, under oath, "What I discovered with Meridian Security network was that, first of all, there was a lack of good accounting procedures. There were many checks that—uh—were—the stub of the check was never filled in. Also, the bank reconciliation had never been—there had been no bank reconciliation prepared for me after the meeting. Checks were bouncing continually—huh—it was just—utter chaos. It was a C.P.A.'s nightmare, if you will.

"We noticed," Kerr, who is also a C.P.A., continued, "some discrepancies between what was listed in the checkbook as the payee and what the actual check was. . . ."

Kerr was being polite. The books and records were a mess. And there were red flags—the accountants' term for questionable transactions—all over the place. What was worse, as Kerr's testimony corroborates, neither he nor Margaret Benson knew anything at all about the existence of Meridian *Marketing*. But, typically, Steven had made the same kinds of errors that had tripped him up in the past. For example, he charged a very expensive desk chair for the Meridian Marketing office on his mother's Mastercard, a less-than-adroit way to hide the purchase.

Kerr's statement also indicated his opinion that for all the problems Steven caused, his mother was not exactly the calmest and most level-headed client a lawyer could desire: "you have to understand that Margaret gets into tirades. . . . She is very eccentric and she goes hot and cold very easily . . . [it is] not unusual for Margaret to go off uncocked [sic]. . . .

"[Margaret] made statements to me concerning some will provisions. . . . Basically, in her tirade of anger she made the statement to me that she . . . had changed her thinking concerning Steven with regard to the will and that maybe he wasn't treating her like a mother. She would never get to see the grandchildren because Steven's wife sort of kept them away, and . . . and I think in a moment of anger she was thinking of disinheriting him. . . .

"I said, 'Well, maybe the better route would be to get an accounting for these loans and treat those as advancements against his share and that would be a more equitable way of handling it.' She just really didn't say anything, but I knew she was thinking and there was no final decision made, but certainly it was part of our conversation."

Kerr also testified that in December 1984 Margaret had asked him to draft a will that would differ from the one he had drawn for her in 1983, a document that divided her estate equally among her three children, Carol Lynn, Steven, and Scott. The changes in this new will, which he said he did draw up but which Margaret never signed, would have pertained "to spreading out payments with regard to Steven and also with regard to Scott."

But not with regard to Carol Lynn? No, said Kerr, because "I think [Margaret] felt . . . Carol was maybe a better money manager."

Kerr said he drafted the revised will and sent a copy to Margaret that same month, December 1984, but they never discussed it until the following June, a month before she was killed. He said when he questioned her she replied that "she had reviewed it, and her mind wasn't made up as to what she wanted to do, and as a result she didn't want to do anything at that point."

A week later, at Carol Lynn's house in Boston, and before she went off to Europe with Scott, Margaret got more specific about both her complaints and her proposed remedies. As Carol Lynn told the police two weeks after the bombings:

> I knew she had a lot of things on her mind—she was worried about getting the stuff for the income tax—and she would do things like get up at two in the morning and start paperwork. And I told her I wasn't going to let her go because if she did she wouldn't get any rest, and she'd never get any better at all. So I finally convinced her to stay up [in Boston] for those two weeks and that we would go every other day for her therapy at the hospital, and that she could rest, which she really needed because she was really sick when she got back, and she still of course had the pneumonia. And you know we talked a lot anyway. . . . She had been talking to Wayne about something; I guess Wayne happened to mention that Steven had bought this house. . . .

That was the discovery which was to trigger the horrendous course of events that followed. It was Margaret Benson's anger, anger that in almost any other parent would have been fury, that made her finally insist on an accounting, a *reckoning*, with her son. Steven had bought a house for himself just when she was seriously worried that her own house plans were in jeopardy, and all because of his financial misdeeds. (Margaret Benson was still, apparently, refusing to admit to herself that what Steven had done, what he was obviously continuing to do, amounted to theft.)

Somehow, following that first moment of discovery, and for days afterward, she was able to contain that anger—or at least to contain its outward manifestations. But then, Margaret Benson had never been one for sustained rage. That was not her style.

Three

The Weapon
of Cowards

"Mother, You'll Never Guess Who That Was!"

On Sunday, July 7, 1985, at noon, Margaret Benson drove her bronze Porsche 280-S to the Southwest Regional Airport between Naples and Fort Myers and picked up her attorney, Wayne Kerr. It wasn't hard to spot the tall, fairly young lawyer, with his full head of dark, disheveled hair and his gawky manner so unlike that of the retired corporate lawyers who stroll the streets of Naples in their lime green sport coats. He put his luggage in the back of the beautiful little car, and Margaret pulled away smartly.

Kerr was in Naples because his client was finally about to make good on her promise to "do something" about Steven. A few weeks before, when she'd said to Steven, almost offhandedly, "I hear you bought a new house," he hadn't denied it; so she knew it was true. She had not yet seen the house with her own eyes, but that was scheduled for Monday, the next day. In the morning, she and Wayne were to stop at the Meridian trailer and go over the books, for the ostensible purpose of preparing Margaret's income tax returns, and after that they'd drive to Fort Myers and

171

find the house. Margaret wanted to *see* it. The reckoning was at hand.

After picking Kerr up, Margaret drove him out to the site of the new house she was planning to build in Quail Creek, and they talked about the advantages of building a new house instead of expanding her present home on White Violet Drive.

Then they drove back home to talk some more business. Kerr brought up several matters that he knew he had to raise, even though he was sure Margaret didn't really want to discuss them. The most important item was the "schedules," the computer printouts of the money owed to Margaret by her three children, which was one of the main things Margaret had been avoiding.

"We had talked about it," Kerr said later, "and it was like everything else—it got put off and put off because it was a delicate subject that she did not particularly care to discuss. I think she was frustrated in putting all these numbers down on paper and seeing what the amounts were."

They'd returned to the house around 2:00 P.M. and had gone right to work on Margaret's personal tax matters. But the question of these "loans" to the children hovered in the background, because the gift-tax laws had recently been changed, and Margaret could not claim everything she'd given her children as a gift— and she had made it quite clear that everything was not.

Carol Lynn made dinner, and the three of them watched some television and turned in fairly early. Scott and Kim Beegle, his girlfriend, were out for the evening. Kim, who had succeeded Tracy Mullins several years earlier, spent almost every night with Scott in his room in the house on White Violet Drive. Margaret denied this, even to such old friends as Judge and Mrs. Newcomer. When they had stayed with Margaret in June, they mentioned hearing noises from Scott's room. They said it sounded like people walking around. No, said Margaret, the room was empty.

Kim and Scott, who seldom returned early when they went out for an evening, had taken the Chevy Suburban, the family workhorse wagon that, despite its broken air conditioner, kept running when all the exotic vehicles, the Porsche and the *two* Lotuses, took turns breaking down. Margaret also owned a dependable Chevy van, but it seemed Steven was always driving that. Carol Lynn had a car in Florida, a Datsun, but it had broken down when one of her brothers was using it, and now it sat at her mother's waiting to be repaired.

On Monday morning, Wayne Kerr got up around 7:15, glanced out the window in his room onto the circular drive in front of the house. He wanted to make sure it was another picture-perfect day in southwestern Florida. It was.

He joined Margaret, who was already up, partaking of a light breakfast of plums and instant coffee, and when Marty Taylor, Margaret's personal secretary, arrived for work, Margaret talked with her for a few moments about specific tasks for that day before leaving with Wayne for the Meridian trailer office, a ten- or fifteen-minute drive from Quail Creek.

The trailer that served as the offices for Steven's various businesses was located at 3739 Domestic Avenue, a rectangular two-and-a-quarter-acre lot in a light industrial area called the Naples Production Park. There was nothing domestic about Domestic Avenue. Next door was a moving company, and up the street a plumbing supply house. The nearest main thoroughfare was Airport Road, two blocks to the west, and there the businesses were almost all commercial, not industrial. Margaret had purchased the lot the previous July for $180,000.

As he and Margaret pulled in around 9:00 A.M., Wayne Kerr noticed a new sign, facing Domestic Avenue, that announced, in bold lettering, "Future Site of MERIDIAN COMMERCE PARK." That would be Steven's work.

Steven Benson was already in his office when they arrived, and Margaret went in and told him that she and Wayne were there to get information for her tax returns; so she needed, for once, a clear picture of what was going in the various businesses. How was the money she had invested represented on the books? *Where* were the books, and were they up to date and properly done? Implicit in her requests were other vital questions, such as "*Exactly* what is going on with these companies? Are they making a profit or aren't they? And if not, *where did all the money go?*"

Steven told his mother he would be happy to answer all her questions and to open all the books for all the companies. But first, he said, he had an appointment he *had* to keep. When he came back, he promised, they would have their accounting. Wayne Kerr recalls him saying, " 'Wait until I get back, and I'll give you everything you need.' "

After Steven left, Wayne began to poke around, but all he could find out in the open were relatively unimportant business records, so then he and Margaret talked with the employees. But it was soon obvious that only Steven could give them access to the kinds of records they wanted to—had to—see. According to Wayne Kerr, "I think I looked at some invoices. I looked at the figure system. I mean, little things. I looked at some jobs to try to get a feel, but nothing connected to what Steven was to provide us with."

There were four Meridian employees present that morning: Brenda Turnbull, Steven's personal secretary, an attractive, articulate woman with dark red hair; Mark Nelson, Steven's second in command in the security business; Steve Dansic, who had more to do with Meridian Technologies; and Mark Patterson, a new employee who said little. The three men were all fairly young, earnest, and clean-cut.

Most of the talking was done by Turnbull and Nelson. From them, Margaret Benson learned the extent of the brand new company that Steven had purposely kept outside the Meridian umbrella—Meridian Marketing—and its office was not in the trailer with the rest of them, but up in Fort Myers, thirty miles away, where Steven and Debby lived—near the new house that Steven had just bought.

As Wayne Kerr put it, "Brenda Turnbull has always been very helpful in terms of information, and she told me about Meridian

Marketing." From her they learned that "Meridian Marketing had an office in Fort Myers on McGregor Boulevard, and that they had just entered into a lease for 2,500 square feet of additional space."

Margaret had barely even *heard* of this company. Now here she was being told that it had already incurred substantial financial obligations. This kind of thing was so typical of Steven that she had to have shuddered inside.

"And then," said Wayne Kerr, "after we got this information, we decided to take a ride up to see the new offices."

They drove directly to the Meridian Marketing office in Fort Myers, and there they found a pleasant but noticeably nervous young man named Steve Hawkins. Neither Margaret Benson nor Wayne Kerr knew exactly what relationship Hawkins had with Steven Benson or with Meridian Marketing. Was he an employee or perhaps even a partner? Margaret remembered that Steven had mentioned Hawkins's name, but she did not know exactly how he figured in. And Margaret hated to have people think she was in the dark about anything having to do with the businesses.

What they had found in Fort Myers was not particularly impressive: a small office with a tiny reception area and a small conference room, and offices for Steven Benson and Steve Hawkins. But Kerr used a smart ploy. He told Hawkins, " 'We were in the area and we were just stopping by to see the new offices.' " Hawkins then took them across the street to see the new space.

What they saw this time *was* impressive. It was a much larger space, and though the work area was still unfinished, they could see the wires for an alarm system (a Steven Benson trademark) and also, Kerr believed, the wiring for a computer system. As he watched Margaret Benson walk around the huge office space, Kerr knew she was dying to ask one simple question: "Is this being done with *my* money?"

She said nothing, however. As Kerr put it, "She would have loved to [ask], but it wasn't proper."

What neither Margaret nor Wayne Kerr knew was that not long

after they'd left the Meridian trailer in Naples, Steve Hawkins had received a call from Steven Benson, warning him that the two were on their way to Fort Myers and that he had better not spill any beans. Hawkins was, in fact, a salaried employee who'd been promised a piece of the business by Steven Benson. Even he wasn't sure what his boss meant.

But he did Steven's bidding, as best he could. Steven had told Hawkins that if his mother and Wayne Kerr saw the new IBM personal computer that had just been bought for Meridian Marketing they would hit the ceiling. He told Hawkins to get it out of the office and take it to his home. Hawkins, who didn't know what to make of all this, put the machine in his car, figuring that would be good enough. He didn't like what was going on, but something told him not to ask too many questions.

After about fifteen minutes, Wayne Kerr and Margaret Benson left the offices of Meridian Marketing. According to Kerr, there was "very little conversation. It was a very awkward situation, and, quite frankly, there wasn't a lot to have a substantial discussion on."

They went out and got back in the car. Margaret was visibly angry. She was, says Wayne Kerr, "quite upset that she had confirmed the fact that there was an office being readied for someone's occupancy. Her number one fear was [that she would end up] being responsible for a lot of these obligations that were entered into by her children, and she didn't want this to happen in this case. And she indicated to me in no uncertain terms that she did not want to be a part of any Fort Myers office . . . she had concerns that the Fort Myers office was much more plush than the Naples office, the trailer, and she thought that the business should be in Naples. She wanted to keep it that way."

And then she saw Steven's house.

Not only did they behold a large two-story home on what had to be at least a full acre, with plush lawns and both a pool and a tennis court visible from the street, but they also saw an automobile in the driveway. It was a Datsun 280Z, the expensive, sporty model.

" 'I was told he sold that car,' " Wayne Kerr remembers an even more upset Margaret saying. She was under the impression, he says, that the car had been sold in order to come up with the money for the down payment on the house. But if the car had *not* been sold, then where did the money for the down payment come from?

According to her lawyer, Margaret made the decision then and there that she would get a lien on that house in order to insure that Steven would have to pay her at least some of what he owed her. "Basically," says Kerr, "she wanted to own that house. She wanted me to prepare whatever documents were necessary, to place liens, or maybe a second mortgage against that mortgage to cover the debts she felt Steven owed her."

It was then, as they drove back to Naples, that a very agitated Margaret Benson told Wayne Kerr that she had been "changing her thinking concerning Steven with regard to the will and that maybe he wasn't treating her like a mother."

They got back to the trailer in Naples about 2:00 P.M. Steven was there and Margaret went right to him, telling him, quietly, that she had to talk with him. They went into his office and closed the door. Wayne Kerr was in there for part of the time. He remembers Steven giving his mother two stories about the blue Datsun 280Z. First he said that he had sold it, then, later, he said it belonged to someone else, " 'a watchman's' or a friend in business."

Margaret didn't press the point of the car, or the house for that matter, because she wasn't quite ready. She believed Steven had accepted her cover story, that Wayne Kerr was down in Naples to help her prepare her tax returns, and that was why they needed to see the books for the various businesses Margaret had funded.

Her intention, says her daughter, was to get the results of the week's work, find the proof that Steven was either dishonest or incompetent (or both) and then present him with a *fait accompli*, the justification for his being relieved of his duties and the leverage that would force him, even if he had to sell his new house and all his cars, to start paying Margaret back the huge sums that he had taken from her, one way or another.

As far as she could tell, Margaret remarked to Carol Lynn later that night, Steven had not figured out what she was up to.

Finally, Steven produced something in response to his mother's request for the books of the various companies. She handed them to Wayne Kerr, and within moments Kerr saw they were a shambles. The checkbooks had incomplete entries and there were checks missing. "I can't work with these," he said.

Margaret told Steven to get all the books and records together, starting immediately. She wanted to be able to go through them with the help of Wayne Kerr, and she said she wanted everything finished and all the books inspected by the end of the week, so that Wayne could do her taxes. She told Steven to get started right away and to expect to work late that night, the usual pattern when Wayne came down to work on taxes. Steven said he'd be perfectly willing to work late, but unfortunately he had an important social engagement already set up for that evening.

Margaret reneged, reluctantly, but told him to be ready to get started first thing in the morning. Then she and her lawyer left.

They were barely out the door when Steven picked up the phone and called Steve Hawkins in Fort Myers to set up that "prior social engagement."

Carol Lynn was surprised when she heard her mother and Wayne come in the door of the Quail Creek house about 4:30. Normally, when Wayne was down to work on taxes they would not be back until at least 7:00 P.M.

Carol Lynn and her mother had had many long talks while Margaret had been with her in Boston just weeks before, and Carol Lynn was well acquainted with the whole situation. Also, the daughter knew that Wayne had told her mother *and* Steven the previous year that, based on what he had found while going over the books, Margaret could have had Steven arrested and sent to jail.

The three of them sat in the kitchen for a while talking about the events and discoveries of the day. Margaret had quite a bit to say about the size of Steven's new house—and how mad she was at seeing, in the driveway, the car Steven had told her he'd sold in order to come up with the down payment. And she also mentioned that she didn't think much of Steven's explanations of whose car it was.

They discussed Margaret's "options," what she should or at least could do to improve the situation, if not remedy it. Wayne Kerr later said he gave Margaret three alternatives: "Shut down the business; second, remove Steven and replace him with Mark Nelson; or, frankly, bring in some new blood to head up the company."

But nothing was resolved. It was all, as the lawyer put it, "just discussion at that point."

Carol Lynn was beginning to think about making dinner when the phone rang. She answered it, spoke for a few minutes, and then came back to where the others were sitting. She had an odd smile on her face.

"Mother," she said, "you'll never guess who that was! It was Steven." Carol Lynn related the conversation: Steven would be down at seven-thirty in the morning to help stake out the lots. "And," she added, "he even wants *Scott* to go along!"

Carol Lynn again suggested that she start dinner, but her mother interrupted her. "Honey, it's your birthday. The least I can do is take you out for dinner."

Although she was tired, Carol Lynn agreed to go. It hadn't been much of a birthday. She'd received no cards, though her mother had taken her to buy some clothes the week before. The three of them went to The Plum, over on "the Trail," which is what most people in Naples called the Tamiami Trail. It's also called Highway 41, coincidentally the same number as the birthday they were about to celebrate.

Once in the restaurant, they picked up the same conversation they'd been having back at the house, but some people they knew came in and sat within earshot, so they switched to safer topics. When they got back to Margaret's house, all three of them were tired, and they agreed that going to bed early sounded like a great idea. Wayne Kerr said later that they must have watched at least some television; he remembered seeing an episode of, as he put it, *"Allen and Katie."*

To the astonishment of his sister and mother, Steven Benson, who was not known either for getting up early or for being punctual, arrived when he'd said he would, at approximately 7:30 A.M. on Tuesday, July 9, 1985.

One of the few bits of conversation that occurred early that morning was Margaret's asking Steven, not long after he'd walked into her kitchen, if he had brought the books with him. He said that he had, that they were in the van.

It was to be a morning for surprises. Not only had Steven been on time at an un-Stevenlike hour, but he volunteered to go pick up doughnuts and coffee. He kidded Wayne Kerr about the lawyer's dislike for instant coffee. Then he left, taking the Suburban. Steven was gone for so long that the others began to joke about it.

Margaret's secretary, Marty Taylor, arrived, and, after a bit of conversation, began to work. Eventually, Wayne Kerr joined her and started to review some of Margaret's tax records. A friend of Ruby Caston, the housekeeper, came by to pick up Ruby's check, got it, and left.

Carol Lynn was working in the living room. She began to wonder what was keeping Steven, because she knew all too well that the longer in the day they waited, the hotter it would be, and the worse the mosquitoes and other bugs would be. Naples in July is a little less paradisiacal than Naples in January.

Finally, a little before nine o'clock, Steven returned. Because Carol Lynn doesn't drink coffee, she hadn't ordered any, so he walked past her and into the other room. He put down a box with the rolls and coffee and then went outside again.

Margaret had not been planning to go with them, and was dressed to go into the Meridian office with Wayne.

"Oh, Mother," said Steven, "I'd like you to go over too."

"Why?"

"There are some things that I need you to see." A discussion followed, but Steven prevailed.

"Okay," said Margaret, "I'll go and change my shoes."

Her secretary then said, "Mrs. Benson, don't forget the pool man is coming."

"Oh, that's right, Steven . . ."

Her son then offered suggestion after suggestion as to how things could be handled by Wayne Kerr. Out of frustration, Carol Lynn, who had been pointing out the impracticality of Steven's suggestions, finally offered an acceptable compromise, and they all filed out. Once again, rather than assert herself, Margaret Benson had given in to what Steven wanted. Earlier, Carol Lynn had seen Steven standing at the rear of the tan van, their mother's Chevrolet van that Steven often drove for company business. She hadn't been able to see what he was doing.

Before he'd left to go for the coffee and doughnuts, Steven had asked if Scott was up. Now, as they were finally getting ready to leave, he asked again. Scott, to borrow Carol Lynn's word, "stumbled" through the kitchen and out the door to the Suburban, which Steven had parked in the circular drive.

Then, moments later, everything and everyone seemed to be ready, and they were set to leave. Almost. Carol Lynn had forgotten her dark glasses and her hat. When she came out to get in the Suburban, she also had a squat plastic glass filled with ice and Coke. She had noticed that Scott was behind the wheel and wondered "why in the world" Scott would be driving when Steven was there. Later, she realized that Steven had arranged the seating.

Carol Lynn carefully set her glass on the back seat so that it would not spill as she got in—she knew how upset her mother would be if she spilled anything on the car's upholstery, even the upholstery of this seven-year-old wagon—and climbed inside the hot car. In the faint hope of catching a breeze, she left the door open.

Steven was about to get in when Margaret asked who had the keys. He walked around to the other side of the car and handed them to Scott. And then he stopped.

"Oh," he said, "I forgot something. I have to run in the house and get it."

"Fine," said his mother.

Steven walked off toward the house, and Carol Lynn reached for her glass. Just then she heard, and *felt*, the largest explosion she had ever known, as a twenty-seven-pound pipe bomb that had been stuffed inside the console between the two front seats went off, obliterating the vehicle.

The windshield blew out, the sheet-metal top peeled back to the rear of the wagon, as if yanked by a monstrous can opener, and both doors blew open, twisting grotesquely in the process.

A funnel of flame and thick dark smoke shot upward. What was left of the inside of the car reverberated with the echo of the blast, but before that could die, it was replaced by another phenomenal noise, one that was somehow even more ominous and terrifying. It was the *sound* of a fireball—a roaring, snapping furnace of sound, as the orange sphere of flame ate its way in every direction at once.

Almost immediately there was no longer a steering wheel, then no dashboard. Only what little remained of the front seats provided any protection—and that just momentary—for the blonde woman in the back seat, who had already stiffened in shock, her eyes stung shut by the force and fury of the blast.

A sky-rocketing shower of pebbles reached its apex and began to descend, striking everything within a radius of more than a hundred feet. Pebbles drummed against the roof and the walls and windows of the house. They struck the tan van and sprinkled the length of White Violet Drive that ran in front of Margaret Benson's beautiful house.

Carol Lynn had not yet tried to open her eyes, but if she had, she would have seen that she and the fireball were now the only occupants of what was left of the Suburban.

Margaret and Scott were blown out of the vehicle and died instantly. He was thrown away from the house and landed on the pebbled driveway, a massive bloodied opening stretching from waist to shoulder on his right side and a knifelike piece of shrapnel wedged in his skull. Margaret, whose body landed near the grass alongside the driveway, had lost her right foot and her left hand. From the forehead down, she no longer had a face.

They had been killed by a pipe bomb—what explosives experts call "the weapon of cowards."

Had her door been closed, Carol Lynn would have been killed. Instead, she soon found herself on fire on the driveway, struggling to get out of her burning shirt. She had lost almost all of her right ear, and there were gaping holes in her leg and smaller shrapnel wounds on her arm and shoulder on the right side. Blood gushed from a huge hole in her chin, and the side of her face was seared. Severe burns covered large areas of her body. Her blonde hair was aflame.

Some 150 yards behind the house, three golfers were about to tee off on the third hole when they heard the blast. One of them, by great coincidence, was Fred Merrill, the real estate man who had sold Margaret and Edward Benson their house in Port Royal and who, with his wife, Bette, had become close friends of Margaret. With him, and helping, was Charles Mayer, also a retired military man who published the community newspaper that served Quail Creek.

Merrill ran the distance to the front of the house as fast as he could, braving a rain of white-hot metal that landed as far as 200 yards across the street and which took off a piece of the chimney of Margaret's house. He saw his friend on the ground, and, hoping against hope that somehow she was still alive, he bent down and grasped her ankles to pull her away from the flaming vehicle. As he moved backward, he tripped on a tree stump and fell.

At that moment, approximately fifty-five seconds after the first blast, the second bomb—another twenty-seven-pound home-made pipe bomb—exploded. This one had been wedged under the back seat—the seat where Carol Lynn had been sitting just seconds before. Again, metal flew everywhere, and the body of the Chevrolet Suburban was jolted off the ground once more. Several pieces of metal struck Fred Merrill in the chest as he was falling backward. Had he not tripped, they might have decapitated him.

Suddenly, people—other golfers, a few neighbors, and some workmen—recovered from their first stunned inaction and began to move toward the vehicle that was blazing in the driveway and the bodies, dead and living, on the ground. A mile away, at the tennis courts of the Quail Creek Club, Stephen Vaughan, Scott Benson's tennis coach, heard the blast. He thought little of it, but drove over anyway to investigate.

Inside the house, at the sound of the first explosion, Wayne Kerr and Marty Taylor looked up at the same instant. The first thing that flashed through the lawyer's mind, as he heard what he thought were pebbles striking the windows, was that Scott's Lotus had blown up.

He got up instinctively and got to the front door as fast as his out-of-shape body would carry him.

At the door he met Steven, whose face was a mask of fear and excitement. "Call an ambulance," screamed Steven Benson, "For God's sake, call an ambulance."

Four

———

The Investigation

"Anything That Doesn't Grow."

It was an atypically quiet morning in the Miami field office of the Bureau of Alcohol, Tobacco, and Firearms. While a normal day does not resemble the familiar near-bedlam of the precinct house in a popular televised police series such as *Hill Street Blues*, the ATF offices are almost always busier than they were shortly after 9:00 A.M. on Tuesday, July 9, 1985.

Special Agent George Nowicki welcomed the quiet. He had paperwork to catch up on, as did one of his colleagues, Terry Hopkins; and they sat at their respective stations, their loosely cordoned off work areas, inside the large airy office of Group One, their unit. Above the desks of all the agents were bulletin boards, and amongst the mug shots of criminals and the occasional Rambo poster were many snapshots. Some were of cars and boats and the kinds of girls who seem to grow only in Florida and California, but most were of family. Nowicki's largest picture was of his twelve-year-old son and only child in a football uniform.

George Nowicki, forty-four, once a starting offensive end for the Georgia Bulldogs, looks as if he would have no trouble fitting into his old uniform. At six-three and a carefully watched 190 pounds, he has the kind of noticeable shoulder-muscle development that only comes from lifting weights. With sandy hair and a slow, easy manner that belies his more than two decades of police work, Nowicki could pass for thirty-five.

Though born in Brooklyn, Nowicki has lived in Florida since he was three years old. After he got his football letter and his degree from the University of Georgia, he went right into the Army, where he served as a paratrooper; then he went to Intelligence School; and later he was sent to the Dominican Republic for the 1965 "police action," and then to Vietnam. Discharged in 1966, he wanted to join the FBI, but couldn't see taking the additional years of schooling that would be necessary in order to become either a C.P.A. or an attorney, then the requirements for becoming an agent. A friend told him about ATF; he took the exam and has never been sorry.

His first assignment was as a still-buster in the hills of Georgia; the biggest still he helped smash was someone's operation on the land of a peanut farmer named Jimmy Carter. He advanced through the ranks and made supervisor but found he didn't like the administrative side and asked to be reassigned to the streets. Nowicki, whose experience spans ATF's metamorphosis from the old moonshine-chasing days to the modern age of law enforcement, refers to himself as a "young old-timer."

His partner, Terry Hopkins, is so quiet he makes Nowicki sound voluble. His straight, prematurely gray hair is worn long and caplike, in the fashion of the early seventies, and at thirty-nine he too appears to be in much better shape than most men his age. While Nowicki has been with ATF since he got out of the army, Hopkins, a former Marine with a degree in criminal justice from Youngstown (Ohio) State, worked part-time as a patrolman during school and found that he liked it.

He passed the ATF exam in 1976, and after three years in the District of Columbia he was sent to Pittsburgh, then asked for a transfer to Miami, which came through late in 1983. By mid-1985, Terry Hopkins had seen more than his share of violence, Florida style, but neither he nor George Nowicki had experienced the kind of assignment that came their way on that quiet Tuesday morning of July 9.

"I heard the secretary pass a call on to Ralph Ostrowski, our supervisor, and then I could hear him repeat a few things, such as, 'bomb blast, automobile, two people dead,' " says George Nowicki. "Of course my ears perked up. I looked at Terry, and he just nodded at me, as if to say, 'Here we go.' And he was right. Ralph called us into his office, told us what he knew, and said we should get to Naples as fast as possible."

They drove to Opalacka Airport, a private field not too far from ATF's headquarters in an unincorporated section of northwestern Miami. Although they moved quickly, they did not speed. As Nowicki said, "The people were already dead, so there was no reason for us to be running sirens and blue lights."

Ralph Ostrowski, Nowicki and Hopkins's superior, is an equally low-key and quiet professional. Technically, he is a Special Agent–Supervisor, which means that although he is an administrator, he is not deskbound. Tall and trim, with the kind of earnest good looks one associates with first-term congressmen, Ostrowski has been with ATF for almost twelve years.

After four and a half years with the Detroit police, he says he had "a desire to get out of local law enforcement." His college degree was in police administration, and he'd always wanted to work on the federal level. He took the Department of the Treasury's enforcement exam, "and ATF was the first one to pick up on me. I was happy about going with ATF, because I knew ATF worked street-level criminals to a large extent. And that appealed to me."

Ralph Ostrowski spent his first five years with ATF in Cleveland. That background provided him with a specialty in arson—

Cleveland's organized crime and unions produced a bombing "every couple of weeks." Once in Miami, he was promoted to group supervisor.

Ostrowski got the call on the morning of the Benson bombing. A detective in the Collier County Sheriff's Department knew well that ATF, which has concurrent jurisdiction with the FBI to investigate bombings, has a reputation for expertise in that area.

July 9 was also Ralph Ostrowski's fourteenth wedding anniversary. As soon as he'd sent Hopkins and Nowicki to Naples, he called his wife and told her to put their dinner plans on hold.

In Ostrowski's discussion with the law-enforcement people from Collier County, it had been determined that ATF would survey the scene of the bombing, and then the normal investigation process—the "whodunit" part—would be done jointly. Ostrowski wanted Hopkins and Nowicki in Naples immediately to evaluate the extent of the damage and to determine the necessary manpower.

"I had discussions with our Special Agent in Charge, Dan Conroy, as to whether or not the National Response Team [a unit made up of specialists in the various aspects of any complicated investigation] would be called out, and it was determined that we would send over two people to see what was going to be needed in the way of manpower.

"Fortunately we had a plane here for another operation, so we were able to fly them over there in half an hour. I chose George [Nowicki] to be the case agent because he has many, many years of experience, and it obviously was going to be a significant investigation. I chose Terry Hopkins because he also has a lot of expertise; he is now known as our cause-and-origin specialist. Explosives and arson investigations oftentimes are very long-term, dry, unfulfilling, and unrewarding types of investigations. It takes a particular kind of agent to work that type of case."

Later that day, Special Agent–Supervisor Ostrowski would have to go to Naples personally. But first he waited for his pair of top agents to give him their initial report.

One thing trained law-enforcement people like Nowicki and Hopkins know is that investigations can take strange and unexpected turns with no warning, and schedules can become meaningless. The first thing they did on the way to the airport was stop for a hamburger. There was no way of knowing for sure when they would have time to eat again.

What concerned Nowicki and Hopkins as they flew to Naples was the whole idea of this kind of crime in a place like Naples. As Nowicki says, "Vehicle bombings are pretty rare. Occasionally, vehicles are bombed with nobody in them, as a warning to somebody. Most of our bombings are property cases. From time to time we got bombings where people are injured or killed, but the vast majority of bombings and arsons involve property damage.

"The drug dealers in this area, for the most part, have quit bombing. Vehicle bombings are down, though there was a lot of it going on in the Cuban population in the late sixties and early seventies, when different factions were angry with one another. And there were Mafia bombings, organized crime bombings. As for the Colombian drug dealers," by far the most dangerous of today's narcotics criminals, "they don't bother with bombs; they just go out and machine-gun somebody."

But a car bombing that involved two—almost three—deaths in a place like Naples, Florida was highly unusual, and the two ATF officers expressed concern to each other as they flew across the Everglades in their government plane; it just could be that they were getting into something weird.

Nowicki and Hopkins were picked up at the airport by Detective Tom Fife of the Collier County Sheriff's Office and driven directly to the Quail Creek subdivision. As Fife drove, he filled the two ATF agents in on some of the details. George Nowicki grabbed a few sheets from his partner's yellow legal pad and took notes. "I had come to work that day," he says, "just expecting to do some paperwork and then later a surveillance, and I didn't have everything I'd usually carry." He scribbled the names of the deceased, Margaret and Scott; the injured, Carol Lynn; and the survivor, Steven.

As they pulled into Quail Creek, George's first thought was that the crime being described to him seemed strangely out of place in the quiet, elegant surroundings. Two things stood out. One was the narrow yellow tape that seemed to be strung everywhere, as if delineating the boundaries of some grotesque celebration. The bold lettering read: "Police Investigation Area. Do Not Cross." The other singularly noticeable item was what remained of the Chevy Suburban. What had so recently been a sturdy, useful vehicle in the driveway of Margaret Benson's handsome home was now a twisted, blackened hulk.

As soon as the two ATF agents arrived and met the officers at the scene, they were taken to view what was left of the Suburban. "We could see by the two distinct blast areas of the vehicle," says Nowicki, "that in all likelihood two separate devices had gone off, and that the devices had been placed inside the vehicle—because the metal had been blasted down under the vehicle. One of the devices appeared to have been right in between the two front passenger seats, right where there would have been a console, and the other appeared to have been under the back passenger seat, if you were only using two of the possible three seats, directly in back of the driver."

And then they viewed the bodies, which were still on the ground under makeshift plastic shrouds. Carol Lynn had already been taken away. Near death, she was the object of frantic and furious attention in the emergency room of the Naples Community Hospital.

The bodies of Scott and Margaret were not where they had landed after being blown out of the vehicle. Courageous bystanders, neighbors and golfers like Charles Mayer and Fred Merrill, had rushed to the blast and pulled them to what they hoped was safety—also hoping against hope that they were still alive. Mr. Merrill, who was struck by shrapnel when the second bomb went off, was not the only one to be injured: Mr. Mayer, a neighbor who'd been on the golf course with the same foursome, came to the vehicle from a different direction and was struck by flying metal. He lost the tip of his nose.

Nowicki says, "They approached a burning vehicle with a gasoline tank. Fortunately, the tank did not blow up, but these heroic people had no way of knowing that it would not."

As George Nowicki and Terry Hopkins surveyed the bodies, the official investigation of the Benson case began.

"We looked to see if the injuries on the bodies were consistent with the physical evidence from the vehicle. In other words, we had been told that Scott Benson had been sitting in the driver's seat, and in fact his body was found on the driver's side of the vehicle, and when we looked at Scott's body we could see that the predominance of the injuries were to the right side of his body, which indicated that the blast device was to his right. He was laid open like a mannequin and you could see his internal parts.

"And when we looked at Margaret, we could see that the very heavy damage to Margaret's body was to the left side of her body. She may even have had her hand on the console because the entire thing was blown off, and her face was just gone."

George Nowicki, a compassionate man, adds, "They probably died in less than a minute—they may not have felt it."

A tragedy of this nature and proportion does strange things to people's ability to recall exactly what happened. When the ATF officers arrived, they were told by Collier County officers that witnesses had placed the two explosions as being anywhere from thirty seconds to ten minutes apart.

The official police estimate was fifty-five seconds to one minute. They made that estimate by reenacting the movements of two key witnesses, where they were at the time they heard the first blast and how long it took for them to get where they said they were when they heard the second. This task was performed by Nowicki along with his counterpart in charge from the Collier County Sheriff's Office, Lieutenant Harold Young. It was an early example of the kind of cooperation between the two different law-enforcement agencies that was to make the Benson case a model investigation.

According to Nowicki, "What we did, two days later, was to get Charles Martin, a roofer who had been working on a nearby roof, to reenact where he was—exactly what tools he had on his body, and exactly where he was on the roof—when he heard the first explosion, and what he did. We ran through the sequence with him. We did the same thing with Fred Merrill, who'd been on the golf course in back of the house, and we ran through it with him. They came out within a second or two of each other."

Special Agent Terry Hopkins, Nowicki's ATF partner, is known for his deliberate and methodical investigative work, traits that carry over to his manner of speaking. He says what he means, step by logical step.

"My first impression when I got there was that I couldn't believe the damage to the vehicle. Something must have been awful big to have destroyed it the way it did. I'd never seen one that bad. Just by looking at the floorboards it was apparent that there were two explosions. We did a preliminary search, and we saw little pieces of pipe. So we had some indication right then that there may have been a pipe bomb in there."

If the bombing had been smaller, and if there had been no fatalities, at that point in the investigation, Nowicki and Hopkins would have done the search of the scene themselves—the careful collection of physical evidence that would become vital if someone were to be brought to court and tried for this crime.

"Because of the extensive damage, and the fatalities," says Hopkins, "we decided to hold off and call the District and get more people out, and do a 100 percent search."

The local law-enforcement people had protected the scene better than most, says Hopkins. "They had the scene secure, and they didn't let anybody in there once the fire was out. They got everybody out of there, had it taped off, and were standing by waiting for us."

Hopkins has a succinct description of how successful the Collier County Sheriff's Office had been in keeping curiosity-seekers away from the scene "Most of the people I saw had badges and guns."

And the press? To their consternation, they, too, had been kept out. "They were mostly up in the air, from what I could see when I got there, in their helicopters. They were no problem."

The police's problem, as they were about to learn, was much closer at hand.

When ATF agents George Nowicki and Terry Hopkins went inside the house they found Steven Benson; the attorney and family friend Wayne Kerr; Margaret's secretary Marty Taylor; an almost inconsolable Kim Beegle, Scott's girlfriend; and the tennis coach, Stephen Vaughan, who had driven over to the house to see what all the smoke and sirens were about. One of the first people Nowicki talked to was Steven Benson, who had been described by some people on the scene as near hysteria—and by others as exhibiting something less than what they guessed would be a natural response for a man who had just lost his mother and brother and had almost lost his sister to a fiery bomb.

At this point, of course, Steven Benson was not even a potential suspect. "When you're talking murder," says George Nowicki, "you think: motive, opportunity, and ability. We knew that he had the opportunity because he was the last person to drive that vehicle.

"I talked to Steven first because I knew that he had already had some conversations with the Collier County Sheriff's Office, and he had told them a certain set of facts. And I went in and talked to him again, and basically I wanted to pinpoint, because it was a little bit unclear to me, exactly where he was—*exactly*—when the first explosion occurred.

"He told me pretty much what he told everybody else—that

he drove there about seven-thirty in the morning from Fort Myers in the beige van that was parked in front of the house, that he took the Chevrolet Suburban to go to the Shop 'n Go to get some coffee and doughnuts for the family and others at the house, and he said that he stayed away for about an hour. And I remember he said an hour, because I went and talked to Wayne Kerr, and he supported what Steven had said about being gone an hour.

"And I also talked to Marty Taylor, and she told me that when she got there about eight-thirty, the Suburban was gone and the beige van was there. So two people supported what he said, and I assumed he was telling the truth.

"When I asked him why was there such a delay," the Shop 'n Go being only a few miles from the house, "he said, well, he had run into a construction worker there at the Shop 'n Go and they had a long conversation."

Other witnesses also supported Steven's story. Wayne Kerr remembered looking at his watch at seven-thirty as he saw Steven drive up Margaret's driveway. He hurried into the kitchen, not wanting Steven to kid him about being late.

Nowicki, the experienced agent, could not help but be struck by what he called Steven's lack of "concern."

"He just seemed concerned for his own situation and what he was going to do next. There his mother and his adopted brother were lying out there in the yard, and he just seemed unfeeling. That's the impression I got. He didn't seem overly nervous, and he didn't seem overly upset. That was the biggest impression that bored into my mind that afternoon, that he didn't seem to have the normal human response to what had happened."

Later that same day, the police, who already knew that Steven Benson had had the opportunity to commit the crime, learned another important fact. "We discovered during the course of the day that he also owned a burglar alarm company and that he was familiar with wiring electrical devices and electrical circuits." Opportunity was now supplemented with ability.

Back outside in the merciless Florida sunshine, the investigative process was unfolding and the cooperation between ATF and the Collier County Sheriff's Office was increasingly evident. Harold Young of the sheriff's office and George Nowicki were co-captains, so to speak. Nowicki's boss at ATF, Ralph Ostrowski, also arrived on the scene that afternoon and stayed for the rest of the week, but early on he placed Nowicki in charge. Ostrowski worked on assigning new tasks to officers in the field as they finished previous ones; and he took on the job of briefing the press, an assignment few officers relish.

Terry Hopkins was named official evidence technician on the case. That meant that as the officers on the scene performed the initial, limited examination of the bombing site and the surrounding areas, they were to bring pieces of evidence to Hopkins for identification and numbering. If there was a question as to whether something found was or was not evidence, he would hold it, and that determination was to be made by Albert W. Gleason, ATF's top bomb expert, who had already been summoned to Naples from Washington, D.C.

Another team member, Mike Gideon of the Collier County Sheriff's Office, was designated the scene photographer. As items were found, he tagged each and then photographed the find. This was another important step in preserving the chain of evidence that could lead from site to trial.

Another important player was the schematic artist, ATF's Tom Dykstra. His work included drawing a rough sketch of the vehicle, and sketches of where the various pieces of evidence had been found within the overall environment.

In addition to these key players, there was a virtual platoon of other officers and agents, fanning out all over, talking to people, finding out what they had seen or heard, what they thought they had seen or heard, and when. At this point, anything was grist for the mill.

The police finally opened the roads to certain limited travel, such as access for homeowners, who were by mid-afternoon becoming less frightened and more annoyed at not being allowed to get to their homes. And finally, the police let the media come a little closer.

Beverly Cameron, a popular and experienced reporter for WINK-TV, one of Naples's main stations located in nearby Fort Myers, was among the mob of reporters on the scene. "From the minute that the murder happened, I was totally caught up in it. Every day, my assignment editor wanted a Benson story, and usually we were able to come up with one every day. But it was difficult because the investigators weren't talking to the press." Cameron says it was every reporter for him- or herself from the very beginning. They were there from every major publication in the country.

One of the people inside the house who was mindful of this was Stephen Vaughan, the tennis coach. At one point in the afternoon, Vaughan says he suggested to Wayne Kerr that he release a statement to the press; Vaughan says his intention was "to stop outside influences from putting words into the mouths of people inside the house."

At four-thirty in the afternoon, Al Gleason, the ATF bomb expert, arrived. The hot, tired detectives and special agents all stood a little straighter when the gray-haired Gleason stepped out of his car. A tall man with a face that seemed to have been marked by all the violence he has witnessed in his long career, Gleason had spent twenty years in the New York City Police Department before joining the ATF. All but two of those years had been on the bomb squad.

From George "the Mad Bomber" Metesky through terrorist bombings involving Cubans, Puerto Ricans, Black Panthers, the Weather Underground, and the Jewish Defense League, Al Gleason had seen it all. There are few, if any, other explosives experts alive today whose experience is as wide or as varied.

When he retired from the NYPD, Gleason was recruited by ATF, which had only recently been given jurisdiction—by virtue of the 1968 Gun Control Act and the Explosive Control Act of 1970, which was implemented two years later—over explosives cases. At the time of the Benson bombings, Al Gleason was set to retire from law enforcement, for the second and final time. The Benson case was to delay that event.

"When I arrived," says Gleason, "the vehicle was covered with plastic sheeting, and I then did a cursory walk through the area, more or less making a mental note as to what would have to be done in the way of search procedures, what type of procedures would have to be laid down for the following morning."

What would Al Gleason tell the team of people doing the step-by-step foot search of the blast area? "I would instruct them," he says in his quiet, almost laconic voice, "to pick up anything that didn't grow."

Gleason says, "My only interest in Steven at that point was *means*—did he possess the means to do something like this?" He knew the answer to that on the first day.

That same night there was a meeting of all the law-enforcement people at the sheriff's office, and Gleason and the others worked out the procedures, figured out who should do what. Then several officers left to conduct more interviews before the day had passed and the memories of certain key people were less sharp. They were working in teams combining one ATF agent with one detective from the sheriff's office. George Nowicki and Harold Young went to the beach hotel where Steven and his wife were supposed to be staying. Debby had been brought down from Fort Myers late that morning by one of Steven's employees.

The interview they had in mind did not materialize; they could not find Steven. But Terry Hopkins and Mike Koors, a giant local detective (at six-five and 220 he made even Nowicki, the former tight end, look small) had better "luck." They went to the Naples Community Hospital and interviewed Wayne Kerr.

Nowicki recalls, "This was the first time anyone had interviewed Wayne Kerr formally. We'd had some conversations with him at the house, but this was the first time anybody was going to sit down with him and talk in any great detail about his knowledge of the family and the purpose of his visit.

Young and Nowicki found Hopkins and Koors just as they were

concluding the interview at the hospital. As Hopkins and Koors walked out to the lobby, "they both, at just about the same time, said, 'listen to this!' " Basically and very briefly, they said that the whole reason Kerr was down there was because Margaret was really unhappy with Steven, and she was considering all kinds of adjustments to his financial picture and to his businesses.

"So on we go. First we had opportunity and ability, and now we have motive. By the end of the first day."

Interior Dialogue

During the day of July 9, 1985, while the world rushed by outside 13002 White Violet Drive, a different, if no less mad and tragic, scene was taking place inside the house.

From all accounts, it appears that when the first bomb went off, destroying the car he had just been driving, seriously injuring his sister, annihilating his mother and brother, and propelling them onto the lawn and driveway, Steven Benson stood near the door and watched for a moment, and then *ran back into the house.*

Wayne Kerr recalls that after he'd heard the explosion, felt the house shake, and heard something strike the windows both front and rear, after he'd gone to the window and looked out at the driveway, half expecting that one of the Lotuses "had blown up again," he then ran to the front door.

But at that very point Kerr was met by Steven, who was coming into the house, screaming—at him, at anyone—"Call an ambulance, call an ambulance."

A few weeks later, Kerr told the police, describing that moment at the door and its immediate aftermath, "I mean he is really shaken by the whole situation, and quite frankly I was shaken and didn't know what had happened.

"The first blast shook the house; it felt like a minor earthquake. And I think while I was on the phone, or right after I got off the phone, the second explosion occurred. By that time—we—him and I, I think, both went to the front door and there were people around—there was some guy with a white shirt—and I, I don't really recall what I saw there. I saw enough to know that I didn't want to see any more."

Wayne Kerr cannot remember how far outside of the house he went, but he does have some memory of what he saw.

"I think, I think I saw the vehicle, and—I think I may have seen Scott on the side—I don't even know where Carol Lynn was. . . . It's all running together now. I know Scott was eventually on the side and Margaret was like—in the flowerbed or where the shrubbery was. And Carol Lynn was across the street. But I'm not sure if that's what I saw when I first came out the door or not. You know we stood out there and went back and forth."

Asked if Steven said anything to him while they stood outside viewing the carnage, Wayne Kerr said, "No. He was really in shock. He was shaking his hands. When the paramedics came he couldn't even pronounce his name, couldn't even hold a cigarette. He was pretty bad off. Making animallike sounds, and, I mean, you know. . . ."

Steven looked out at the car. "He was going back and forth—from in[side] the house out to the front where the pavement, or where the walk and driveway run together. He was walking there and back and I tried to sit him down and give him cold towels. I think he was in a state of shock."

But did Steven ask Wayne to come out and help the people in the burning vehicle, or did he ask Wayne to help him provide help?

"No, no comment was made. I thought I was helping by the fact that I was calling the ambulance."

According to Wayne Kerr, only about fifteen seconds elapsed from the time Steven rushed in until the second explosion occurred. He also says that to the best of his recollection, when Steven came in the front door, he closed it behind him.

Kerr says that at some point—just when, he isn't sure—Scott's girlfriend, Kim Beegle, came out of Scott's bedroom. "I don't know if Scott had been moved or Scott was where he was when it originally happened, but he was lying—there's an island or something there and he was lying on the island—and she came out and said, 'Oh, my God. He's dead.' We tried to sit her down and calm her, but she couldn't believe it."

More than six months later, Kim showed no hesitation when a lawyer asked her in a deposition, what was the first thing she remembered about the morning of July 9, 1985. "The bomb," she said. "That's it."

Kim had met Scott in a bar about four years before. According to her, they "planned to marry after he got through the U.S. Open . . . he wanted to better his tennis career first."

Two nights before the killings, she said that she and Scott had one of their usual nights out on the town. They had made the rounds of the Brassy, the Mason Jar, the Caddy Shack, Sutton House. The next night, he had removed his cache of marijuana from the Suburban. He didn't want Margaret or Steven to find it.

On the morning of the bombing, she says she didn't even remember Scott getting up because of how soundly she sleeps. When asked, "On a scale of one to ten, with ten at the soundest, where would you put yourself?" she replied, "About ten, like a rock."

She was not asked to describe how she felt when she learned Scott was dead. Clearly, as Wayne Kerr said, "She was expressing a lot of emotion . . . and couldn't believe it."

Another person who was having trouble believing the tragedy had occurred was Stephen Vaughan, Scott's current tennis coach. At the moment he heard the explosion, he thought "they were drilling for water or something."

He had driven to work that morning. "I hadn't seen Scott for several days, and I had told him I would call him and let him know what time I wanted him to come up, because my summer schedule was very light and therefore I had more opportunity to work with him—I remember thinking that I should just go by the house, but I didn't. I went straight to the courts. That struck me as strange a couple of days later, why I would want to go over there; but I ended up going [straight] into the shop.''

Just prior to opening the tennis shop at Quail Creek, which he does at nine each weekday morning, Stephen Vaughan phoned the Benson home and talked to Scott. "He said, 'I have to go stake out some property with my mom, and then I'll come right over.' And I said, 'Fine.'

"I went out on the court with my nine o'clock lesson, and at some point, 9:10 or 9:15, we heard this explosion. Sometimes there's cap rock that they have to blow out of the way when they drill a well, and I'd heard explosions before and it didn't faze me. The only thing was, I knew where Scott's house was, and I saw the smoke come up, and, just proximitywise, I got a picture that it was coming from that area. Whether it was closer or whether it was beyond, I couldn't really tell, so I saw the smoke go, and said, 'Well, they must be drilling for water, or something, and I went on with my lesson.

"Then there was another explosion, and more smoke, and I didn't have any idea what happened. But as I'm finishing my lesson around 9:30, sirens began to come up, and there was a lot of activity going on. So when I finished my lesson and walked into the shop the ladies were arriving to start to play, Tuesday being Ladies' Day. I asked what was that, and what's going on.

"They said, oh, it's not even on Quail Creek property, it's way back beyond. And then a lady who lived on Butterfly Orchid, a street that, right after you enter Quail Creek, also goes back to the Bensons' street, said that the ambulances or fire trucks, whatever she said, were going down her street, that way. And so I immediately said, 'I'm going to go see what's going on.' I am curious by nature.

"I drove up and parked on Butterfly Orchid, and walked across the vacant lot, so I was coming up to the side of the house. The police were there, and they were roping the area off, and they were putting Carol Lynn in the ambulance when I arrived.

"One thing that got me was, I could see that the Suburban was blown up, and the Suburban never ran very well, so my first thought was maybe the engine blew up, and no big deal, nothing was that major. As I walked across the vacant lot I came across one of the windows of the Suburban. It had blown five hundred feet, but it was still intact, and I really didn't think that much about it.

"But as I got to where I could get to the yard, I could see one body lying in front of the vehicle, covered, and it happened to have a foot, his left foot was exposed, and I knew it was Scott. I knew it was Scott. I couldn't see Margaret's body, because it was blocked by the side of the house, but I knew Scott was dead right then.

"I walked up, and Steven was sitting on the front steps with Wayne Kerr, and Kim was on the front porch, and Kim was crying, and Steven was shaking back and forth, doing whatever he was doing. He wasn't crying. It was more or less a shocked kind of a rock, I guess. I had never seen anyone devastated by such a thing before, so I had no way of knowing if his reaction was genuine."

Later, something caused Stephen Vaughan to form an opinion. "When I got there, obviously I was a little in a state of shock myself; everybody else was so panicky that I was trying to stabilize, as much as I could, what was going on. So when I walked in, the only thing I could do was ask Steven if there was anything I could do for him, and that sort of thing.

"Steven said he wanted a cigarette. Wayne Kerr said he would light it for him, and, well, Wayne Kerr is not a smoker,"—the tennis coach is, ironically—"and he took a cigarette out and a lighter, and he held the cigarette out and tried to light it without putting it in his mouth. And it wouldn't light. Steven laughed, at that point, and took the cigarette and said, 'I'll do it myself.' It could have been a hysterical laugh, but that shocked me—that he would be able to laugh at anything at that point."

From that point, says Vaughan, he had difficulty understanding why Steven, in his opinion, "was not sad. Kim was sad. She was very distraught. And Wayne Kerr was just thankful it wasn't him."

Stephen Vaughan, who had probably arrived at the house within half an hour of the blasts, then went inside and tried to, as he put it, "stabilize things." No one else seemed capable of fulfilling that role. "I went inside and started to do things like getting the policemen drinks. Marty [Taylor] was a basket case, she couldn't do anything, and I just let Wayne handle Steven. I tried to control Kim as much as I could, and just keep everything intact."

At one point, probably when Nowicki and Hopkins, the ATF agents, arrived, the police came to the door and told Stephen Vaughan to get the others away from the windows, as they were going to have to uncover the bodies. He did so, but then went back to the windows himself and watched.

"Half out of nonbelief, and half out of wondering what it would take to kill Scott [who was] in that good a physical condition, I had to see it for myself. Well, I saw it. Scott [was recognizable], other than half his side was missing. Margaret was *destroyed*. She was so bad that I couldn't tell which way she was lying, whether on her back or on her stomach. All I saw was that her clothes were completely blown off. All that was left was a pair of panties—and threads. She was so obliterated that if I hadn't known it was her I would never have been able to distinguish who it was."

But as the morning progressed, Vaughan noticed two things that bothered him, especially on reflection. The first was that Steven Benson showed no interest in going to the hospital to visit his sister, who had to be, at that moment, in very critical condition.

"As the morning went on, I asked Steven if he would like to go and see Carol Lynn. After all, there was absolutely nothing they could do for Scott and Margaret. I kept asking him if he'd like to go see Carol Lynn, and his answer was no. And I probably asked him half a dozen times. All he would say is that he wanted to wait for Debra, his wife, to get there."

When Debby Benson arrived, Stephen Vaughan witnessed the second thing that bothered him. She had been picked up in Fort Myers by Steve Hawkins, who worked for Steven Benson at Meridian Marketing, the company Steven had been trying to keep secret from his mother and, possibly, also from Wayne Kerr. Hawkins was the same employee Steven Benson had called and told to get the IBM personal computer out of sight before Wayne Kerr and Margaret arrived on their surprise visit, the day before.

Vaughan was standing nearby when Hawkins and Debby Benson arrived. Before Hawkins could even offer his condolences, Steven Benson shot out the question, "Did we get any money in today?"

By four-thirty in the afternoon, when Gleason, the ATF bomb expert, arrived, things had settled down inside the house. Sherri Vaughan, the tennis coach's wife, who for a brief period had been Margaret's secretary, was there, her husband having summoned her. She helped to calm things. At one point in the afternoon, she took what was left of the coffee and doughnuts that Steven had brought, reheated it in the microwave, and passed it out to anyone who wanted any. Unknowingly, these people ate and drank what might well have been evidence.

Later, when an officer came in and asked if there were any pictures of Margaret and her children, Sherri remembered that Margaret had kept a file with personal data on her three children. She got it and gave it to the officer, who flipped through it and, finding no pictures, tossed it on one of the kitchen counters. Mrs. Vaughan never saw it again.

During the afternoon, someone realized that they ought to be notifying the remaining family members, such as Margaret's father, Harry Hitchcock, and Janet Lee Murphy, her sister, and of course Carol Lynn's two boys. Because he had given Travis Kendall, the younger of the two, a tennis lesson, and because he could say that his mother was *alive*, Stephen Vaughan made that call himself—"I felt like I could handle that one." On the others, he placed the call and then gave the phone to Wayne Kerr, who, from all accounts, was having difficulty speaking in a normal manner. But he got through these difficult calls. One couple, friends of Margaret's whom he called later on at the request of Carol Lynn, said his voice was so high they thought he was "a woman. When we called his office the next day we asked for '*Miss* Kerr.' "

All through the long day, Stephen Vaughan was the person who was getting things done, whether it was the phone calls or making funeral arrangements or getting out the press release or even calling the developer of Quail Creek and having the contract for the purchase of land rescinded. Wayne Kerr spoke the words, says Stephen Vaughan, but the ideas were not his.

Like certain others who knew Margaret and had the opportunity to meet the people she hired, Stephen Vaughan had never been overly impressed with Wayne Kerr. As for Kerr's conduct on the day of the bombings, Vaughan says that the lawyer was "a basket case." And Steven? "He was worthless."

Steven's behavior continued to bother Vaughan, especially as it related to Carol Lynn. "He didn't seem to care about what state she was in and whether she needed support. After all, that's the only member of your family living. You don't just cast that aside. It seems like, to me, you would want to see the surviving member. But he seemed to have the opposite reaction, that he didn't want to see her at all."

Late in the afternoon, Stephen Vaughan drove Wayne Kerr over to the hospital to see Carol Lynn, and the lawyer was allowed in to see her. "Sometime later," says Stephen Vaughan, "I called the house and asked Sherri to drive Steven to the hospital to see Carol Lynn, if he wanted to, and he finally accepted. This was pretty late in the afternoon."

Sherri Vaughan says the ride to the hospital was rather strange, with Steven hardly saying anything. But at one point, she recalls very distinctly, he said, "I guess I never really got over my father's death."

After they left the hospital, having had to wait for Wayne Kerr to be interviewed by the two police officers, the group talked about plans for the night. According to Vaughan, "Steven Benson said he didn't want to go back to his own house in Fort Myers that night, so I said I could get them rooms in a motel. In fact, I said I could get an adjoining room for Wayne Kerr, if he wanted to stay with them."

Vaughan also suggested dinner arrangements, which involved meeting Debby Benson, who had gone up to Fort Myers to get their three children, at a McDonald's restaurant halfway between Fort Myers and Naples. Vaughan made reservations at La Playa, a nice motel near the beach, and then called a Chinese restaurant to have food sent over.

Then a slight hitch developed. "When Steven [went] into the McDonald's, Wayne Kerr came over to me," recalls Stephen Vaughan, "and told me that he didn't want to stay wherever Steven was."

Vaughan invited Wayne Kerr to spend the night with him and his family at their home in Naples. When Steven Benson heard that Kerr was not going to stay at the La Playa, he said he would go home. Vaughan called the La Playa and canceled the reservations.

Late that night, after long discussions about the horrendous events of that day, Wayne Kerr told the Vaughans the police had suggested to him that it might not be a good idea for him to spend the night in close proximity to Steven Benson.

Closer and Closer

One day after the bombings, Steven Wayne Benson stopped talking to the police. To this day, he has yet to tell anyone on the record why he (or whoever counseled him) thought this was a good idea. But whatever his reasons, the effect of that decision was to make the law-enforcement people even more curious about this young businessman who, in their opinion, had displayed anything but the normal human reaction to the death by bombing of his own mother.

Experienced law-enforcement personnel, if they go by the book, are not supposed to get emotionally involved in a case. They are not supposed to "fix" on one suspect and get upset or angry when they can't connect him to the crime. Many of the police officers who were after the killer or killers of Margaret and Scott Benson broke this rule. Early on, they *knew* he had done it, and it drove them crazy to see him driving around Naples and Fort Myers in the same beige van that had been in the driveway on the morning of the killings, wearing the same placid expression on his round, innocent-looking face.

One of the professionals most bothered by Steven's freedom of mobility—by his freedom, *period*—was George Nowicki. Yet it bothered him to be so bothered. "I know it's unprofessional to concentrate on one guy like that and let it get to you, and I know we were not supposed to want to zero in on him until we had eliminated everybody else, but damn, here's a guy whose own *mother* has been blown to bits and he would not talk to us."

Another cop, this one a local, who had that same feeling from the very first day is Mike Koors, the big detective from the Collier County Sheriff's Office and one of the first officers on the scene. He and his boss, Lieutenant Harold Young, took a statement from Steven in the master bedroom of Margaret's house within an hour of the bombings. Steven's manner bothered Koors right away.

"It was bullshit nervousness, so to speak. The overexaggerated shaking, is the best way to put it. I've seen a lot of people come out of a lot of hairy situations, and he was so nervous that he couldn't even put a cigarette to his lips, he shook so badly—that's the impression he gave. Then he grabbed his hand with his left hand, to be able to smoke, and I just thought, 'What's this shit?' It didn't look right. I thought, 'How many people have I talked to in similar situations? What's this guy doing?'

"And then, listening to him talk about what he did from the time he got there until the explosion, well, your eyebrow goes up a little, and you think, 'Hmm, that's odd.' And then as things progressed, it got even odder."

"We continued with the investigation," says George Nowicki of ATF, "and we received different kinds of information"—in a case like this, information comes from all over, by way of letters that may or may not be written by cranks, anonymous phone calls and tips, and for-sale information from regular police sources on the streets or in the jails, people in jails being especially interested in trading favors—"such as the information that Scott had been in an argument of sorts with Kim Beegle's brother over a boat that Scott had sold him, and supposedly the brother wasn't going to pay him the rest of the money. But it wasn't the sort of deal where the brother would kill Scott. Heck, he owed Scott the money; it wasn't the other way around.

"We heard about an altercation over a watch or a piece of jewelry that was stolen. We heard about Tracy Mullins, the mother of the illegitimate child. So we keep getting information that might take us away from Steven, but every time we do, we keep coming back to Steven.

"And this is why: at the end of the first week, we knew that the devices were two four-by-twelve-inch pipes; we knew that one of the end caps was U Brand, which used to be Union Malleable, up there in Ashland, Ohio. We knew that another one is manufactured by Grinnell, ITT Grinnell, and oddly enough, one of their plants is in Columbia, Pennsylvania, right outside of Lancaster, right there.

"So we know we have end caps from two different manufacturers, and we've got two separate devices. And then Mike Koors and Terry Hopkins, who had been circulating around the plumbing supply houses, found out that somebody bought two four-inch end caps on Friday, July 5, in the afternoon, from a big plumbing supply place in Naples called Hughes Supply. The person who sold the end caps doesn't remember much about the sale. Somebody in the store thought he remembered that somebody called and asked if they had *four* end caps—they were looking for four but they settled for two, which turned out to be the U Brand end caps.

"And in this visit to Hughes Supply, they also found that someone had bought two four-by-twelve-inch pipes, which is the same size that we have from the scene—and Hughes Supply is right around the corner from Meridian Security Network, Steven Benson's workplace."

In addition, the officers found the receipts for both of these purchases, and each one was made out to a "Delray Construction." But the name of the company was spelled differently on each receipt, and on each receipt the signature was badly scrawled. "Just a chicken scratch," says George Nowicki. Of the two salesmen who handled the transactions, one couldn't remember any-thing, but the other recalled the buyer as being "large, heavy-set, with sunglasses." He could remember nothing else.

The police then set up a mug-shot photo lineup. One of the pictures in the lineup was of Steven Benson, but it was not a very current one. (Nowicki had borrowed the shot from the family al-bum, courtesy of Marty Taylor, Margaret's last secretary.) But no one at Hughes Supply could identify anyone from the photos.

As soon as the receipts were discovered, Terry Hopkins, the evidence technician, insisted they be kept in plastic "document protectors," just in case they contained any prints. The fact that the receipts had been handled by several people did not worry George Nowicki.

As he says, "A convicted felon may come in to buy a firearm, which of course is illegal, and give a false name or some other false information, but he can be tracked down because of a fin-gerprint or a palm print. And that's true even if, as in this case, the invoice or receipt has been handled by the dealer, his book-keeper, and one or more clerks. Invoices may sit around for months, sometimes years, but we are still able to get prints off of them. So we knew, in this case, that finding a print was at least a viable possibility."

As Hughes Supply was only one of 270 different outlets that police eventually contacted in their attempt to discover where the pipe had been purchased, Terry Hopkins did not attach undue significance to finding the two receipts. Nonetheless, as Nowicki pointed out, he was not about to discount their potential impor-tance—especially when Hughes Supply was right around the cor-ner from Steven Benson's office.

On Friday he had merely photocopied the receipts; on Monday he went back and asked for the receipts themselves. Once he got them—in cases like this, businesses usually hand over the ma-terials willingly; if they don't, the police have to get a court or-der—he put them carefully into the plastic document protectors.

Let the lab determine their possible importance. It was all part of the routine.

By the end of the first week, Al Gleason and his team of ATF agents and officers from the Collier County Sheriff's Office had made some progress. Using the standard crime scene search procedure, he reduced the perimeter of the search area bit by bit, and as he did, the men found more and more pieces of pipe. They also found bits of human flesh.

On the second day of the search, and after the carcass of the Suburban had been removed, Al Gleason having probed and studied it for hours and hours, the search area was reduced to a circular area of twenty to twenty-five square feet, the immediate area of the tragedy. Then they began both a visual search and an actual sifting process that resembled the work of scavengers on a beach.

They found more bits of flesh, more "minor parts, but nothing recognizable." Gleason said the scene began to get "a little raunchy, so we actually spread lime on the ground before we shoveled up the material we would sift through."

Every evening after the bombings there was a general meeting of all the law-enforcement people back at the sheriff's office, and by Wednesday night, Gleason was able to report that they had found enough pieces of pipe to be able to say with certainty that it *was* pipe. The same was true with the end caps. By midday Thursday they had enough pieces of pipe to confirm that it had been four-inch diameter pipe. Fragments also indicated the length of the pipe to have been twelve inches.

So they knew that inside the Chevrolet Suburban there had been at least one twelve-inch pipe with two four-inch end caps. "And," says Al Gleason, "that is a container, and what else could it have contained but a bomb?"

They also discovered, on reconstructing the pipe bombs, that at least one of them had a hole drilled through it. And that meant a wire, which meant an electrical charge, which meant some sort of electrical detonating device. "We know that there was a wire, and we know that it wasn't burning fuse because any type of burning fuse would have left some residue in the vehicle. Plus, we had batteries, and you don't need batteries to burn a fuse."

How "good" a bomb was this? Says Al Gleason, "It was sophisticated. The use of a pipe may not have been deemed sophisticated, but the pipe, keep in mind, is only a container. However, in the United States, when people make bombs, pipes are the most common containers."

But what did all these discoveries mean? Gleason explains, "Based on all the fragmentation we collected, we knew we had parts of three four-inch caps. Possibly four, but by putting them together we could only readily identify three. We knew we were dealing with two bombs. That was no mystery: we had two craters in the car, we had two explosions, we had two bombs. Now, were the bombs similar? Well, based on the diameters, they were similar. And the only thing that would tell us that the lengths were similar was the fact that the damage—the internal damage, and the damage to the vehicle—was similar.

"So we knew they were both four-inch, we knew that at least one was twelve inches, and the other could very possibly be twelve inches.

"When we got all the pipe frag together, and we knew what the standard weights were—for a cap, for example; the pipe cap weighs 4.3 to 4.5 pounds, four pounds, three ounces, to four pounds, five ounces. And we recovered 10 pounds, 10 ounces, which is more than two [caps]. With the pipe, four-by-twelve standard weight would be 10.7 to 10.11—we recovered 11 pounds, 9 ounces, more than one.

"So we had one-plus pipe, and we definitely had two-plus end caps in weight. We did the reconstruction, and that gave us someplace to go as far as trying to find out who had pipe, who sold it, who bought it. And that's how Hughes Supply was identified as having sold certain things, and of course how, eventually, the palm print came out."

The sifting operation also produced something else of significance—"a lot of electronics," says Al Gleason. "Now what you try to do in a situation like this, or with any bombing, is to try to identify what was normally common to the scene, and what's there that wasn't supposed to be there. Well, certainly pipes don't belong; no mystery there." But the sifting process also produced "a lot" of small electronic parts such as resistors, transistors, diodes. "All these little components," says Gleason, "and we were also coming up with burned pieces of circuit board. Small pieces."

The point is that once Gleason and his teams had accounted for everything that was *supposed* to be in the vehicle, they still had a number of these electronic pieces, and the bit of a circuit board, that did not belong, that were foreign. They may well have been parts of the detonating device.

One "foreign" element turned out to be part of a circuit board and a switch from one of several identical citizen-band radios that they learned Steven had bought. But that's all they were. And they went through the same process with what was left of a lantern that Scott had bought and which had been, they learned, seen in the vehicle as recently as the Friday before the explosions.

A sloppy or less ethical investigator might have stopped there and said he had found the triggering device.

Gleason's standard is higher than that. "I've been in this business a long time and I am not going to testify to something unless it's right. . . . As an expert I have to be right; morally, I have to *believe* that I'm right."

But despite the CB radio and the lantern, when all the sifting and investigating was done, there were still some things left over: "Two things we were never completely able to eliminate were one small piece of circuit board together with an IC chip—neither the CB nor the lantern has an IC chip, which is a memory-logic-timing type of chip. And we did have additional electronics, plus a piece of board, and a very, very small piece of relay.

"The small piece of relay we couldn't tell what it came from, other than that it did not come from the CB. So we had some electronic components that did not belong in the car. We also had batteries—beyond the six that were in the lantern—that did not belong in the car.

"So what did we really come up with? Well, I know I have a bomb, I know it was pipe, I know it was smokeless powder, and I know that they blew up. Okay, so how did they blow up? I examined that car [and] I know it wasn't in the ignition switch . . . so in my mind, it had to be an independent device placed within the vehicle. And that device was electronic, and did contain a timing and initiating circuit—these are all burglar alarm things, by the way," he adds, reminding one that Steven's security company was in the alarm business.

Gleason continues, "and this circuit would involve a system that would have an IC chip. And nothing else in that vehicle had an IC chip. And we did have an IC chip intact. So, little by little, we put the whole scenario together—and it takes a lot to convince me, but I'm pretty much convinced that it was done by activating a switch that had been placed on the outside of the car. The activation could have been done manually, or by an electronic device, or simply by touching two wires together and closing the circuit that would activate the timing and ignition device.

"I couldn't get on the stand and testify that that was *exactly* how it happened, but there's enough to tell me that most probably there was an independent electronic device in the vehicle and it contained a timing and initiating circuit."

What Gleason means is that the killer either stood next to the Suburban after everyone else was in it and flipped a switch he had previously installed in an out-of-the-way place on the outer body of the vehicle—or he did the same thing using some other device (a beeper? a garage door opener?) while standing near the vehicle. That action would trigger the timer, and because he knew (having set the timer) how much time he had to get clear, he could then walk, stroll, or run a safe distance away before the first of the two *twenty-seven* pound bombs exploded.

―――――

While all of this was happening, the press was having an unusually difficult time trying to get someone to talk to them, to
give them anything more than the official law-enforcement line.
Steven wasn't talking, Wayne Kerr wasn't talking, and Carol Lynn
couldn't talk.

The Naples *Daily News*, an afternoon paper, managed to run
its first story on the same day as the tragedy: "Vehicle Blast Kills
2 at Quail Creek Home." That understandably skimpy story was
followed the next day by one that lived up to its headline. "Mystery Surrounds Cause of Fatal Vehicle Explosion." It began by
quoting a police official who said, "What we've got at this point
is something that's unknown." As so many of the early stories
did, this one got a few of the facts wrong, such as listing that
Scott Benson still lived in Lancaster, Pennsylvania; but it supported its label of "mystery" by stating that "authorities are providing Steven Benson and his wife with unspecified security at
an undisclosed location" and that the sheriff's office had posted
a guard outside the door of Carol Lynn's hospital room in Naples.

A companion story, headlined "Second Blast, Flames Hampered Aid Effort," provided more color. It quoted several witnesses, including Charles Mayer, the golfer who had lost part of
his nose. According to the paper, he said, "I don't remember
anything after the second explosion. I was knocked to the ground
on top of her [Carol Lynn Kendall]. All I remember is getting up
and asking somebody for a towel."

The story also said that "Residents of Quail Creek Community
agreed that the blast was substantial. 'It sounded like dynamite,'
Victoria Beaudry said. Beaudry and her mother, Carol, live almost
100 yards from the Benson home near the third green of the golf
course. 'It shook the house, but I just took it for granted that it
was something to do with the construction,' Carol Beaudry said.
Carol and Victoria Beaudry said emergency crews were at the scene
within ten minutes of the initial explosion."

The story concluded by stating, "Authorities say they are not

sure what caused the explosion, adding that if it was set inten-
tionally they do not know what the motive for a bombing might
have been."

Several days later, the legwork of Naples *Daily News* reporters,
with Denes Husty in the lead, began to pay off. A front-page
story on the Benson case (in those early days and weeks, almost
every single story on the Benson case was front page) was headlined, "Surviving Son Drove Truck Prior to Blast." It began, "Investigators looking into the deaths of Margaret Benson and her
youngest son Scott say the truck they were in Tuesday when two
pipe bombs exploded had been driven earlier in the day by Mrs.
Benson's oldest son."

The account, which quoted Lieutenant Harold Young, whom
Collier County Sheriff Aubrey Rogers had put in charge of the
investigation, continued, "Investigators do know Steven Benson
had walked out to the truck with his mother, brother, and sister
as they were preparing to view a piece of property, but he had
returned to the house just before the explosion. He was not injured. 'We're not really clear on why he walked away,' Young
said. 'We haven't had a detailed interview with him yet.' "

Another story, which ran two days earlier in the Naples *Daily
News*, gave one of the first indications that this was going to be a
most unusual day. It broke the news that unbeknownst to Steven
Benson—and apparently to her own attorney, Wayne Kerr—
Margaret Benson had a second will.

2 WILLS FILED FOR VICTIM OF PIPE-BOMBING

by David Flechsig
Staff Writer

Two very different wills appeared Thursday in Collier County
Probate Court, both signed by tobacco heiress Margaret H.
Benson for the distribution of her estate.

Mrs. Benson, 63, and her 21-year-old adopted son Scott
were murdered in a July 9 pipe-bombing in front of their Quail

Creek home. The blast also critically injured Benson's daughter Carol Benson Kendall, 40, while Steven Benson, 33, and Mrs. Benson's personal attorney were inside the house.

Wayne Kerr, Mrs. Benson's attorney and an investment advisor, submitted a will he authored for Mrs. Benson May 11, 1983. According to that will, all "tangible personal property" would be dispersed "in as nearly equal portions as may be practical" to Scott Benson, Steven Benson and Carol Benson Kendall. The estate was estimated at $10 million in 1983.

That will also created a trust by a supplemental agreement that has not been made public, providing an income for each heir. Kerr was to have full control of the trust, according to the will.

Within five hours of when the first will was filed, local attorney Guion DeLoach filed a second will, dated Jan. 29, 1985. The second will makes no mention of a trust and splits all property equally among the three children.

DeLoach said today that it would be up to the surviving heirs and the courts to decide which document should be enforced.

"I got the impression that the only one who knew of this will was Margaret and the witnesses, as is frequently the case," DeLoach said.

Sharon Hester, a witness on the will DeLoach authored, was a neighbor of the Bensons when they lived in Port Royal.

"I thought the one I signed was the last," she said.

Mrs. Hester said Mrs. Benson asked her who was a good attorney and she directed her to DeLoach. DeLoach's office is adjacent to Mrs. Hester's husband's business.

Harry Hitchcock, 88, the founder of the Lancaster [Leaf] Tobacco Company and Mrs. Benson's father, said he was surprised to hear of a second will.

"I was very surprised to hear it," Hitchcock said.

The retired executive is still living in Lancaster, Pa., where all three children were raised.

He said he did not know why his daughter would change attorneys or write a new will.

She met Kerr after her husband died," Hitchcock said. "He became her tax attorney and an investment advisor. She was one of his principal accounts."

"This completely bewilders me," Hitchcock said. "I can't get any rest and I keep thinking I'm just going to wake up and it will have been a bad dream."

DeLoach said the significance between the two wills is substantial.

"It cuts him (Kerr) out of it," DeLoach said. The old will would have provided a steady income to the three beneficiaries and the attorney administering the will, he said. The new will allows the beneficiaries to do as they wish with equal shares without Kerr having any authority, he added.

"He would have controlled the children through the trust," DeLoach said.

Kerr was unavailable for comment about the wills Thursday and today.

Margaret Benson was married to Edward Benson, former chairman of the board for the Lancaster Tobacco Company, who died in 1980. His 1980 will provided for assets of $910,733 to be awarded to his wife.

The executors of that will were released by the court— completing the full terms of Edward Benson's will—on July 5, 1985, just four days before the bombing [in Naples].

A number of people who have been in on this case from the beginning say that one of the most important points in the foregoing story is represented by the sentence that read: "The old will would have provided a steady income to the three beneficiaries *and the attorney administering the will.*"

Sherri Vaughan, the wife of Scott's tennis coach Stephen Vaughan, has a vivid recollection of Wayne Kerr's reaction when

BLOOD RELATIONS / 223

he got the news of the second will. Kerr, who had stayed with the Vaughans the night of the tragedy and who knew that Mrs. Vaughan had worked briefly for Margaret Benson, asked her to work for him in the house on White Violet Drive until things got settled.

"I ought to send Wayne a bill," says Sherri Vaughan. "He still owes me, never paid me. He left town without saying good-bye or anything, just took off. After I went over that day," the day of the bombing, Wayne Kerr "asked me if I would start working from that point forward, and I went every day until Friday, and he left at around one o'clock on Friday and never came back. So I never went back either, when we found out that he'd left town."

Why did he leave so abruptly? "I was there when he got the call about the other will. It was a total shock to him. He just put down the phone, and he left. That was the last I saw of him."

At 2:00 P.M. on Sunday, July 14, 1985, a funeral was held for Margaret and Scott Benson at St. James Episcopal Church in Lancaster, Pennsylvania.

Tracy Mullins was there, the girl who claimed Scott was the father of her two-year-old girl, and she cried loudly and uncontrollably. Steven and Debby were there, and he cried, quietly. Earlier, however, at Janet Lee Murphy's house, Debby had complained about the heat and left a roomful of relatives to seek fresh air, and Steven had complained about some of the people chosen as pallbearers.

Before the day was out, Steven, citing financial reversals, had asked his grandfather for a loan of six thousand dollars. Harry Hitchcock said yes.

Almost all of Margaret's old friends were there. Mary Miller Glose and her husband, Ed, the van Huystees, Judge and Jane Newcomer, the Goldsmiths from Lake George. And her father, her sister, her nieces, her grandsons Kurt and Travis, but not her daughter.

After the funeral, as they were driving away from the church, one old family friend and his wife discussed the expression on the face of Steven Benson as he walked down the aisle of St. James. It was not, they both agreed, grief. What it was, in their concerted opinion, was fear.

Gotcha!

On the first Sunday after the bombings, the southwestern Florida papers were filled with Benson case stories. One of the most accurate had to do with the press itself. "Officials at the Sheriff's Department," reported the Naples *Daily News*, "say the gaggle of reporters covering the Benson murder hasn't hampered their investigation."

According to the paper, Deputy Chief Ray Barnett also said, "the case has generated more nationwide interest than any unplanned Sheriff's activity in [my] years with the department." He added, "There's more media coverage on this than any event I can think of in the last fifteen years. . . . It's phenomenal. I guess it's because it's a bombing." He than added a professional aside: "The 'Operation Everglades' drug round-up in 1983 and 1984 drew more reporters, but those raids were pre-publicized to the press."

By this point the press had learned that the search for the pipe had turned up some early leads. On July 16, one week after the deaths, the *Daily News* reported: "Investigators say a recent purchase of galvanized pipe from an area supply house may yield clues to who placed the two pipe bombs in a truck owned by the slain heiress, Margaret Benson. . . . A construction supply company employee, who spoke to the Naples *Daily News*, on the condition he not be identified, said investigators asked him about a recent purchase. The purchase was made in the week prior to the blast, the salesman said. He stated a 'heavy-set' white male entered the store late one afternoon and bought a 12-inch section of 4-inch galvanized pipe. . . ."

Having taken two steps forward, on the next day the newspaper took one step back . The lead story, headlined "Puzzles Plague Pipe-Bombing Investigators," said, in part, "Six Collier County Sheriff's investigators working full-time to solve the pipe-bomb murders of Margaret and Scott Benson are finding more questions than answers as they delve into the past of the wealthy tobacco family. 'We don't really have "a" suspect. We have a lot of suspicions,' [said] Deputy Chief Ray Barnett."

Four days later, the news was more positive. Or at least more interestingly suggestive. On July 21, a story headlined, "U.S. Combed for Sources of Bomb Parts," stated, "ATF agents won't tell the media what type of detonator was used to trigger the blasts, but Barnett says the devices are 'fairly rare,' leading authorities to believe they may be able to track down the buyer." Barnett was also quoted as saying that the investigators—six men from the Collier County Sheriffs Office and six from ATF—all of whom had been working nonstop since July 9, would get a "weekend break."

The next day's headline story in the *Daily News* reflected some real progress, whether the police were admitting it or not. "Lt. Harold Young, chief detective of the Sheriff's homicide unit, was tight-lipped this morning about how the case is progressing," said a story that carried the headline, "Bombing Investigators to Meet Prosecutors." It continued, " 'We're meeting with representatives of the U.S. Attorney and State's attorney to look at all the legal aspects of the case,' Young said. 'We are getting sub-

poenas for several things, but I'm not going to say (for) what,' he
added. . . . Our list is not as long (as it once was).' . . . More
than 100 people were questioned about the Benson case last week
and that many could be questioned in the next several days,' Young
said."

While the media were battling one another and the police for
information, there was, as Lieutenant Young indicated, a great
deal going on behind the scenes. Young, who came to Collier
County from police work in Ohio, is actually a native of Ken-
tucky, and his opinions are delivered with traces of a twang and
a colorful directness. "And from the interview [at the hospital]
with Kerr—we had already become suspicious of Steven, because of his attitude, and him being the last person to drive the
vehicle, I mean, shit, it had two *big* bombs in it, and that place
up there is pretty secure. And the possibility of him driving around
all morning with a damn bomb in the vehicle, well, it just didn't
sit too good at that time.

"And then after we talked to Kerr, and found out what all was
going down with momma and him, and we knew she was having
problems with Steven stealing money and she was going to remove him, disinherit him, take his house, and, hell, Steven became a real strong suspect then.

"So then our object was, [because] he was about the strongest
suspect we had, we have to go through the process of eliminating
him [as a suspect]. And, shit, that never happened. [Our suspi-
cions] got stronger and stronger."

What about Wayne Kerr? Did the police ever suspect that he
was the killer, or was in some way implicated? "Yeah. At the
time, definitely. He and Steven were real close, and he was even
claiming at the time that he and Steven were best friends, that
they were best man at each other's weddings, and shit like that.
But there was never anything we could pin on or stick Kerr as
being a suspect. He was in the house, more or less during all the
time that Steven was gone. And we never did come up with any

evidence of a conspiracy or that Steven acted other than on his own."

Ralph Ostrowski, the head ATF agent, says the same thing: "We never seriously considered Wayne Kerr as a suspect."

Young, nonetheless, did not particularly like the youngish, rotund attorney from Pennsylvania, who was, by all accounts, extremely frightened by the events of July 9, 1985; Stephen Vaughan, the tennis coach, said, "The night of the bombing, when we were leaving the [Benson] house, I gave Wayne a ride, but he stood about a hundred yards away when I started my van."

"At one point I talked to Kerr," said Lieutenant Young, "and I guess we tried to put a little fear into him. I told him we thought we'd better get a statement from him 'fore something happened to him. So I guess we shook him up pretty good."

As for Steven, his behavior continued to send off warning bells in Harold Young's mind. "He probably went home that night," says Young, "and rested probably pretty good. . . . My experience with guys that do premeditated murders is that they are very calm, never show any emotions, and they can sit through a trial without showing any remorse or any human emotions. And that's what this crime was—a cold-blooded, calculated homicide."

What did Lieutenant Young, a homicide specialist, see as the motive in the Benson killings? "That he had just bought that house up there [in Fort Myers], and the possibility of mother closing down all the businesses that he had started up, and maybe losing the house, and I think he was getting pressure from Debby, his wife, and I think the prospect of losing everything. You know, he'd had so many failures. And the possibility of being cut back down to nothing was probably bothering him. . . ."

The day after the bombings, Harold Young and George Nowicki told Wayne Kerr that they wanted to talk to him. They wanted to get further verification of some of the things the lawyer had told Detective Koors and Agent Hopkins the previous night. "But," says Young, "he was running around and being kind of hard to deal with, so we went over to Steven's little trailer," the office of the Meridian Security Company, among others, "and Kerr was playing the big businessman. 'Have a seat, I'll be with you in a minute,' shit like that.

"Well, I didn't go for that shit, and finally he said, 'Okay, I'll talk to you now,' and he pulls out, I guess it was Steven's desk, he pulls out a chair and puts his coat on the back. And I said, 'Now grab your damn coat, you're going with me.'

"I didn't get any objections. He just grabbed his coat, and put his big ass in the car with us, and we hauled him down here and interviewed him again."

As Lieutenant Harold Young well knew, and the press to its consternation did not, a number of important investigative efforts were beginning to bear fruit in the second week after the bombings. One was the effort to interview the sole survivor, Carol Lynn Benson Kendall, who by the third week was in serious but no longer critical condition. The police had made polite but frequent requests to interview her, but would wait only so long before insisting. After all, she was the most central witness to a double murder and almost a third, her own, and the information she possessed might be all that stood between the police and an arrest warrant for Steven Wayne Benson.

There was, however, a problem. Carol Lynn was not ready to talk to them, both from a physical standpoint, and because she was uncomfortable with the idea of talking "about my brother to the police." It wasn't that she had no sense of duty; Carol Lynn Benson Kendall had a very strong sense of right and wrong, an almost outdated sense of right and wrong. Nor was it that she didn't want to avenge the death of her mother, with whom she had struggled for years to come to better terms, to reach an accommodation based on their mutual love and respect, if not always mutually agreeable behavior. It was that she did not want to be the main witness against her own brother. So the police kept in frequent touch with her, through her doctors.

Fortunately, they were making more progress in other areas.

For example, as George Nowicki says, in addition to learning that someone had bought four-inch end caps on the Friday afternoon before the Tuesday bombings, and the twelve-inch pipe on Monday afternoon, Mike Koors and Terry Hopkins got a description of that person as being a "heavy-set white male with little glasses and a hat." What made that important was the information other detectives got from talking to employees of Steven's that on that same Friday afternoon he had been asking anyone in the office if they had a hat or a cap he could borrow. They had remembered the request because it was so unusual—none of them had ever before seen Steven wear any kind of hat or cap.

That information made Nowicki and company all the more eager to get the results of the ATF crime-lab tests on the invoices. If they contained fingerprints, and if those fingerprints matched . . . well, perhaps that was too much to hope for. Nonetheless, the invoices did come from Hughes Supply, and Hughes Supply was right up the street from the Meridian trailer on Domestic Avenue. . . .

Another factor that George Nowicki added to the equation was his impression of the visit he and Harold Young had made, the day after the bombings, to Steven's home in Fort Myers, the home that Margaret Benson had, reportedly, considered the "last straw."

"Right after they got through talking to Wayne Kerr in the hospital," on the evening of July 9, the day of the murders, says Nowicki, "I called Steven at home, and asked him if he'd talk to us, and he said, 'I'm tired, I'm really exhausted, and I'm a little disoriented, and I'd rather not.' I said, 'How about tomorrow?' and he said, 'Yeah, fine, tomorrow.'

"So we go up to see if we can talk to him, and we arrive [in Fort Myers] the next day, and he says, 'You know, I'd rather talk to my lawyer first, before I talk to anybody.' "

That *bothered* George Nowicki. "If somebody had just killed my mother and adopted brother, you wouldn't need a lawyer to talk to me. I'd be on your front doorstep, trying to knock the door in to find out what you're doing next and what I can do to help. But he had this defensive posture, and there shouldn't have been one."

Interestingly, the detectives did talk to Steven's wife, Debby, or, as Nowicki calls her, glancing at his notes in a November 1986 interview, "Debra Jean Franks Benson." She agreed to talk to them in her backyard, in a kind of free-form interview. Nowicki says, "Steven's three little children were running around, and the interview took a great deal of time, because Debra was always running off after the kids, and then coming back and sitting down. We finally finished the interview."

What did they learn? "She made it very clear that she and the rest of the family were on the outs."

But George Nowicki also says this about Debby Benson, the object of so much criticism regarding her relationship with her former mother-in-law: "The first time I saw her [on the day of the bombing] she was crying. And she was the only one."

On July 11, Nowicki and Young went to the office of Thomas Biggs, the lawyer Steven had chosen to speak for him. Biggs told them what Steven had authorized him to say, that the reason he was gone so long on the morning of the bombings was that, at the Shop 'n Go, he had run into a construction worker he knew, someone who worked for Sand Kastle Construction, and they'd had a long conversation. Other than that, the police learned virtually nothing new from the statement, and if anything, the idea of using a lawyer to transmit such a bland exchange of information made them more wary of Steven, and more suspicious.

Armed with that information, however, a number of investigators were sent out to see if they could find the construction worker. Nowicki and Young interviewed the manager of the Shop 'n Go, who said he was very busy that particular morning, and he had no recollection of talking to anyone who resembled Steven Benson.

As far as the Sand Kastle employee was concerned, no one at the company could identify who that might have been or who might even have been that far north of the city at that time on a Tuesday morning, as most of their construction workers were already on the job by that hour.

Nowicki says, "We can't take [the search for Steven's alibi witness-construction worker] to the ridiculous, but we took it as far as a reasonable person would take it. We wanted to see if we could find this individual in order to give [Steven] the benefit of the doubt. But we could never find him."

The police also performed such tasks as timing the drive from 13002 White Violet Drive to the Shop 'n Go and back, in order to see what portion of the absent hour could be attributed to travel time. They clocked the trip, made at normal speeds, as taking five to seven minutes.

On Monday, July 15, Nowicki and Young talked to Mark Nelson, Steven's main employee at Meridian Security Network. They asked him, on the basis of what Terry Hopkins and Mike Koors had learned from other employees, if Steven ever wore a cap. According to Nowicki, Nelson responded by saying, " 'It's funny you should ask that, because on Friday, I think it was Friday'— he wasn't sure—'Steven said he was going to be working out in the sun and asked if anyone had a hat or a cap he could borrow,' and," said Nowicki, "we found that he had asked two other employees the same thing.

"And of course," adds Nowicki, "the person who bought the pipe showed up with a cap, a baseball-type cap."

That same person had asked the clerk for a pipe and end caps on two separate days, and Nowicki explains the significance of that: "If a person buys a section of pipe and one end cap, they're going to cap something off. But if you buy a section of pipe and *two* end caps—" he laughs, letting the obvious sink in—"then you're making a bomb. You don't want to do something like that that's going to attract attention to yourself."

On July 24, the police ran into another roadblock when they tried to take a formal statement from Wayne Kerr, now back in Pennsylvania. The lawyer surprised them by refusing to allow them to tape-record the interview, insisting that all they could do was take notes, which then had to be reduced to a "Written Report of Interview." And then, when George Nowicki and Harold Young got started, Kerr began to claim an "attorney-client privilege" for almost every question.

Kerr claimed, according to George Nowicki, "that he couldn't tell us anything about Steven because he was Steven's attorney. But when we'd say, 'Okay, then tell us about Margaret,' he'd say, 'I was Margaret's attorney.' Finally we had to go to the judge to get it resolved."

The judge was Florida Circuit Court Judge Hugh Hayes, who was to handle the case from beginning to end. The young, highly respected jurist was not the type to agonize over this kind of decision. He ruled that Wayne Kerr could not, in effect, claim either privilege as the spirit—or the disinclination to answer a particular question—moved him. The next time Wayne Kerr sat down with the investigators, his answers were, at least by comparison, full and cooperative. Nonetheless, there were no bombshells dropped in that interview.

As it turned out, Wayne Kerr was saving his bombshells. For, two days later, he walked into the Naples office of Dean Witter Reynolds, the nationwide investment firm, and, stating that he was the personal attorney and representative of Margaret Benson, attempted to withdraw one *million* dollars in cash and securities from her active assets account.

John Melick, Sr., the Dean Witter man in charge, remembered that he had read something in the paper about Margaret Benson having left *two* wills and that one of them failed to mention attorney Kerr. So he balked. And he called the courthouse and asked to speak to a judge who might tell him whether he should hand over such a large amount of money, under the circumstances, to Wayne Kerr. The answer was *no*.

The next day's Naples *Daily News* screamed: "Benson Attorney Demanding Control of $1 Million Dollar Account."

By then, however, several of the chief investigators were no longer in Naples. They were on the road. And the trips made by both teams—detectives Mike Koors of Collier County and Billy Riehl of ATF, and George Nowicki and Lieutenant Wayne Graham of Collier County—turned out to be quite productive. In fact, when the four of them got back to Florida and turned in their reports, the police had *almost* everything they needed to arrest Steven Benson, and to charge him with the pipe-bomb murder of his mother and adopted brother and the attempted murder of his sister.

Koors and Riehl, a former Pennsylvania cop who was raised in the Lancaster area, were sent to the city where Steven had been raised to see what they could find out about his background (along with that of the whole family, to a lesser extent) and his habits, as well as to see if he had any police record. They struck out on the last count, but they did very well on the others.

The picture that developed from their dozen or so interviews was not at all complimentary to Steven Benson. "There was one guy," says Detective Mike Koors, "who said he'd take me and Lieutenant Riehl out to dinner if we found one person in Lancaster who said he was Steven Benson's friend—and we didn't.

"We talked to a woman who had worked for Margaret right after Benny died, and she didn't like Steven one little bit. She said he was the reason she quit, because he was such a pain in the ass. And then we talked to Nancy, Steven's first wife, who is such a nice person, and when I walked away from that interview, I thought, 'What a bastard Steven is, what a bastard he was to this girl.' I didn't feel sorry for Steven; all I could think was what a prick he was."

Koors admits that he became more emotionally involved in this case than was his professional norm. "My wife always would say to me, 'You just can't handle the fact that somebody killed their mother,' and I said, 'I know I can't.' It's so hard to believe that somebody would kill their own mother."

Nancy Ferguson Benson said in the autumn of 1986 that the only way she could explain what had caused Steven to do what

The Benson clan adds a new member when Steven
marries Nancy Ferguson.

Edward Benson and Scotty.

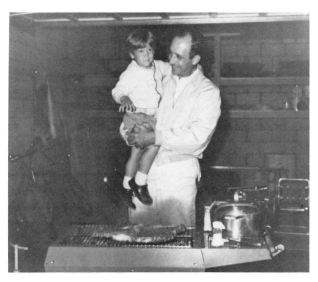

Margaret and Benny at a graduation ceremony for a
U.S. Coast Guard course. Margaret, who graduated at the
top of her own class, went on to become the Flotilla's
Training Officer. Benny became a commander.

Carol Lynn's children. Left to right: Travis,
unidentified friend, Kurt, and Scott. Scott's dog,
Buck, is in the foreground.

Benny, surrounded by
Margaret's Louis XIV decor.

Steven marries
Debby, 1980.

Father and son.

Scott at fifteen.

Mr. and Mrs. Harry Hitchcock
("Boppa" and "Mom-mom") with
granddaughter Sheryl Murphy Murray.

Benny, near the end of his life.

The Steven Benson family.

The Benson home in Port Royal. Benny never got to enjoy it.

Margaret at the Chantecler ski
lodge, near the family's
Canadian home. Benny kept
this photo in his office.

Scott.

Carol Lynn, posing for a
fashion layout in Lancaster
News. (PHOTO COURTESY OF
CAROL LYNN BENSON
KENDALL)

Janet Lee Murphy.

Margaret (in hat) with Sherry Hester, on their Israel trip in the summer of 1984.

The last photo taken of Margaret and Scott. Janet Lee
is at left. Harry Hitchcock and Brenda (Janet Lee's
daughter) are at right.

Harry Hitchcock at home in his garden.

The Bensons' Chevrolet Suburban in police custody.
(AP/WIDE WORLD PHOTO)

Carol Lynn at Massachusetts General Hospital,
July 29, 1985. (PHOTO BY RICHARD MATHESON)

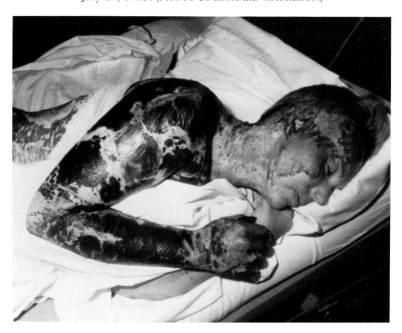

Top, left to right: George Nowicki, Terry Hopkins, and Bill Riehl. *Bottom, left to right:* Al Gleason, Ralph Ostrowski, and Michael Koors—six of the investigation team.

Carol Lynn explains where everyone was when the bomb exploded. (AP/WIDE WORLD PHOTO)

Richard Cirace. (PHOTO BY RICHARD MATHESON)

Judge Hugh Hayes presides over a bench
conference. Carol Lynn waits to continue her
testimony. (AP/WIDE WORLD PHOTO)

Steven Wayne Benson, defendant.
(ERIC STRACHAN, NAPLES *Daily News* PHOTO)

 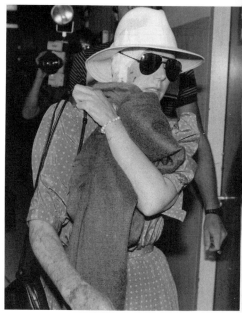

Above, left: Kim Beegle, Scott's girlfriend, recalls the fatal morning. (LAURA ELLIOT, FORT MYERS *News Press* PHOTO)

Above, right: A badly injured Carol Lynn goes before the grand jury. (ERIC STRACHAN, NAPLES *Daily News* PHOTO)

Steven during pretrial hearing.
(JOE BURBANK, FORT MYERS *News Press* PHOTO)

Wayne Kerr, attorney and family friend, testifies for the prosecution while Assistant District Attorney Dwight Brock looks on. (BRUCE MOYER, NAPLES *Daily News* PHOTO)

"Every night I go to bed praying that I will wake up in the morning and find that it was just a very bad dream, a nightmare." (THOMAS PRICE, FORT MYERS *News Press* PHOTO)

Michael McDonnell,
Steven's defense lawyer,
after the guilty verdict.
(ERIC STRACHAN, NAPLES
Daily News PHOTO)

Steven Benson shedding a
tear upon hearing his
mother's voice on tape.
(GARTH FRANCIS, FORT
MYERS *News Press* PHOTO)

he did—and she agreed with the jury verdict of guilty—was that "he just lost it," that a combination of pressures had become too much for him. Mike Koors agrees, but with the reservation that it was a false dilemma.

"Yes, he was on the verge of losing house, car, and everything. But from the way Wayne Kerr talked, momma was going to do nothing more than slap him on the wrist, and he should've known it. But he had probably got tired of that—short-term gain, no problems with mom; long-term gain, a rich man. I think there's no beating that motive."

One of their "finds" on the Lancaster trip was a notation in the senior high school yearbook of a girl with whom Steven had shared an adventure. To commemorate it, he wrote in her book: "Till we go bombing again." The investigators were understandably intrigued, until they learned that it referred to a night when she and Steven were driving around and he had thrown firecrackers at a parked police car.

Somewhat more to the point was an interview they had with a man named Tom Schilling, a roofer who had worked for the Bensons. They found him working on a building across from the charming new town square in downtown Lancaster. Koors says, "We walked across the street and sat on a park bench, and it was cool. I thought, 'Jeez, this is the way all our interviews should be.' "

But as they were crossing the street to get to the bench, Schilling said to the detectives, according to Mike Koors, " 'I want to tell you guys one thing up front—I think Steve's a fucking asshole.' And I thought, 'Oh, good, we *want* to talk to you,' but before we started I said, 'Couldn't we just tone that down a tad for the tape recorder here,' as we were about to turn the tape on and we didn't need to hear that kind of shit right off the bat!"

Schilling told them—and Koors says it was "neat" because he could remember exactly when the incident he recounted had occurred because it was the same week in 1981 that John Hinckley shot President Reagan—that he was up working on the roof when he saw Steven walk out holding two "small 'firecrackers,' " Says Detective Koors, "That's what they call them up in Lancaster, 'firecrackers,' and apparently they play with them up there. They fill copper tubing up with black powder, and make fuses, and blow the shit out of stuff."

According to the roofer, Steven's appearance with the devices was followed by a very loud explosion. "What amazed Schilling," says Mike Koors, "was the fact that he—Steven—had set them off remotely," using some kind of electronic device.

"He said he remembered Steven from high school, and how Steven would deliberately forget his gym clothes so he wouldn't have to work out, and the coach made him come out in his underwear. And Schilling said, 'Here we are in high school and the guy's crying because he's got to come out in his underwear.'

"I said, 'Well, what did you do about it?' and he said, 'I beat his ass every time I seen him on the street.' You mean you'd just walk up and smack him? 'Yeah, he's such an asshole, a spoiled rich kid. I mean, who drives a *Lincoln* to high school?'

"Schilling just did not like him. But he liked Scott, told me Scott was a 'party guy,' when Scott would come to town they'd party at his house. I said, 'What do you mean "party," drugs and all that stuff?' and he said, 'A little marijuana, a lot of alcohol, not hard drugs, not what you'd call drug addict stuff. We're talking party stuff. Scott was a party guy. If Scott was going to party, everybody partied. If you wanted to borrow Scott's car he'd tell you when he'd need it next. If he didn't need it for a month, he'd tell you to keep it for a month. That's the kind of guy Scott was. Everybody liked Scott; Steven sucked.' "

Koors sums it up: "He just *didn't like* the man."

Special Agent William Riehl, Koors's partner on the Lancaster fact-finding trip, also has a vivid recollection of that investigation. Having grown up in the area and having been a police officer in Philadelphia and then, for three years, an ATF agent assigned to Lancaster, Riehl was able to get faster cooperation from the local authorities than perhaps anyone else would have. Still, that connection did not produce any startling revelations.

Special Agent Billy Riehl is a member of the Southeast National Response Team (NRT), one of the "SWAT" units of the Bureau of Alcohol, Tobacco, and Firearms Bomb and Arson Response. As he explains it, the NRT is composed not of specialists but of experienced officers who can do a variety of tasks. "Everybody can do everything. Everybody on the team is capable of being a schematic artist or photographer or crime-scene search or interview team or whatever it is. But the concept is a team concept. There's twelve guys on an NRT, including a lab technician and an explosives guy."

Assigning a National Response Team to the Benson case was considered, initially, but it was not done because so many of the officers already involved were NRT members that, in effect, they functioned as one.

Of the trip that he and Mike Koors made to Lancaster, Special Agent Riehl has this to say of its genesis: "At some point we had heard that Carol Lynn was hesitant to cooperate with the authorities, for some reason or other, and we had heard that her grandfather, Harry Hitchcock, was going to be going up to Boston to talk to her. So the time was ripe to go talk to him before he went to see her, in order to solicit his help in asking her to cooperate with us, because she was *there*, she was a very important witness."

They got to Lancaster and Harry Hitchcock the day he was to leave for Boston to visit his granddaughter, and he agreed to speak to her on their behalf and urge her to talk to them. Hitchcock was, according to Agent Riehl, "simply the nicest and most impressive person I met in the whole investigation."

Billy Riehl's opinion of Steven's record as a businessman was as negative as Mike Koors's opinion of Steven's personality. "From what we heard, he was just a lousy businessman. He was a guy who wanted to be a millionaire by the time he was thirty-seven, and [even if he were] given a million he couldn't do it. According to some of the guys who knew him up there, he was destined to be a loser. All his [Pennsylvania] business ventures were down the tubes."

While they were still in Pennsylvania, they learned that Tom Perret, the ATF agent in Boston, having tried and failed to reach them, had sent word to Collier County that Carol Lynn was ready to talk.

George Nowicki and Lieutenant Wayne Graham of the sheriff's office made a mad dash for the airport. In a mix-up worthy of Clouseau, first one officer and then the other caused them to miss a Boston flight. Finally, having packed only carry-on luggage, they scrambled aboard in haste and were in the air headed north. The interview they were about to conduct was clearly the most important of all the interviews, by all the law-enforcement personnel, to date.

Just before they left, Nowicki had discovered that Steven Benson had hired a private security guard to keep the curious—and the cops, as it turned out—from entering the development where he and his family lived. When Nowicki heard this, he was torn between direct action and going to the United States attorney for a ruling on the legality of the situation.

The "direct action" he'd contemplated? "I thought hard," says Nowicki, "of cuffing the security guard and throwing him—it may even have been a 'her'—into the back of the squad car while we got the answer. You know," he says, grinning, "the old hot back seat routine."

Once in the air, the officers pulled out yellow legal pads and began to jot down questions to ask Carol Lynn, talking animatedly as they wrote—until the businessman sitting next to Nowicki said, "That wouldn't be the Benson case you're talking about, would it?" They put away their pads and made small talk for the rest of the trip.

It was a reunion of sorts for George Nowicki and Wayne Graham, who had worked together fifteen years earlier when Graham was a Naples city police officer. Now a lieutenant in the Collier County Sheriff's Office, Graham held ATF in general, and George Nowicki in particular, in extremely high regard. His opinion did not change as a result of the investigation into the Benson case. "Those ATF guys, all of them," he said in an autumn 1986 interview in his neat-as-a-pin special response team office, "came to work. No partying, no fooling around. They came to *work*."

Graham, an easy man to talk to on his own terms, nonetheless gives the impression that he would be a bad man to cross. One of the first of the Collier County authorities on the scene on July 9, 1985, he was in the house when Steve Hawkins, who brought Debby Benson down from Fort Myers on the morning of the bombing, was asked by Steven Benson first thing, "Did we get any money in today?"

That shocked Wayne Graham, but not as much as a conversation he himself had with Steven Benson only moments later. "Steven came up and asked me if he could go into his tan van. I asked why, and he said, 'I've got to get in there and get some equipment out, because I've got an installation in the morning.'

"I said, 'You're not getting anything out of that van until it's been checked by the bomb disposal unit.' He said something about the van having been moved, and I said, 'You won't go in there, Mr. Benson, until it's been cleared by Harold Young, who is in charge of this crime scene, and by ATF, who's responsible for the security of this crime scene. You won't go in there.' And he didn't.

"There came a time when he did"—and here Graham hesitates, aware that what he is about to say could well be misunderstood, could be considered insensitive. But he decides that it is important for him to say it. "His mother, for lack of a better way of describing it, was kind of spread out down the side of the van. The door was spread with blood, and bone matter, and, ah, skin. And he never had it washed.

"Being a law-enforcement officer, we have a rather, I don't

really know how to say it, we look at things a lot differently than the regular Joe on the street, because we see so much of it. And maybe we've got a tainted [view] or our vision becomes tainted, somewhat, but we even made comments [when we'd see Steven driving the unwashed van] like, 'Well, there goes Steven this morning. He must be taking Mother for a ride and showing her around.' I mean, every time he got in the van he's opening a door," and here he lowers his voice, "*that his mother's spread out on*! But he never washed it off. Now that's cold."

The first thing officers Nowicki and Graham encountered when they arrived in Boston was an 11:00 P.M. midweek traffic jam in the tunnel leading from Logan Airport. Welcome to the big city. All the scene needed was Dennis Weaver playing McCloud goes to Beantown.

ATF's Tom Perret, who had picked up the two Florida cops at Logan, drove them to a motel on what Nowicki recalls as the "south side of Boston." The next morning they went to Massachusetts General Hospital, where Carol Lynn was recovering in the Burn and Trauma Center.

"The first people we met were Harry Hitchcock and Janet Lee Murphy, and we had some conversations with them down in the security office. My first impression of Harry Hitchcock," says George Nowicki, "is that he reminded me of my wife's grandfather, who is a very direct man, and when he talks to you he looks you right in the eye."

And Janet Lee Murphy, Margaret's younger sister? Nowicki says, "She was very attractive, and I thought she looked more like she could have been closer to *Carol Lynn*'s age than Margaret's.

"Both of them seemed struck by the tragedy in the family, yet they seemed like they wanted to make us comfortable, to help us. That's the impression I got from both of them. And then they told us that Carol Lynn was ready to talk to us."

Wayne Graham also has a vivid memory of his first meeting with Harry Hitchcock and his daughter Janet Lee. "We were talking with the chief of security there at Mass General, and I didn't know who they were when they came in. [Hitchcock's] kind of a grand gentleman to see, with that white hair. I mean he just fits the profile of the patriarch. And Janet Lee is a *nice*-looking lady.

"The chief of security, who had ushered them right into his office, said to me, 'That's Mr. Hitchcock and Janet Lee, and I think you should go and talk to them because they have some questions.'

"So I walked in, and I started to introduce myself, and Janet Lee stood up, and she said, first thing, without even saying who she was, she said, 'Steven did it, and I want him to get the death penalty. He killed my sister, he killed my nephew, and he tried to kill my niece, and I want him to pay.' And then she got emotional, she got tears in her eyes. But it wasn't, in my opinion, sadness; it was anger. She was *angry*.

"Mr. Hitchcock said, '*If* Steven did it, then he should pay, under the rules of our law and the rules of God,' and that was my first indication of Mr. Hitchcock's religious beliefs."

What the Florida detective so liked about Janet Lee Murphy was that, "She let me know her feelings right away." Graham appreciated that trait because it is one he very much shares, as he proved minutes later when he and George Nowicki met Ric Cirace, Carol Lynn's lawyer. They had barely begun to talk when Graham decided that their three-way cooperation would be facilitated if he let Cirace know how he felt about most lawyers.

Says Wayne Graham, almost proudly, "George and I both feel that you have to be extremely careful till you get the ground rules set, and you have to understand where [lawyers are] coming from and what's going on. So we were very standoffish with Mr. Cirace. We liked Ric okay, but we treated him simply as a matter of business." But they could see that Cirace, a naturally friendly person, was somewhat surprised by their stiffness.

Finally, Lieutenant Graham decided to let the lawyer in on the situation. He said, "Look, I want to explain something to you.

We have a certain attitude when we're dealing with people, in particular attorneys.''

Cirace asked, "What do you mean?"

"Well, let me just put it this way—and I think I represent George as well in this matter—and that is, I think I'd rather have a sister as a whore than a brother as an attorney."

Cirace gaped. *"What?"*

Graham told him again, and asked, "Do you understand what I mean?"

Cirace said he thought he got the picture, so Graham grinned, and said, "Okay, having that in mind, let's start to work together."

Graham and Nowicki had flown up from Naples expecting to stay overnight on Thursday, interview Carol Lynn on Friday, and return to Florida on Saturday. As things turned out, they did not go back until the following Monday. But the results of the interview—which turned out to be interview*s*—exceeded their greatest hopes. And those meetings became an intense emotional experience that would bind the police, the victim, and the victim's lawyer into a common force aimed, with differing degrees of anticipation, at the conviction of Steven Benson.

Neither officer could ever forget that first meeting with Carol Lynn Benson Kendall. Says Wayne Graham, "In the solarium there, outside the elevators, we met with the legal department and the chief of surgery and the chief of staff, and their hospital representatives. And we informed them that we wished to go in and take a statement from her, and upon conclusion of the statement we would return to Florida. Whereupon they advised us that we would have fifteen minutes every two hours, and that in between those two hours they would assess whether anything had occurred that might cause her discomfort or might not be to her advantage for recovery.

"And we tried to negotiate that somewhat, because our plans

were, as we had packed clothing for one day, to interview her Friday and go home on Saturday. But we respected what they said, because it was very obvious that they were going to stick to their guns. Their first concern was for her, and they didn't *care* about our problems."

At that point Carol Lynn's condition had stabilized, and her doctors had performed the emergency skin grafts, but she was still listed as "critical."

"We're talking about a lady," says Lieutenant Graham, "who, when I walked in the room, her hair was gone, so was her ear, and she looked, as the orderlies were saying, like French toast. Definitely a crispy critter."

However, with Cirace's help, they were able to get the fifteen-minute edict modified to the extent that they could continue the interview beyond that point if Carol Lynn was not tired. And under that arrangement the interviews began, with the doctors coming by every quarter-hour to see how their patient looked. If they thought she was tired, then a nurse would appear in the doorway and tap on the face of her watch, a polite way of telling the police to beat it.

As they settled in to begin the initial interview, Wayne Graham fought a momentary feeling of revulsion, brought on by the combined smell of burn medicine and burned flesh. Crowded into the private room were the patient, the two detectives, Ric Cirace the lawyer, and Tom Perret of ATF.

George Nowicki began, in his slow, southern semidrawl, by identifying himself and naming the other people in the room, and giving the date and the time.

Then he said, quietly, "We are going to interview Carol Lynn Benson concerning her knowledge of," and then he corrected himself, saying, "Carol Lynn Benson *Kendall*, of the events of July the 9th, 1985, and the prior thereto. . . ."

Then he looked over at her on the bed and said, in a voice that managed to blend authority and concern for her feelings, "Carol

Lynn, what we want to do now is to question you first about the most difficult part to talk about, and get that out of the way, talk about July 9th of 1985, if we could.''

And so she did, in a voice that was to go through many changes, from soft to quaveringly firm to weak but angry, all the way to tearful and barely understandable. There were pauses, breaks, and cessations, but throughout it all there was information—information provided through a heavy emotional screen.

And not only was this information wearying to impart, it was also very tiring to receive.

Said Wayne Graham, "She was so emotional, I mean, it was so *pitiful*, you just wanted to make everything all right for her. And we got so involved with her emotions, the same as . . . the 'Stockholm Syndrome' will start between the negotiator . . . and the hostage taker. And the same thing was happening to her. We started trying to calm her down and help her mentally.

"We would come out and we were as emotionally drained as she was. George looked at me, and he said, 'Are you whipped?' and I said, '*Yes*.'

"And the odor in the room of that burned flesh was strong, and the [smell of] the medicine. And there was a guy in the next room, a fireman, and he was just, aw, was he *burned*. And I have a fear of fires. . . .

"And in the meantime, while we're doing this, there's Steven driving around in the van and calling grandpa, wanting money. And grandpa's trying to figure out how to reach Steven to get him to cooperate, because he can't figure out why he won't cooperate."

If Harry Hitchcock had heard his granddaughter's testimony in full, he would have realized why his grandson would not talk to the police. He didn't dare.

The doctors allowed no interviews on Saturday, but the detectives were there by eight o'clock Sunday morning, and they continued, this time in slightly longer sessions—even Carol Lynn was asking the doctors to let her talk for longer and longer periods, because she wanted, as Graham said, "to get it said and done."

"Everyone knew," said Graham, "how important this thing was, and that it would play a major part in how we were going to continue the investigation. Because now we were starting to *see*, and this had to do with *motive*. She had so much background to give us, things that had happened back in his life, that we just had to keep going."

When it was all over, Carol Lynn had a question for her questioners. "She asked us," says Lieutenant Graham, " 'How did my mother die? Did she burn up inside or was she on the ground? I can't remember. I don't know how she died and no one will tell me.'

"George and I looked at each other, and I said to her, 'Let me just tell you this. There was an explosion, that you are well aware of, and your mother was blown from the vehicle, and she died instantly. And she was not burned.'

"She started crying, but you could tell she was really relieved because she said, 'It's been in my mind all this time that my mother burned up. I could see Scotty, and I could see him lying on the ground, and he didn't look like he was hurt. But I didn't know what had happened to Mother. I just didn't know.' "

Wayne Graham answered, "Your mother never, ever, ever knew. There was no way she could have known."

George Nowicki summed up the import of Carol Lynn's testimony, as it affected her brother Steven: "She just eliminated everybody else as a suspect."

On July 30, Frank Kendall, ATF's fingerprint expert (and no relation to Carol Lynn's former husband) called to tell George Nowicki that he had some "interesting news." He had found two very clear palm prints, one on each of the receipts from Hughes Supply Company.

On August 16, armed with a search warrant "for the person of Steven Benson to produce finger and palm prints," Nowicki and

Young watched as Lieutenant Jack Gant took Steven Benson's prints in the office of attorney Tom Biggs in Naples. Saturday morning, a very concerned George Nowicki took the prints personally to the ATF lab in Atlanta to see if they matched the prints on the receipts from Hughes Supply. He was met at the airport by Frank Kendall. Kendall drove Nowicki directly to the lab and went right to work.

Two developments made Nowicki increasingly excited. First, it became clear that the same print was on each receipt. That meant the prints could not have been those of an employee, because there had been two different salesmen. Second, one of the palm prints appeared to be of a writer who was left-handed—and Steven Benson was left-handed.

When he had the results, Kendall prolonged telling Nowicki what they were, just to tease him. Finally he said, peering into this scope, "It looks like him. It *is* him!"

On August 22, at the Fort Myers office of one of his civil attorneys, Barry Hillmeyer, Steven Wayne Benson was arrested and charged with the first-degree murders of his mother and adopted brother, and the attempted murder of his sister.

When Steven Benson fell asleep in the police car on the way back to Naples, Wayne Graham, who was also in the car, thought to himself, "Now there's one cold son of a bitch."

Five

The Trial

Hurry up and Wait

The trial of Steven Benson was a series of anticlimaxes punctuated by moments of high drama and culminating in a conclusion that seemed, but was not, foregone. In other words, the long-delayed trial just managed to live up to its advance billing. It also means that he almost got away with it.

The chief players in the drama were the following: Steven Benson, the defendant; Michael McDonnell, his chief defense lawyer; J. Delano Brock, the lead prosecutor; Carol Lynn Benson Kendall, the main witness for the government; and Hugh Hayes, the trial judge. Others were to play important secondary roles, mostly behind the scenes, and there were several who almost played major roles but who, for one reason or another, did not get to strut their hour upon the stage.

In the end, despite what was said or was not said by Steven or his sister or Brock or McDonnell, and despite what ruling Judge Hayes made or did not make, there was only the jury to decide what had happened. To say to Steven, go or stay, and, if "stay," then live or die.

But it was a long time—certainly as far as the public mind and appetite were concerned—before anything was resolved. From one July to the next, and then some. And during all that time, the questions continued to reverberate. Did Steven Benson try to kill his sister? Did Steven Benson kill his brother Scott? And, in a sense the worst question of all, did Steven Benson kill his mother?

When her brother was arrested and charged, Carol Lynn Benson Kendall was still in the hospital. While her physical condition was slowly improving, she wasn't so sure about her mental and emotional stability. For one thing, she had so very much to *worry* about.

Steven, for example. She recalls the time, while she was still in the hospital in Naples, when she looked out toward the empty nurse's station and saw him standing there. "I was absolutely certain that Steven had come to the hospital for just one reason—to finish the job of killing me. I could just see him coming in and putting a pillow over my head to suffocate me. I was so wrapped in bandages that I was immobile, so sedated and weak that even if I'd known where the call button was, I could not have used it. I was totally vulnerable. Then a nurse came to the station; Steven spoke to her briefly, and turned—and left."

And Carol Lynn had only been in the Burn and Trauma Center at Massachusetts General Hospital for a day when her younger son, Travis, reported that his "Uncle Steve" had called to find out how packages were delivered to Carol Lynn's hospital room. Cirace, her attorney, immediately contacted the bomb squad of the Boston Police and security at Massachusetts General, which placed an armed guard outside her door.

Richard Cirace had only been Carol Lynn's lawyer for a matter of hours, but he was already beginning to realize that he had walked into a case that comes to a lawyer only once in a lifetime, unless he's lucky—and then it never comes at all.

Without a doubt, it would be a big-fee case—Margaret Benson's estate was worth ten million dollars, everyone said—but it would also be a major headache case, one after another after another caused by problems in widely disparate areas of the law, until he actually questioned whether the whole thing was worth it.

When Carol Lynn Benson Kendall went to Florida early in July to stay with her mother, she didn't even have a lawyer. Since she didn't own any real estate or have much money of her own to speak of, she seldom *needed* a lawyer. On those rare occasions when she did, her mother would "lend" her Wayne Kerr.

Yet it had been Wayne Kerr who'd suggested she get a lawyer of her own in Boston, just as it had been Wayne Kerr who had asked her, as he was putting her on the hospital plane to Boston, if she had "considered the possibility that Steven may have done it?"

There were any number of pressing reasons why she needed a lawyer who would be concerned with her needs alone. First of all, at the time Carol Lynn retained Cirace, Steven was a prime suspect in the killings; less than a month later he was arrested and charged with those crimes. Cirace, who had worked on a lot of criminal cases with John Albert Johnson during the eight years he had worked in his office and for his own clients in the two years he'd been on his own, knew she would be the government's key witness in any case against Steven.

Then there was the matter of Margaret Benson's estate. The day after the bombings, Steven, through Wayne Kerr, had petitioned the court to be named executor of his mother's estate. One of Cirace's first legal tasks was to get his client named as executor, to get her in, as he phrased it, "the power position."

Finally, there was a matter that had not yet surfaced, but which he learned about early on. And when he did, he saw its importance immediately, even though it involved a legal claim that seemed to have been languishing at the time of the murders. It was the paternity suit filed against Scott by Tracy Mullins in 1983. At the time of Scott's death it was not being "aggressively pursued," which is legalese for a case that no one cares about at the moment. But the deaths of Margaret and Scott would almost certainly change that case into an enterprising lawyer's dream of a "contingency case" (no win, no fee; big win, big cut to the lawyer).

For one thing, if a judge ruled that the little girl *was* Scott's, as his only heir she would certainly be entitled to a large portion of his estate, if not all of it. And that estate now included, or would eventually include, his share of Margaret Benson's, Edward Benson's, and Charlotte Hitchcock's estates, just to list those who were already deceased. It could be quite a substantial estate, and Cirace had the job of seeing that Carol Lynn's rights in all these estates were not just protected but aggressively promoted.

Then, as if all of that was not sufficiently complicated, Cirace had yet another possibility to keep in mind—what if Steven were convicted? The likelihood was that he'd be tried in state court; he'd been arrested and charged by the Collier County Sheriff's Office personnel, working hand-in-glove with the ATF people. Florida has a Killer Statute, which says that a killer cannot profit by his crime, either by inheriting or by reaping proceeds from anything like a book or movie contract. So if Steven were convicted of killing his mother he would get nothing from her estate.

That would mean that Scott's share would be *half* of his adoptive mother's estate, not one-third. And if Tracy Mullins won her paternity suit, then Carol Lynn would "lose" a great deal of money. Cirace was retained to fight that battle as well.

His final charge was similar, but sadder. As the family had not believed that Tracy Mullins's child was also Scott's, Carol Lynn had no qualms about opposing the paternity suit. The next legal problem was a different matter, however. The question was: what rights to Margaret Benson's estate did Steven's *family* have? Even, for the sake of argument, if his wife were to receive nothing, what about the three children? What share, if any, would they get? What share, if any, did they deserve? They of course were not culpable, yet their father could be said, if convicted, to have "created" the estate. Should they, as an extension of their father, be allowed to profit?

What made this issue even more poignant was the existence of Carol Lynn's children. If all the various legal battles were lost, those two boys, aged fifteen and sixteen in 1985, stood to lose a very great sum of money, at least indirectly. Was that fair? Did "fairness" even enter into it? Cirace had a lot to do. For the first time in his professional life, Ric Cirace began to work eighteen hours a day, *every* day. "I moved my office into the hospital," he says. "Basically, I practiced law out of Carol Lynn's hospital room."

One of the first things he realized was that the two police officers from Florida knew one hell of a lot more about the case than he did, and that he had better "go to school on them." So on Friday night, following their first day of taking Carol Lynn's statement in intermittent sessions, Nowicki and Graham were treated to a native son's tour of Boston, starting with dinner in the predominantly Italian north end, where Cirace, whose family owns a liquor store and an importing business in the neighborhood, is well known. The greetings (and toasts) were many and effusive. After that he gave them a fast tour of some of the Boston sights, including "Cheers," the bar where the popular television show of the same name is set. (The next day the doctors ordered a full day of rest for Carol Lynn, so Nowicki and Graham went sightseeing. Nowicki, a history buff, was ecstatic; Wayne Graham said, "If I'd a let him, George would've dragged me around the whole goddamn town.")

On Monday night, Cirace and the two police officers took the same flight down to Florida. It was the first of dozens of similar flights the lawyer took before the Benson case was over.

"When you have a case like this," says Cirace, "you have to look at the total picture. It's a big case; it's not a quick in-and-out. And whatever judgment you make, whether it's in regard to [legal] issues or not, you have to be making your chess moves in consideration of what's going to be happening in six months or a year. And how well you advise the client now may well affect how those issues come up later on."

That point of view became Cirace's lodestar. For the next year and even longer, he was to repeat it, or a version of it, over and over again to Carol Lynn: "You have got to think of the big picture!"

That phrase became almost a mantra for the intense young lawyer with the damaged client who had to pull herself together so that she could testify on behalf of the State of Florida, when it attempted to prove that her brother Steven was guilty of murder. So from the very beginning, she accepted what she later referred to as a "May I?" relationship. That became *her* mantra.

Shortly after Cirace arrived in Florida, there was an interesting development in the case. On July 30 there was a ten-minute hearing in Naples before State Circuit Court Judge Charles T. Carlton. As a result of the hearing, all assets in the estate of Margaret Benson were frozen "until further notice." The Benson case had already been assigned to Judge Hugh D. Hayes, but with Hayes on vacation, Judge Carlton entered a temporary order pending his colleague's return.

The hearing was called for the simple reason that things were getting rather complicated. There were two wills, one of which named Wayne Kerr as executor and one of which did not; but there had been no judicial determination as to which will was valid. Also, there was the question of Margaret's liquid assets, for example the money in the Dean Witter Reynolds active assets account.

Kerr's attempt to take control of that money had resulted in newspaper stories that implied he was up to something, but at this hearing, his attorney said that Wayne Kerr was simply acting to transfer the brokerage account into Margaret Benson's estate, which he felt—on the advice of counsel—he had every legal right to do because the first will had not been declared invalid. As things turned out, that was the correct position.

Present at that hearing was E. Richard Cirace, of Boston, counsel for Mrs. Carol Lynn Benson Kendall. But Mr. Cirace was a silent party. Speaking on behalf of Mrs. Kendall was Edward Cheffy, a Florida attorney with the Naples office of Frost and Jacobs, an Ohio firm Cirace had chosen to help him handle issues relating to the estate of Margaret Benson. That was the first of Cirace's many "chess moves."

"I was adamant," said Cirace in an interview early in 1987, "that nothing be done to pit Carol Lynn against Steven—or to link them in such a way that it could be said, if and when she had to testify against him, that she had a conflict of any sort."

When Cirace went to Florida for the first time, Steven Benson had not yet been arrested, but he was represented by an attorney, Thomas Biggs. Mr. Biggs, who was no stranger to criminal-law work, knew by the time of the hearing at the end of July that Steven was the prime suspect—by that point, headlines in the local press were saying things like, "Benson Refuses Questioning," followed less than a week later by "Benson Probe Nears End."

As a result, Biggs was tenaciously trying to link his client to Carol Lynn in as many perfectly legitimate ways as he could, on the theory that if the two of them had, or even appeared to have, conflicting financial interests, that fact—or apparent fact—could be brought out on cross-examination and could be useful in attacking her testimony, should Steven ever be brought to trial for the murders.

As Cirace says, "Following my first meeting with Carol Lynn in the hospital, it was clear that she wanted me to go down to Naples and handle the estate matters, and that she did not want to be cut out of anything. I think she anticipated that Steven was going to take charge because that had always [been] the way things were.

"With the allegations that were going on [involving Steven], it was critical that Steven not get in that slot as personal representative. She certainly did not want him in it; and neither did Janet

Lee Murphy or Harry Hitchcock. Nor did they want Wayne Kerr to be the personal representative. They wanted me to do whatever was necessary to protect Carol Lynn's rights and to protect the rights of Margaret's estate. They wanted me to work with Wayne Kerr; and I welcomed his help, as I would have been foolhardy to think I could walk in and take over everything on such short notice.

"Carol Lynn's interest was foremost in my mind, and my ego was not going to get in the way, so I said I would go down, and I would not just welcome Wayne's help but would solicit it."

At that point Cirace knew that Wayne Kerr had petitioned the court to be named the personal representative of the estate. But Cirace was not yet clear on who could serve lawfully as a personal representative. When he got down there he learned that you had to be a family member or a lawyer who either was a member of the Florida bar or had a residence in Florida.

"I also learned that Wayne Kerr had given his residence, on the petition to be named personal representative, as '3739 Domestic Avenue in Naples.' That's Steven's *trailer*," the business office of the Meridian companies.

When the Boston lawyer got to Florida, he hired both local counsel, Robert Hagaman, and the Naples office of Frost and Jacobs. Cirace says that instead of making the kind of fee arrangement whereby the lawyer or law firm gets a percentage of the value of the estate—which is still the way it's done in most areas of the country—Cirace worked out a deal with Frost and Jacobs that set a cap on what they could earn for their legal representation. The amount? "A quarter of a million," says Cirace. "I knew that to be a good deal for Carol Lynn."

He found out that lawyer Biggs wanted Steven and Carol Lynn to be appointed *co*-personal representatives. "To me that was insane. I said I wouldn't be a part of it, and Carol Lynn wasn't going to be a part of it. I did not want to pit brother against sister. Besides, he had not been arrested yet.

"Biggs kept arguing the presumption of innocence and everything else. That's how I focused in on Frost and Jacobs as being the personal representative. I knew I needed local counsel down there, and initially that's what Frost and Jacobs was going to be.

"Then, when I saw where Biggs was coming from, I didn't want Carol Lynn to be a part of it. After knowing her for two weeks, I knew just where she was coming from. Plus, I knew she wasn't as yet physically or emotionally capable.

He says that, in effect, he had to save her from herself. "Because she would have wanted to do things with the estate, and Steven and Biggs would have used that to their full advantage— questioning things Carol Lynn might have done. And I wanted somebody to protect Carol Lynn, and play it superstraight."

Cirace says, "I wanted Frost and Jacobs as a buffer, so that nobody could point the finger at my client, prior to the criminal trial, and say that she was doing things [that were] improper.

"My ultimate concern was that this was a sister who was going to have to testify against her brother. And, as she was the only percipient witness to the event, her testimony was critical. That being the case, I knew that any defense lawyer who came in was going to have to walk a fine line between not abusing Carol Lynn and taking her to task as to why she did certain things, or make it look as if she had an ulterior motive or a self-interest."

By transferring those concerns from a seriously injured Carol Lynn to what Cirace calls "a legitimate big firm which I knew was going to play it straight, I knew that that was putting the client in the best posture, in light of the fact that my first priority, as was hers, was to see justice done."

Cirace was concerned that they not "engage Steven head on." If Carol Lynn's lawyer had pushed to have her named "P.R." (personal representative) then Steven's lawyer would do the same.

"We had a choice of making them *both* P.R., but in my mind that would have made Carol Lynn's testimony totally unbelievable—why would you consent to having your brother become the personal representative of your mother's estate when your testimony is going to be: 'He stood there and watched me call for help,' or, 'He gave Scott the keys and walked away and then the car blew up,' or, 'I thought Steven's behavior was odd that morning; why the hell did it take him so long to get the coffee and doughnuts?' or, 'I knew Mother had caught Steven with his hand in . . . doing things with this Meridian Marketing Company.'

"So it didn't make sense to me to have her connected with Steven in any way. And what Tom Biggs was trying to do was trying to get Carol Lynn's imprimatur, in any form."

When Biggs countered Cirace's moves away from joint representation by suggesting that Carol Lynn was not physically capable, by virtue of the injuries she'd suffered in the bombing, Cirace offered to produce a videotape he'd had made of Carol Lynn, in her hospital room in Boston, walking around and talking with her doctor—who then turned to the camera and gave his opinion that within six weeks she would be able to handle the physical elements that the job of personal representative required.

At that point, Cirace petitioned the court to have Carl Westman, a lawyer in the Naples office of Frost and Jacobs, named as interim personal representative, with Carol Lynn to take over the job six weeks later. Cirace may have had the ulterior motive of giving his client that length of time in which to see that perhaps this was something she should not do.

His fear was based on his "big picture" strategy. "Tom Biggs said he would back off if Carl Westman was P.R., but not if Carol Lynn was." According to Cirace, Biggs kept maneuvering to build a defense for Steven by pulling Carol Lynn closer and closer to her brother.

"And then [late July 1985, three weeks before Steven was arrested] they wanted legal fees—for Steven. Biggs wanted the estate to release some money. First Biggs wanted Carol Lynn to give him some money, and then—as I said, he kept looking for ways to tie her in to Steven. They were looking to get some fees from Carol Lynn, and I said, 'Absolutely not.' "

But Carol Lynn also needed money at that point. It was discovered that she had no money to pay her hospital bills! As a part-time consultant, she was supposed to be covered by the overall Meridian Securities Company policy—but someone, either Steven or Wayne Kerr, had "forgotten" to pay the insurance premiums.

As Cirace put it, much later, "Not only does he blow his sister up, but he doesn't give her coverage!"

After Steven had been arrested and indicted, the lawyers were able to work out an agreement with the court that would release some money to the advantage of all concerned.

"Carol Lynn has always had a fondness," says Cirace, "for Steven's children. She regards them as Bensons. She was concerned about their being supported. So we worked out an agreement whereby a distribution was made of $100,000—and agreed to by Judge Hayes. It was like a pass-through: the money went to Steven, through his hands, to his children, into a guardianship with Barry Hillmeyer."

Another legal task that Cirace performed was to figure out what would happen if the Killer Statute or any of the other controlling legislation should be overturned: "Suddenly it dawned on me that somewhere down the road there might be a challenge to the Florida statutes, both the Killer Statute and what is known as the Anti-Lapse Statute, which governs estates, on Carol Lynn's behalf, and, if successful, whether she could get Steven's children's share."

What made this question potentially important was not, says Cirace, any desire on Carol Lynn's part to deny money to or take money back from Steven's children. It was caused by his (and her own) concern over the possibility that if Tracy Mullins should win her paternity suit against Scott, *and* those statutes overturned, Carol Lynn might have to stand by helplessly and watch both Steven's children and herself and her children lose money to Tracy

Mullins and a child that Carol Lynn does not believe is Scott's. ("I have seen pictures of that child," she says "and there's no *way* that's a Benson.")

Cirace said he didn't want to have his client come back to him, should the situation described above come about, and say, "Why did you give away $100,000 of my money?" In order to protect against that eventuality, "We structured the agreement so that the money would go into a guardianship, *and*, if it was determined later on that Carol Lynn was entitled to the money, that money which was not used to support Steven's children would go back to Carol Lynn."

In this situation, as in several others at the time, Cirace had to exercise great care not to let it appear that by helping Steven's children, Carol Lynn was in any way taking a position on his possible guilt or innocence. "She was one step removed. She was showing concern for Steven's children, but not necessarily condoning Steven—or helping him build a defense fund. Steven had not been arrested yet, and I was keeping her at arm's length, always.

"My biggest concern when I got into the case and saw what was going on was to have Carol Lynn neither *help* nor *judge* Steven, but to remain totally impartial; and that's how I tried to maneuver everything from the beginning."

Cirace recognized his client's dilemma. "She felt a responsibility, a moral obligation, to Steven's children. *And* she felt a moral obligation to her brother. She wanted to give him the presumption of innocence. However, if it was determined that Steven had done it, she did not want to participate in being an active part of his defense. So, these were the things that I was juggling, over and above her immediate questions about the estate."

All of this is not to say that Carol Lynn Benson Kendall and E. Richard Cirace did not have some sharp differences of opinion. His exuberance is a tribute to his heritage, and Carol Lynn, for all her gentility, knows how to make her position known. Her voice is a multiranged instrument capable of producing the softest of communicable tones, but also a full-volume, crystal-clear shriek. Her voice befits her avocation of appearing in what used to be called closet dramas, private readings of plays in someone's home. In fact, when detectives Graham and Nowicki had first met the principals in the Benson case, they used to discuss who would play her part in any eventual dramatization, and they decided on "a younger Carroll Baker type." As for Cirace, the first moment they saw him, they turned to one another and said, at the same time, "Baretta!"

The loudest arguments had to do with Carol Lynn's desire to get certain items out of her mother's estate, specifically furs that belonged to her and some jewelry her mother had promised her in the first will but neglected to mention in the second. Cirace said no.

"Of course there were times when I would have liked to have given in and made her happy, but I knew that if I made a claim on Carol Lynn's behalf for those items which she thought were hers, like some of the furs and her mother's jewelry, Steven's lawyers would have loved to have stirred up the waters and gotten that into the newspaper, and then claimed that those were not gifts but assets of the estate, and that Carol Lynn was full of. . . .

"I wanted to avoid all of that, because there were already enough headlines. I wanted to keep Carol Lynn the victim, and keep people's sympathy. I was afraid that they would misunderstand her concern for the personal property. It would *look* wrong.

"Being a trial lawyer, my mind was always on the day when Carol Lynn was going to take the stand and people were going to *see* her and assess her credibility and how sincere her feelings were. She can't come across as having sincere feelings about the loss of her mother if it looks like she's more concerned about the personal property.

"And I knew that Mike McDonnell [the lawyer who represented Steven at trial] would have just *loved* to use that kind of publicity against her.

"But as a result of our strategy, when McDonnell took her deposition, there was nothing that he could focus on with regard to Carol Lynn's involvement or interest in the estate. All he was able to talk about was 'the incident.' "

Once again, she had put her life in the hands of a take-charge male. And she and Cirace were, according to anyone who observed them, from Harry Hitchcock and Janet Lee Murphy to Wayne Graham and George Nowicki, a hell of a good team.

Once Steven had been arrested, on August 22, things began to move quickly—for a while.

On September 3, Judge Hayes (who had already approved the second will the week before Steven's arrest) ordered Wayne Kerr to answer the prosecutor's questions regarding Margaret and Carol Lynn, ruling that his attorney-client privilege, as far as the prosecution's interests were concerned, did not extend to them. He also ruled that Kerr had to answer questions about Meridian Security Network. As a result, it was learned that while Margaret thought she was the sole owner of the company, Steven had never filed the proper documents to back that up and had let people believe he was the owner.

On September 5, Steven was indicted and charged with two counts of murder in the first degree and one count of attempted murder. Judge Hayes set the trial for November 13, 1985.

Steven had been locked up since his arrest, and his lawyers moved to have him released on bond. One of the letters the judge received opposing bail apparently had an effect on his decision. The letter was from Steven's grandfather, Harry Hitchcock, who wrote, "Anyone who is capable of murdering his mother for money is capable of murdering his grandfather for the same reason. . . . A substantial sum of money will be available to Steven on my death from my late wife's estate and I am afraid for my own safety if Steven were free."

Janet Lee Murphy, Steven's aunt, also wrote to oppose letting him out on bond. "I am greatly concerned that Steven would be a threat if set free. I sincerely feel that Carol Lynn's life would be in danger, as well as that of my dad."

On September 12, Judge Hayes refused to allow Steven Benson to post bond.

The day before Carol Lynn was to be released from the hospital, a nurse came in and told her the facts of life with skin grafts. "Until that day, no one had told me that skin grafts shrink. But now I was hearing that, over the next year, the grafts would be constantly pulling one way, so I would have to be pulling in the other. If you don't constantly pull them in the other direction, they'll just shrivel up. It's hard work."

Holding up her right hand, she points to the spaces between fingers. "The skin between here will grow up and form webbing, and they have to cut it away. Eventually I was going to both an occupational therapist and a physical therapist every day. And there were constant massages to keep the skin pliable. And I could only turn my head a little bit.

"I forced myself to do things on my own. I forced myself to sleep at night in a certain way so that the skin would stretch, and I forced myself not to turn while I slept. All of these exercises were things I had to think of, and do, constantly."

Carol Lynn's resolve, which Dr. Burke, her main burn doctor, says was to amaze everyone in the hospital, must have been something to behold. "I made up my mind that I was not going to allow this thing to change my life."

Eventually she did not just regain the finger mobility she had before the bombing, she *exceeded* it.

What about her facial appearance? How did she deal with that? "I just decided that I wasn't going to let—that as far as my face was concerned, that I wasn't any different inside—and I was just going to go ahead, and go out, and that's it. And I don't care if people want to look.

"I know that's one of the things you have to deal with—look-

ing different. I look different than I did before. But it's not something that you can dwell on. . . .

"It's not as difficult now," she said in the autumn of 1986, "as
it was when I first got out of the hospital. I remember a day when
I went to Jordan Marsh to do some shopping. I needed to get
some clothes, because I didn't have anything, and I needed
something that was easier to get into, because at that point I could
not straighten my arms up enough to put anything over my head.
I had to have help. I needed a couple of 'dress dresses.'

"They had a three-way mirror—and then my hair was really
short; I looked like a punk rocker—and on the one side of the
mirror, I looked like my normal me. And on the other side of the
mirror it was just, of course, all, ah, yucky. It was . . . upset-
ting."

But she didn't give in to it. "What good would it have done? I
wasn't going to go shut myself up in a corner. I figured if other
people could stand looking at me, well, I just won't think about
what I look like on the outside.

"One very strange feeling that I had, when I was in the hospital, I can remember thinking about this. . . . I had always been
an attractive girl. I never really thought of myself as being 'beautiful'; there are so many beautiful girls. I was just 'above average
attractive.'

"But I had spent my *life* being that. And I was used to having
men react to that kind of thing . . . being able to *use it* to get
something accomplished . . . the kind of thing that you can get
somebody's attention—because if people are normal the first thing
is usually a physical thing, and I'm not even talking boy-girl sort
of thing, but even a business thing in certain respects. People
like attractive people.

"And the 'inside' me, all of [my] ways of relating to people,
take into consideration how one looks. Normally, you don't think
about it, and certainly I had never really consciously thought about
it, at least not quite in these terms, before. And suddenly now I

find myself a 'beautiful' girl *inside*—inside I'm the same person—but on the outside I look different now."

It was like being one person trapped inside another's shell.

On September 20, 1985, Carol Lynn Benson Kendall had her deposition taken by her brother's defense counsel, Mike McDonnell. The scene was a room off the main section of the Naples City Jail in the Government Center, a few hundred yards away from the bay and the section of quaint shops and restaurants that line the dock and reel in the tourists. It was a beautiful day, outside.

Throughout the entire deposition, Steven, who did not greet Carol Lynn or ask about her health, which should have been an obvious question as she was still heavily bandaged and had almost no hair, passed notes to his attorney. "Maybe fifty times," recalls Ric Cirace. "It was just terrible the way he was trying to intimidate her. And here she hadn't even wanted to tell the police what she knew about him."

Cirace had prepared his client in general for what he was certain would be an ordeal. And he prepared her in particular for one area of questioning. It came up about halfway through the session.

Cirace was sure that McDonnell knew that Scott was, in reality, not Carol Lynn's adopted brother, but her son. And he was sure that McDonnell wanted to disguise that knowledge so that he could get Carol Lynn, on the record, to say "brother." If he could get that statement on the record, he would have a powerful weapon to use in attacking her testimony when it came his turn for cross-examination.

He phrased his question rather subtly.

"Now, Carol Lynn, would you please tell us how many times you have been hospitalized in your life, and for what reasons?"

She answered slowly, and in one of her quieter voices she listed approximate dates of hospital stays for medical problems as a child.

Then she said when she was in the hospital for childbirth, for Kurt, and for Travis.

And then, just when Steven and his lawyer must have thought the jaws of the trap had clanked shut, Carol Lynn Benson Kendall added, "And in December of 1963 I went into the hospital for the birth of my son Scott."

"Jesus!" says Cirace, "you could feel the electricity in the air. Mike McDonnell was some kind of *pissed*, and Steven, Steven!— he looked at his sister as if he wanted to kill her."

Sex, Drugs, and Rock 'n' Roll

"Even Merv May Get Pre-Empted" read the headline in a box on page one of the July 14, 1986 Fort Myers *News-Press*, the day Steven Benson's thrice-postponed murder trial began.

The story beneath that headline said:

Southwest Floridians will have ringside television coverage as news cameras from across the nation start focusing attention on the Steven Benson trial that begins today.

Reporters and camera crews from Florida News Network, Cable News Network (CNN) and local ABC, NBC and CBS affiliates are in Fort Myers to cover what could be the largest media event to hit Southwest Florida in some time.

"It's going to be a nightmare," said Jim Bennett, news director of WINK-TV (channel 11). "Probably Monday will be the worst day of all."

The burden of organizing that coverage has fallen on himself, Bennett said. Besides the big-name national news organizations, other regional and state networks are expected in Fort Myers to cover Benson's trial, he said.

"I honestly think that once they get a taste of what's going on, there will be a lot of foreign coverage," he said. "Once the sex, drugs, and rock 'n' roll get going, I bet even the BBC (British Broadcasting Corporation) will get involved."

Reporters and a camera crew sent Sunday from Atlanta-based CNN (Cable News Network) will have the capacity to cover the trial live, assignment editor Jim Hedges said.

"We're so hot on it we may end up going live," he said.

Hedges said CNN editors will decide whether to cover the trial live once jury selection is finished and the trial is under way, probably later this week.

WINK is planning heavy coverage and will broadcast live reports from the courtroom at noon, 5:30 P.M., 6 P.M. and 11:00 P.M. every day, Bennett said. The station has special permission to have a live report from the courtroom at 10:30 every day, interrupting the Merv Griffin show.

"We also plan on breaking into programming with live testimony when we think it merits it," he said.

Duane Sulk, news director of WEVU (channel 26), said the station will carry live coverage of the trial.

"Right now we plan to have hourly updates Monday through Friday on the hour, every hour," he said. "We plan to go live as warranted. If that means in between programming, you bet. The trial takes precedence over any programming."

WBBH-TV (channel 20) doesn't plan to break into regular programming for the trial, but will have live reports when necessary, news director David Cromwell said.

"We won't break programming unless it's an issue that is life-threatening or crucial to the audience," he said. "We won't even break for a verdict usually."

Cromwell said the station plans less extensive coverage because he believes television audiences will get tired of the heavy trial publicity.

"This (trial) is of interest to a narrow spectrum of the audience," he said. "There is usually a loss of interest in a big hurry after so much coverage. But we will be live at 6 and 11 (P.M.) if it warrants live coverage."

Mr. Cromwell sounds like an intelligent man with a good sense of priorities. Unfortunately, in this case, his prognostication—that television audiences would get tired of the heavy trial publicity—was dead wrong. Even when it was over, they were still asking for more.

It took more than a year from the date of the murders to bring Steven Benson to trial. At first the date was set for November, then it was postponed to March, then April, and finally Judge Hayes told both sides to be ready to begin by July 1986, or else. Some of the reasons for the delay were interesting.

For one thing, Steven had no money. In fact, he not only claimed to be an indigent, but in December 1985, after the first postponement, his lawyer got Judge Hayes to agree, and for more than a month Mike McDonnell was paid by the taxpayers of Collier County for the legal work he was doing on behalf of tobacco heir Steven Benson.

On January 13, Judge Hayes reversed his earlier ruling. He said he was influenced by the fact that Carl Westman (of Frost and Jacobs, the Naples firm Cirace had found to act as personal representative) had testified that Steven had been given $100,000 from his mother's estate for his children, and that the money was being held for them by a guardian. The judge said he couldn't understand how a man who had at least some control over $100,000 could be termed indigent.

"As I stated on December 2, I'm concerned and perplexed as to whose money it is and who's entitled to it." He felt that having access to that amount of money "clearly takes Mr. Benson outside the arena of indigency." While Carl Westman had testified that Steven could receive no money from his mother's estate until he was cleared of all criminal charges against him, Judge Hayes maintained that the money was actually Steven's: "The money is and was his. I doubt that because he set up a guardian fund that he couldn't get it back."

"However," reported the Miami *Herald* on January 14, "Hayes ruled that all expenses incurred for Benson's defense between the December 2 hearing and Monday's [January 13] hearing will be paid by the county. McDonnell said the bulk of the work putting together Benson's defense took place during that time."

One of the local papers, the Fort Myers *News-Press*, went a bit further, pointing out that Judge Hayes seemed to be having a little difficulty with Mr. Westman's testimony.

"The court does not feel very comfortable about the way (that) evidence was presented," Hayes said Monday about the December hearing. "Quite frankly, every time a question was asked Mr. Westman, there never really was a clear answer on whether he (Benson) could get those funds."

Hayes said his opinion is that Benson can legally obtain those funds for his defense unless a challenge is upheld in court. . . . McDonnell said following the hearing that he was slightly confused by Hayes' reversed ruling and that he will probably ask the Second District Court of Appeals in Lakeland to review the decision. Westman was referring questions Monday to his spokeswoman, Myra Daniels, who said that Hayes was in error and that Benson cannot benefit from the estate funds. "Those funds are for the benefit of his (Benson's) children," Daniels said. Barry Hillmeyer, a Fort Myers attorney and the legal guardian of Benson's children, declined comment Monday.

Another interesting pretrial development involved the press. On February 6, 1986, Judge Hayes issued a gag rule on the press, which the prosecution had been wanting for quite some time.

J. Delano (Jerry) Brock, the chief assistant state's attorney who prosecuted Steven Benson, now says, "The first week of the case, the local newspapers were my main source of information." He feels that Steven was aided, and the prosecution hindered, by the fact that Steven was able to learn, from newspaper and television accounts, that a "print" had been found on the sales receipt from Hughes Supply. Brock's point is that the investigators might have been able to get a set of Steven's prints much sooner, and without having to go the extreme of obtaining a search warrant to do so.

He also feels that Steven's rights would not have been violated in any way if that had been the case.

"Without that knowledge, he might have just *given* us the prints," said Brock. "And then there was the business of Steven running around with a private investigator talking to people whose names had been in the papers, like the people at Sand Kastle Construction. That should not have been in the newspaper."

Apparently Steven and a detective had been seen all over Naples, talking to many of the same people the police had been talking to in an effort, the defense later explained, to find the Sand Kastle employee with whom Steven claimed he'd had a conversation on the morning of the murders, but whose name Steven could never recall.

Disclosure of such information, in Brock's opinion, has "the potential for jeopardizing the amount and quality of information that law enforcement is able to obtain." He also feels that without all the leaked information, "Steven Benson *might* have talked to the police, early on."

The longer Brock talks about the issue, the more worked up he gets. "I read the whole damn investigation in the newspaper!" He says that while "it is not an unusual phenomenon to have the details of the investigation in the newspaper," in this case it is the "extent of it" that bothers him.

"Several strategic decisions were undone," Brock says, "by details being printed in the newspaper. In one case we had a search warrant that contained deleted names, and yet those names got in the paper anyway!"

The question of how Steven was going to pay for his defense was finally settled in early March 1986, almost eight months after the date of the bombings. Judge Hayes agreed to a partial distribution of the estate of Margaret Benson. He gave $244,974.39 to Steven and an equal amount to Carol Lynn. Approximately $80,000 of Steven's share went to pay the case-preparation costs of Mike McDonnell and his partner Jerry Berry, a former assistant state's attorney, who was also defending Steven Benson.

Not long after that, the defense requested a delay, which the Judge granted; but when summer arrived, Judge Hayes said that was enough. He set the trial for Monday, July 14, 1986, in Fort Myers. He told the attorneys that he had a judicial conference to attend later that month, and by damn he was going to attend it.

The lawyers knew that there would be no more delays. They'd already seen the trial postponed, for one reason or another, three times, and seen its site moved from Collier County to adjoining Lee County and then back to Collier County and then back to Lee County. The defense lawyers had also tried to get Judge Hugh Hayes off the case, but without success. After more than a year of backing and filling, a year in which the public appetite remained primed for this trial, it was time to get down to it. Let's get going, said Judge Hayes, and let's get going in Fort Myers.

The media heaved a collective sigh of relief. Fort Myers was by no means Naples, but at least it was a *real town* with a nice Holiday Inn and several other well-known chain motels, not to mention the classy accommodations available a short drive away in Sanibel Island or even Fort Myers Beach. After all, at one point, when Judge Hayes was losing his patience with all concerned, he asked the press how they'd like it if he moved the trial to LaBelle, a tiny, midcounty crossroads town without so much as a two-story motel, much less a HoJo's. Beverly Cameron of

WINK-TV, to whom the judge directed the question, remembers shuddering at the thought.

The old courthouse in Fort Myers is a beautiful, moss-draped relic, in front of which several ancient trees, also covered with moss, stand as if at attention. The building, while not truly antebellum, nonetheless looks the part perfectly. One could see any number of heavy trial dramas being played out here, something quintessentially southern, like *To Kill a Mockingbird*. What one could not see, however, was the trial of Steven Wayne Benson.

That took place across the street, in the new and almost antiseptically clean Judicial Center, the kind of government building that honest politicians point to with pride. It has that "Your Taxes at Work" heartiness.

Even before 7:00 A.M. there were enough people in the hallway outside of Courtroom A to constitute a crowd. When there was less than an hour left before the opening time of 8:30 A.M., they fell almost automatically into a line. Strangers became friendly, all washed in the same quiet tension.

At the appointed hour, Val Everly, a thick-armed bailiff in a handsome short-sleeved uniform, opened the door to the first 225 or so spectators who were lucky enough to get a seat. They moved in, chose quickly or were directed to seats, and sat down. Soon the clean new courtroom with its simple, governmental accoutrements was settled, and the air became filled with the familiar thrum of a roomful of nervous, excited spectators awaiting a public trial of some notoriety. In not too many minutes, the murder trial of Steven Benson was to begin.

Unfortunately, criminal trials, whether they are highly publicized or not, always begin—unless the two sides agree to let the judge hear and decide the case—with the slow, careful, and very often boring process known as jury selection. This one was no different.

In order to choose a jury, the lawyers for each side question potential jurors drawn from a panel of locally resident citizens about a variety of topics. In a murder case, one of the obvious questions is how the potential juror feels about the death penalty, which the state of Florida has, and another basic question concerns the effect of pretrial publicity. The lawyers, whether defense lawyer or prosecutor, want to know if the possible juror can eliminate from consideration what he or she may have heard or read about the case, and make a judgment on the basis of the evidence presented during the course of the trial. In the Benson case, that process took almost three full days.

There were a few light moments; there always are in criminal trials; otherwise, the tension would become unbearable. They provide the same kind of relief as the grisly jokes told by law-enforcement people.

People can be rejected as jurors either peremptorily (without having to explain why) or for cause, though in the state of Florida the number of peremptory "challenges," as they are called in a capital case, is limited to ten. By the end of Tuesday, the second day of jury selection, a good many people had been rejected.

One man was so clearly hard of hearing that it was obvious he couldn't serve. Later, he was candid with reporters, who swarmed after all the rejects like chickens after corn: "I would have liked to have stayed on," because, as he put it, "This thing is going nationwide." He also admitted that the lengthy selection process was "monotonous as hell."

Another man who was excused—because his long-planned vacation was only a few days away—said on being questioned by court officials that he had expected perhaps a day or two of jury duty in traffic court, not the Benson case. "When I walked in," he told them, "I said, 'I'm in the right church but the wrong pew.' " He too admitted that he would have liked to be on the Benson jury. "It's the intrigue. Everybody has a bit of the whodunit in them."

A woman who was excused had expressed strong opposition to the death penalty. She accepted her dismissal philosophically. "I have definite opinions. Maybe they wanted people who are more flexible. You never know what they are looking for, so you can't take it personally." Unlike the men, she didn't at all mind not being chosen. "It's a relief," she said. "I would hate to judge a human being. You can never really be sure."

Sitting next to Mike McDonnell and near Steven, at the defense table, was a striking woman who was being paid to "know what they are looking for." Her name was Margaret Covington, and she has both a law degree and a Ph.D. in psychology. A Texan, Dr. Covington is a known expert in the relatively new field of jury-selection assistance, and she has worked with the famous criminal defense lawyer Richard "Racehorse" Haynes of Dallas. She had also worked with Mike McDonnell on an earlier murder case. Viewed from the spectators' section, Dr. Covington's full head of light blonde hair provided a striking contrast to the dark-haired, dark-suited, and dark-miened defense lawyers.

In a brief interview she gave the Fort Myers *News-Press*, Dr. Covington said that while the effects of pretrial publicity can be hidden within a person's mind, this problem is seemingly balanced by the fact that people forget what they've read about a case: "It doesn't mean that much to them." But the problem arises, she said, when something happens during the trial to dredge up that memory; it's at that point the pretrial publicity can do its damage. "Ideally," she said, "you want people who have a clean slate."

And that, as both sides were learning, was particularly hard to find in the case of Florida versus Steven Wayne Benson.

One woman was rejected as a juror because she'd recently had a traumatic experience that she couldn't get out of her mind. The week before, she'd been jogging on the beach when she heard someone call for help, and looked up to see a woman in the water. She went to help her, and got caught in the undertow herself. They were both pulled to safety, and they became, she said, close friends almost instantly.

The prospective juror said she didn't think she could serve

because she kept having "flashbacks of myself and that lady. My first duty in my mind and my heart is to make sure that she's okay. My concentration and my emotions are not with it."

By late Wednesday afternoon, however, there was a jury. Ten women and two men, most of whom appeared to be at least in their sixties, plus two alternate jurors, were seated and ready to hear the case.

Florida law forbids the media to use the names and addresses or even the ages of the jurors, but there was no law against printing their occupations or their hobbies. One paper mentioned that among the folks who were to sit in judgment of Steven Benson were two nurses, a retired industrial safety engineer, an inspector for a construction company, and two "avid readers of murder mysteries."

Once they knew that they were the jury and that no one would be added and no one who'd been seated temporarily would be replaced, they had, as the heroic beach jogger put it, their "minds and their emotions" totally concentrated on the arduous task before them.

Judge Hugh Hayes made things official by welcoming the newly sworn jurors and thanking the others in the jury pool for "helping us try to select the jury, even though you may not have been selected." Then he gave them the first of what would be many warnings about avoiding outside contact.

"It's really important, obviously, at this point, that you remain totally free from any exposure to the press, either in newspapers or TV, or radio or any other type. There is always the possibility," he said, with an added note of concern in his voice, "that if the exposure became great enough it might be necessary for the court to have you sequestered. In other words, in order to make sure that you are not unduly, quote—tainted—unquote."

From the looks on their faces, it seemed highly unlikely that any of the jurors failed to get Judge Hayes's message.

With that, the court was ready for Assistant State's Attorney

Jerry Brock to make his opening statement. Seeing him walk toward her side of the courtroom to the lectern, the court reporter interlaced her fingers and then stretched her arms in front of her to limber her fingers, cracking her knuckles in the process, just another professional getting ready to go to work.

The courtroom was of course the focal point of everything that had taken place in the one year and eight days since the bombings. A few of the people responsible for that effort were in the courtroom, especially prosecutor Jerry Brock and his brother Dwight, but the great majority were not. A number of them, however, were in the building, such as ATF agent George Nowicki and several of the Collier County detectives who had worked so many hours to get the indictment against Steven. They stayed around, waiting for the word that it had really begun, making small talk, and pretending not to be apprehensive.

There had been some feeling a few months earlier, on the part of the law-enforcement people, that Jerry Brock and the state's attorney's office were not as eager to prosecute, or as sure of their case against Steven Benson, as were the men who'd put the case together.

"Not true," said Brock sometime later. "Prosecutors aren't satisfied unless they have twenty-seven eyewitnesses and a bushelful of confessions. We're always searching for that. Law enforcement and prosecutors look at things differently. We look at it from a conviction standpoint, and they look at it from an arrest standpoint." Apprised of that comment, one law-enforcement officer who'd worked on the investigation editorialized, "What crap."

In any event, by the time the trial finally started, the police and the prosecutor were as one. Some of them would be called on to testify as to what they had found, but they'd already done their main job. Now they were waiting for the chief prosecutor to do his.

"Mr. McDonnell, your honor, ladies and gentlemen," said Jerry

Brock. He put a sheaf of notes, in two piles of legal pads, on the lectern, shot his cuffs, and began, with only the slightest of tremors in his voice.

"I trust that everyone is doing well this morning," he said right off the bat. "As we indicated earlier, of course my name is Jerry Brock, I'm an assistant state's attorney, and I'll be prosecuting the case along with my brother, Dwight Brock. Now, as the judge has indicated to you, the purpose for my making an opening statement at this particular point in time is not to offer to you, ah, testimony. The testimony will come solely from the witnesses that appear and testify. My purpose is only to give you," without warning he corrected his course, "and I like to look at it in terms of the picture on a [jigsaw] puzzle. Whenever you buy a [jigsaw] puzzle, it comes in a box [and] you always have a picture of how the puzzle is going to look once you've put all the pieces together. So that is my purpose for making a opening statement. . . ."

Slowly and carefully, in his heavy Florida accent, and delivered in his natural, down-home way, the tall, gawky, thirty-eight-year-old career prosecutor—he'd come to the state attorney's office right out of law school—worked his way up to what it was he was promising the jury in the way of proof.

He told it in the form of a narrative. He did, and then she did, and then he did—laying out, flatly, the whole story of what the government believed had happened, and why. For well over an hour, he told the jury, whose interest never flagged, what the state felt it could prove had transpired. There were no histrionics, and he hardly ever changed his tone of voice from the flat monotone in which he began. But anyone who heard what he said had to steal a glance, from time to time, at the defendant.

And then, just when one would have expected him to pick up the pace, perhaps to point fingers, to call Steven names, Jerry Brock lowered his voice a notch, mentioned quietly that "of course" what he'd just presented was nothing but an overview, and, thanking the jury for its attention, went and sat down.

As openings go, it was either not much of a job—for such a high-profile case—or it was wondrously subtle.

Michael R. N. McDonnell, Steven Benson's chief defense lawyer, could hardly have looked or sounded more different from Jerry Brock. A graduate of the same Florida law school as Jerry Brock (Stetson), the forty-five-year-old McDonnell had a much less parochial Florida background. Born in New Jersey, he grew up in Michigan as well as in Florida, but graduated from West Point, served two tours in Vietnam, and came out of the Army as a captain in the infantry.

Where Jerry Brock is something less than sartorially splendid, his courtroom opponent could pass for a middle-aged male model. His suits, mostly dark, are well cut and look expensive, and his shirts and ties complement them nicely. Where Jerry Brock is fighting a losing battle with his thin, sandy hair—he has marshaled what's left up front into the remnant of a forelock—Mike McDonnell has a full head of dark hair shot through with gray, which somehow looks both combed and casual at the same time.

Even their voices are different. Brock's accent is rooted in mid-Florida, but McDonnell's is hard to identify. It's simply a very good voice, and he uses it well.

There was also a marked difference in their faces. McDonnell has a strong, jutting jaw. His other facial features are thin, almost patrician, and his glasses enhance his seriousness. There is a touch of Robert Redford about him. Jerry Brock, by contrast, is plain folks. His long face is made up of equally long features. He has a disarmingly pleasant and sincere grin, but it was seldom if ever in evidence during his opening remarks. In the business world, it would not be hard to imagine Mike McDonnell as a company president and Jerry Brock as his plant foreman.

What effect any of these superficial differences might or might not have on the Benson jury is strictly conjecture. But as McDonnell got up to make his opening statement on behalf of his client, he certainly looked like he had, and was, the right stuff.

"As you are aware," he said, getting down to business after the briefest of greetings, "these statements that we have heard this morning must be proven by evidence. These inferences from circumstances must be established to you beyond and to the exclusion of all reasonable doubt. And that is the issue for you to decide, and I trust that you will remember to look to the witness stand, and not to the attorneys, for the evidence in this case."

In a firm, confident, and sincere voice, McDonnell continued. He characterized Brock's account of what had happened, of a murderous Steven Benson, as an "interesting story," with the emphasis on the "story," adding, "I suggest to you that the evidence as it unfolds in this trial will *not* establish the story that's been told to you."

He continued with a description of Steven Benson so different from the picture painted by the prosecutor that the jurors, even though they'd certainly expected divergent views, might well have wondered if they were talking about the same person.

"I suggest to you that the evidence will show that Steven Benson was the loving son of Margaret Benson, the peacemaker in the family, the man who took over for the family when he lost his father, the only one who did not fight, physically, tooth and nail, drawing blood. And he was called upon to settle the disputes between the rest of his family members. The evidence will show that Steven Benson is a family man, married with three delightful children, twins and another child. . . ."

Some jurors may have raised an eyebrow at that last comment, as there was no one seated in the first row of the spectator section, reserved for family members, who could have been Steven's wife. Nor did she ever make an appearance during her husband's trial.

McDonnell went on to suggest not only that the prosecutor was wrong about Steven's actions on the morning of the murders, but that Steven had actually performed heroically, by going back out to the Suburban after the first explosion and trying to help.

At one point, he walked over to Steven Benson—who was seated at the defense table, wearing a light gray suit, a white shirt, and a dark tie—and put his hand on his shoulder. "I'd like you to look at this man," he said, "my friend, Steven Benson." He kept his hand in place as he continued, "The state is saying that Steven Benson, the man who never became angry, the man who never, ever fought with his family, on July 9th of 1985, walked out in front of his house in broad daylight, and *destroyed*, or attempted to destroy, every single member of his family.

"For no good reason."

And then he released his grip on his client's shoulder and went on with his opening statement. He mentioned what later developed as the first line of Steven's defense—that Scott Benson had been involved in drugs and that the bombing was in some way related to that activity—by saying that Steven was a wonderful big brother to "Scotty . . . and [Steven] helped him all the time, because Scotty had a lot of problems." In a belittling tone, he said, "Why did he want to kill these people? Because his mother wanted to look at the books"—suggesting that this was hardly, under the circumstances and history of this family, an adequate motive for murder.

But then McDonnell said something that may have been a slip, and if it was, it was an interesting one. He mentioned, ". . . when Steven's father died," and then, after the slightest of pauses, he added, "of natural causes." As there had never been any suggestion that Edward Benson's death had been anything *but* a natural cause, it seemed an odd subject to broach, even in passing.

Shortly before he came to a close, McDonnell accused the law-enforcement people, whom he called "my friends, most of them, and for whom I have respect," of having botched the investigation. And because of that bad job, he said, the defense had been prevented from finding out who the *real* killer was: "That prevents us from ever knowing with any certainty in the foreseeable future why this happened and who did this tragic thing.

"But one thing remains clear, from the evidence that you have *sworn* to adhere to, Steven is an innocent man. And as you see the evidence unfold, you will see that had Steven not gotten out to help his sister in the car, the state would be trying to prosecute three murders instead of two, because Steven would have probably died in that bomb blast."

After stating several specific areas in which he was sure the state would fail to produce convincing evidence, McDonnell returned to the theme of Scott and drugs. He said that he did not intend "to speak ill of the dead," and then he proceeded to do just that. "Scotty was off in the wrong direction, and you will hear of his involvement in the use of, the sale of, and the smuggling of illegal drugs."

McDonnell had planted the hook, the seed of doubt, and now the jurors had at least a vague alternate explanation of what had happened, and could await the evidence.

He closed neatly by saying, his voice still even and steady with no hint of overdramatization, "You have told me and I believe, that you now regard Steven Benson as an innocent man, that in each of your minds, the slate is clean. That you will now receive the evidence, such as it is, and I beg of you to pay close attention to it. There is not one thing that *I* don't want you to hear. I want you to hear it all. And when all the evidence is in, and all is said and done, you'll be able to look at Mr. Brock and say, "Steven is an innocent man.""

Carol Lynn had been brought to the courthouse on Thursday, the day the attorneys made their opening arguments, in case the government wanted to put her on the stand right away. Instead, they opened with a string of law-enforcement witnesses who almost put everyone to sleep.

The evidence they presented, such as photographs of the "crime scene," were essential, but it was closer to what trial lawyers call "housekeeping matters" than the vital open-court testimony the general public is used to reading about or seeing in television shows and the movies, distorted as those may often be.

Several of the first Collier County police officers to arrive on the scene in front of 13002 White Violet Drive took the stand. One testified that he saw both Steven and Kim Beegle. She was crying, he told the jury, but Steven "appeared to be calm." Another officer testified that part of his job was to lock up the Benson home and patrol the grounds each night after the crime; the idea behind this testimony was, in part, to counter McDonnell's promise to prove that the investigators had destroyed evidence and made it impossible to find the "real killer."

The first few witnesses were so "flat" and their answers so rambling that the impression given was hardly one of a tight, well-molded prosecution case. Even the judge later said, "After the first few witnesses, I really wondered about the government's preparation of its case." Judge Hayes was well aware that with the massive amount of media coverage, the Florida state judicial system was also, in a sense, on trial, and he wanted a well-run, fair, and efficient trial.

Of all the people in the courtroom, Jerry Brock was probably the least worried about the way things were going. He was putting his witnesses on the stand and the evidence was getting in, and the record was being built and protected. Also, he knew that he had a couple of "high-visibility" witnesses waiting in the wings.

The first one he called, on the heels of all the police officers, was Kimberly Dawn Beegle, who for three years prior to his death had been Scott's girlfriend. The next witness was to be Scott's natural mother, Carol Lynn.

Carol Lynn remembers the waiting. "Kim was on the stand much longer than had been expected and I had to wait through the entire morning. About 10:30 I was brought down to a room near the judge's chambers. The waiting was more difficult there because I was completely by myself, in a windowless room without so much as a bar journal to read. I remember I could hear voices, not distinguishable words, just an undercurrent of sound. Each time there was a long pause, I would wonder if it were now my turn. Kim came back there at one point, but while she was in there, there was someone else in the room with us at all times. I assume [that] she was there so there would be no conversation between us, but she and I just spoke briefly. She said she had some pictures for me. There was no conversation about her testimony or the trial or anything like that.

"And so she went back on, and I was not taken into the witness area, I guess not at all, except for when they took a break when I was on the stand."

Was she worried about testifying, scared? "No, I didn't have anything to say except facts. I wasn't doing any accusations, I wasn't making accusations. The only thing I could testify about was what I saw, what I heard, what I experienced, the way I felt during the bombing, things that seemed out of the ordinary to me—strictly really factual things.

"Oh, there was a certain amount of apprehension, though I'm not sure apprehension is the right word. It was certainly a very stressful situation, I mean I know my brother Steven is going to be sitting out there. There's all these people. It's going out over national television. It's not an easy situation to find yourself in.

"In any court case it's not easy, but certainly to be put in a situation where you're having to testify . . . I don't want to say 'against' Steven, and I didn't like any suggestions by anyone that I was testifying 'against' Steven. That was not my position, and I didn't feel that was what I was doing, though it could be construed that way. I took umbrage at finding in the newspaper comments that I was the prosecution's 'star witness,' or that my testimony was going to help 'convict' Steven. That may have been factual, but if it was a portrayal of me as 'the one who was out to get him,' or that it was my testimony that was going to do it, I found that very offensive. Because I didn't like to be portrayed as that, [and] I certainly didn't want *Steven* to feel that.

"I was not testifying *against* Steven. All I was doing was relating facts as I saw them or heard them or felt them. That was my attitude toward my testimony. It was before, it was during, and it is now."

The spectators and press alike all craned their necks when Kim Beegle entered the courtroom from stage left. Neither short nor tall, at twenty-one, she was simply a very attractive young lady. Dressed rather demurely in a white on white brocade suit and red, V-necked blouse, her blonde hair parted down the middle and falling just below her shoulders, there was something open and even a little cocky about her demeanor on the stand.

Occasionally, when it was warranted, she'd flash a charming smile, as if she'd forgotten and dropped her guard, and when she did she seemed almost a girl. But most of the time her jaw was set, and she looked straight ahead, probably quite nervous to begin with, but increasingly confident of her ability to "handle it."

All that composure broke, however, when the prosecutor asked Kim to identify a picture of Scott. It was a picture taken in the morgue, and she burst into tears.

Yes, she said, first on direct examination and then again when the defense cross-examined her, Scott did use marijuana and had used cocaine. But if McDonnell was going to paint Scott as a heavy user of drugs, he was not going to do it through *this* witness.

Early in her direct testimony, there was a bit of poignancy. Brock asked her what her relationship was with Scott, and she said she was his fiancée. He then asked her when this had been determined, and she replied, "the night before he was killed."

A slightly different picture of Scott from the one that had been painted in the defense lawyer's opening statement emerged a few moments later.

Q. Did Scott have any hobbies, or things that I would have considered hobbies—he may have looked at it differently . . . ?

A. Yes. His sports car. Golf. Tennis.

Q. Okay, let's talk for a moment about tennis. What was his involvement in tennis?

A. He was a professional tennis player.

Q. Had there been any recent events that had occurred in respect to his tennis, which were notable during the month of July?

A. He was accepted to the U.S. Open. That was very important.

Q. Do you recall when he had received this invitation to the U.S. Open?

A. I believe it was a couple of weeks before he was killed . . . the beginning of July.

Q. Okay. As far as Scott's desires, was this an important event in his life?

A. Yes, very.

Q. What was his reaction? Could you describe his mental attitude as it manifested itself in his activities?

A. He was very happy, skipping around the house. He was acting like a little kid.

Brock elicited testimony from Kim that Buck, Scott's dog, usually barked in the night, at such occurrences as the "security guy in his little car" going by. He also had her testify that when she had checked the console in the Suburban the night before the killings there was no "twelve-inch piece of pipe" in it.

Then he began to ask her about the morning of the deaths, and asked if anything had awakened her.

"Yes, she said, a loud noise, a——" and with that her thin but hard-won resolve was gone. She put her hand up to her face and began to cry. It appeared to be a very natural and unaffected response.

She recovered quickly, but almost started again when the prosecutor asked her, "In what room were you sleeping?"

"Scott's."

"And where was Buck?"

"With us."

Just moments later, Brock asked her what she did on the morning of July 9, 1985, after she was awakened by the "loud noise" she'd just mentioned.

Through the entire interchange, her testimony about the horrible events of that morning, she would have to fight back tears.

On occasion, Jerry Brock would tell her she could take her time, rest if she needed to, but Kim would press on.

"Upon hearing that loud noise, what if anything did you do?"

"I got up and went to the window."

"And that was the window, where?"

"In Scott's bedroom."

"After looking out the window, what if anything did you do?"

"I, what did I do?"

"Yeah."

"I looked out the window."

"Okay, but after you'd looked out the window, did you do something else?"

"When I saw the golf players looking toward the driveway," then, she said, she looked in that direction too, ". . . I saw that the truck . . . was all . . . engulfed in flames."

Kim Beegle was having a little difficulty speaking at this point, and Brock waited for a moment before asking, "And what did you do upon observing that?"

"I got dressed and went out of the room."

"Where did you go?"

"Outside."

"And what did you do when you went outside?"

"I went up to Scott."

"What did you observe, if anything, whenever you got outside?"

"When I got outside, the first person that I noticed was Carol Lynn, and she was standing across the street . . . and she had blood all over . . . she had . . . she had blood. . . ."

"Okay," said Brock, "just take, just take your time."

". . . she had blood all over her."

Kim regained the composure she had lost in trying to say that Carol Lynn was covered with blood, but she didn't have it for too long before losing it again.

"I seen, Steven was sitting on the steps and he had his hands in his head"—realizing what she had just said, she smiled a wan little smile and corrected herself before going on—"head in his hands. And I went to Scott, and then I went back into the house."

"Okay, whenever, whenever you saw Scott, what was your re-action? Or what did you know at that particular point?"

"It was obvious that he was dead."

"Okay. So then you went back into the house?"

"I stopped and told Steven that Scott was dead, and he didn't even look at me, and he wouldn't even say anything."

It was at that exact point that Jerry Brock handed something to Kim Beegle and asked her to identify it. It was a picture of Scott. She identified it, her face caving in, and then she had to identify another one. As the prosecutor walked away, the court stenographer stood up and handed Kim some facial tissues. The witness took them, blew her nose quietly, and then waited just a moment before wiping her eyes.

Kim then testified that her next act was to go into the house and call her mother; she asked that someone come over and get her. A friend of her brother's came right away.

Brock's final question and answer established one more fact: that when Kim Beegle left the Benson residence for the last time, she took the dog, Buck, with her.

McDonnell must have been at least somewhat concerned after Kim Beegle's direct testimony. After all, the jury had now heard one police officer and Scott's girlfriend say that Steven's reaction to the tragedy was, to say the least, odd. McDonnell managed to repair that somewhat by bringing out on cross-examination that, in an earlier deposition, Kim had said that when she first saw Steven he was crying.

At one point, Kim did manage to slip in an explanation for why there were some conflicts between her testimony in court and statements she'd given during a deposition taken by McDonnell the previous December. She said she was "nervous" then, and when he asked her, perhaps unmindfully, *why* she'd been nervous on that occasion, she replied—in a voice so soft it's possible none of the jurors heard her—"Because Steven was there."

McDonnell's cross-examination of Kim was forceful on the few occasions when that was called for, but generally he took it easy on her. That may have been just as well, because he was to need his energy for the next witness, Steven's sister.

"I'm Not Going to Have
You Distort My Answer!"

The word had spread almost instantaneously. One minute no one was sure when Carol Lynn would take the stand and the next moment everyone seemed to know it. Those spectators and others—local lawyers and law clerks, courthouse aides, relatives of one of the principals—who were lucky enough to have seats, squinched down in them as if to make sure nobody could move them and prayed they wouldn't have to get up and go to the bathroom and lose their seats under the no-saving-seats policy.

Those still lined up in the hall talked nervously to one another or listened intently to the various television and radio reporters who were moving up and down the hall to and from the makeshift control room. A few people in line gave up and went down the corridor hoping to find standing room in or near the little cubbyhole room that contained a television monitor which provided a better picture of the witness than 80 percent of people inside the courtroom would have.

Steven Benson, who'd barely glanced at Kim Beegle as she walked to and from the stand, did look up and seemed to stare at his sister as she went by, but once she was past, he didn't bother to turn his head. He kept his eyes forward and his body in the same rigid pose it had been in all week.

Commenting on Steven's stiffness and lack of facial expression, or what psychiatrists call "affect," one young newspaper reporter said to another, "What do you expect? The guy's been in jail for a year. He's brain dead."

She looked every inch the daughter of a proper, well-to-do family from the Northeast. Dressed in an off-white linen suit, over a cream-colored silk blouse, she wore very little jewelry—a large diamond engagement ring that had been her mother's, two gold bracelets, and a simple gold necklace. Her hair was very blonde, but in a tasteful shade and style, parted down the middle and brushed back to the sides in a way that was both serious and attractive. It made the more obviously blonde shade and style of attorney-psychologist Margaret Covington, who had been sitting at the defense table since the first day of the trial, look somehow girlish and dated.

No eye in the courtroom was anywhere but on the witness. For, evident to all was the reef of scar tissue that ran across the right side of her jaw. Equally red and obvious was the scarring on her right hand.

Jerry Brock, his manner suddenly more forceful and his voice more confident, as if her appearance were giving him new energy, began the questioning.

Brock wasted no time getting to the true relationships involved. Carol Lynn testified that Steven was her brother, that Margaret "had been" her mother, and that Scott, who had been her son, had been adopted by her parents. There were to be no doubts up front, and no trying to sugarcoat anything. McDonnell would have nothing to gain, or reveal, on cross-examination when it came to Carol Lynn's family skeletons. The jury would know from the start that this is who she was, and that neither she nor Mr. Brock was attempting to hide anything as relevant as Scott's real identity.

Within minutes, he had her outlining the important details of the events that led up to July 9, 1985. She explained why Wayne Kerr had been asked to come down on Sunday July 7, and she testified that on Monday, Steven had called to ask where Margaret and Wayne were. And then she testified—or began to— about her opinion as to why Steven wanted Scott to be sure and come along on the family outing.

Here, Mike McDonnell asked if he could approach the bench, and one of the central oddities of this otherwise near-perfectly run trial was again highlighted: Judge Hayes did not allow the lawyers to say, "I object."

Later he explained that he felt his ruling kept the lawyers from using the wording, or simply the tone, of their objections to make or score a point with the jury. "Jerry, for example," said Judge Hayes in reference to the chief prosecutor, "likes to cite the statute or code section when he makes an objection, and the problem is that even if I overrule him, the jury may be impressed by what he said, and the case citation he may have mentioned, even though his objection failed." Thus he had the lawyers come to the bench, and the more knowledgeable spectators could figure out, from the answer that followed, or didn't follow, which side had prevailed. It may have made for greater fairness and fewer histrionics, but it was not the kind of trial that fans of Perry Mason know and love.

As they returned to their places and Jerry Brock repeated the question (it appeared that he had won this time), McDonnell asked to approach the bench again. And back they went.

While all this went on, Steven showed a little more movement than was his norm, leaning forward in his chair, adjusting his glasses, and once actually leaning over to answer something asked him by Margaret Covington, his full head of dark hair and her very blonde one contrasting nicely for the television cameras that, from their vantage point in the booth behind the jury box, caught almost all angles of the slightly U-shaped room.

The third time around, Brock, who professed for a moment to have forgotten the question, got to ask again about Carol Lynn's impression of Steven's request that Scott come along for the ride.

Mincing few words, she said, "I couldn't see what point there was for Scott to go along, because it wasn't really a job that took three people. And to get him up at that hour in the morning . . . it just seemed like a dumb thing to get Scott up at that hour to go out there."

At least several members of the jury had to have had the same thought.

In case anyone had missed the significance, he had her explain that the request that Scott go along was solely Steven's. Also, the very idea of Steven himself being up and about at 7:30 in the morning was truly out of character. She emphasized that it wasn't normal for Steven to be "up and functioning at that hour."

While Carol Lynn was on the stand, any number of people in and out of the building were holding their breath. The police officers, especially Nowicki and Graham and Wayne Kerr and Harold Young and Mike Koors, all knew that her performance might very well make or break the case they had put together.

Since the first week of the investigation, they had been fairly sure, then quite sure, and then *positive* that Steven was guilty. But they knew all too well the dangers of a case that relied so heavily on circumstantial evidence. If Carol Lynn "did well," they had a very good chance of convincing the jury. If she did poorly, or if McDonnell "destroyed" her, to use the parlance of the profession, on cross-examination, their case would be badly damaged.

Another behind-the-scener who was biting his nails, figuratively if not actually, was Richard Cirace, Carol Lynn's lawyer. As far as he was concerned, a large part of his job—as far as the criminal trial against Steven and his client's role in it were concerned—would soon be over. He had managed to keep Carol Lynn together, emotionally, and also to keep her out of the news except for her legitimate appearances. The latter was of extreme importance to him. He felt that any unwarranted publicity was potentially damaging. If he could have kept Carol Lynn under glass until the trial, he would have done so happily, and with a sigh of relief.

As for the cops, they had developed a genuine affection for the sister of the accused. Nowicki and Graham and Harold Young acted like slightly older brothers, and Koors in particular liked to kid with her, though he did it somewhat gingerly at first. "Maybe she was spoiled and all that," he once said, "but you look at Carol Lynn, and you talk to her, and you gotta see that's a class act."

With Cirace, the relationship was different—and more complicated. From the first day he walked into her hospital room he was—certainly in her mind—far more than her lawyer. He was her protector, the man, as she put it time and again, "who takes care of me." And while he seemed to relish the role, their proximity got to him at times. Ever mindful of "how things looked," he considered it improper to be seen alone with her unless it was in transit to and from court, and even then he usually relied on someone else to get her there and back. His job, as he saw it with the trial drawing ever closer, was to be protecting her interests, not holding her hand.

As she got "better," she let him know what she thought of this arrangement. "The only time we ever had dinner together," she recalls easily, "was once when I had to bring a document to his room as he was ordering dinner from room service and he asked if I wanted him to order for me, and then one night during the trial we went out for Chinese food—which he made me go in and get—and then we sat in his car eating it, and listening to Dr. Ruth on the radio!"

Also extremely concerned for Carol Lynn and what she was undergoing as she sat on the stand were her grandfather Harry Hitchcock and his remaining daughter, Janet Lee Murphy. And too, for better or for worse, their thoughts were also with Steven.

All of these lines of force, however, were converging on a single point: Carol Lynn on the stand.

———

Carefully and precisely, in her excellent diction—all the more noticeable in counterpoint to the prosecutor's twangy pronunciations and occasional mispronunciations, plus the odd "y'all" that he would drop in from time to time—Carol Lynn drew a very definite picture of what she believed had taken place that fateful morning. She told of awakening at about 6:15 or 6:30, of her mother getting up a few minutes later, and of them talking for a while before anyone else arrived on the scene. Then, she testified, as she and her mother were eating their breakfast, Wayne Kerr came into the kitchen area. Not long after that, Steven arrived, and Carol Lynn said she had looked out the window and seen him doing something as he stood at the open back of the tan van he had just arrived in.

Before she was asked to describe what happened once Steven had arranged the seating of the other family members in the Chevy Suburban, Carol Lynn testified to another point the prosecution considered to be essential: she explained how her mother had almost not gone along that morning, how she had dressed to go to the Meridian office with Wayne, and how Steven talked her out of that idea and into going along.

A juror would have had to be very dense not to feel the cumulative effect of all this evidence from the most crucial witness in the case.

Finally, she was brought to the point of telling the jury what had happened once they were all in the Suburban, supposedly on their way to do mother a favor.

Q. At the time that you were proceeding to get into the automobile, where was Steven?

A. As I was setting the things on the seat of the car, my mother had inquired of Steven where the car keys were. Or she said, 'Who has the car keys?' And Steven indicated that he had them. And then he walked from that side of the automobile—he was partially in the car, sitting on the edge of the seat; he wasn't all the way into the car when my mother said that—and he got out of the car on the passenger side and walked around the back of there, or the other, coming on to the [driver's] side. At that point, as he's coming towards me, I'm starting to boost myself up. Steven . . .

Q. What was your position, as far as boosting yourself up into the automobile?

A. I had one foot inside the car and the other was still on the ground.

Q. Okay. Now, at that particular point in time, as you're getting into the automobile, and you got one foot in the car and one foot still on the ground, what, if anything, happened?

A. Steven helped me up, boosted me up into the car. As I was going up, he kind of gave a little boost up—in.

Q. Okay. Then what happened?

A. He started to close my car door, and I told him that I wanted to leave the car door open——

"Oh God," muttered a middle-aged woman in the spectator section to no one in particular. She had realized immediately that if what she was hearing was the truth, and if that action—Steven's closing the car door—had been completed, then in all probability the attractive witness would not be up on the stand recounting this tale. She would be dead.

"The car was really hot inside, and when a car is built like that, with a lot of doors, I leave a door open to get it cooled off. . . . So I asked him to leave the door open."

According to Carol Lynn, her brother Steven then walked up to the driver's side and gave the keys to Scott. And then,

A. He said something to the effect that he had forgotten something, and—I don't remember specifically what it was, it was, a tape measure, something he would have needed to go with us—and that he'd be back in just a minute.

Q. Okay, and after he'd made that statement, what did he do?

A. Then he headed towards the house.

Q. Now what were you doing during this time period? Or what did you do after he made the statement and headed toward the house?

A. Then I, I reached over to pick up my drink, because I didn't want it to spill—I had it sitting on the seat and I didn't want it to spill—so I was reaching over to pick up the glass.

Q. Did Steven disappear from your sight?

A. Yes, he did. . . . He was walking towards the house when I leaned over, ah, reached over to pick up my glass . . . and [when] I sat up, he wasn't in view at all. . . .

Q. Okay, after you had turned your head, looked straight ahead, and seen that Steven was nowhere in sight, what was the next thing that you recall happening?

She explained that she noticed, or was aware of, Scott moving his body as if he were leaning over to turn on the ignition. "And then immediately following that was when I was suddenly surrounded by this orange thing . . . and I was——"

She paused, momentarily. She was by no means confused, though it was more likely that she was searching for the right, maybe even the exact, word. But the prosecutor, knowing they'd come to the crucial point, was taking no chances. Up to this point his witness had been perfect. He stepped in with a fast question. "Did you have any sensations by virtue of being surrounded by this orange thing?"

"Well, I felt like I was pressed back in, I felt like I was being pressed back into the seat. And it was——"

Again, Brock interrupted her: "Did you know what had caused that 'orange thing' that you were referring to?"

"No, I didn't. Ah, my, I thought I was being electro——" She was testifying a bit more slowly now; "—electrocuted. And I remember calling for someone to help me. And I remember thinking to myself, I wonder what I touched on the car that I could be being electrocuted. Because I was, I was, I kind of felt stiff, and like this for . . . I could feel something going through my body, sort of like an electric shock kind of feeling."

Q. Okay, could you describe the orange sensation that you were perceiving?

A. It was kind of like lying down, and I wasn't lying down, but it was that feeling as if you were lying down in a tunnel, and this thing was all around me, and there was like an air space, and then there was this, this orange thing all around me and I——

Q. Was it like that orange light?

A. I guess. It was just there. And there was something about it, it was like "malevolent." I don't know how to explain it, but, it, it was just there, and it was awful.

Q. Okay. Now, what was the very next thing that you either did or perceived?

A. I called for my mother to help me. And nothing happened, and then I called again, and still nothing, nobody was coming to help me, and I thought to myself, well, nobody's coming, I'm going to have to do something for myself.

So, my eyes were squished shut. I wasn't conscious of them being shut, I was just conscious of opening them, and I just opened them a little bit, carefully, and I could see the body of my son lying there on the ground. And, he just looked so, I knew something was wrong. It wasn't that——

Q. Did you have, other than something being wrong, did you know what had happened at that particular point in time?

A. No, I didn't. But right after, when I saw him, and . . . he had his eyes closed, and it wasn't, there was just a little blood on his face, and, and it's not that I thought he was dead, it's just that, I don't know, maybe my brain knew it, and that what, and then right after that then I could see tongues of flame coming up around the front seat, and I guess that seeing Scott's body and seeing the flames, it kind of woke me up, and I realized that the car was on fire and I had to get out.

For another five minutes, Jerry Brock carefully brought out from his witness that she somehow got herself out of the car and onto the ground, rolling once or twice to put out the flames on her right shoulder, and pulling off her shirt. And when she had accomplished all that, she looked up.

"The next thing I remember is sitting up partially, and seeing my brother Steven standing on the walk."

At this point, Brock chose to interrupt again and to ask her to explain *exactly* how she was sitting up, and Carol Lynn Benson Kendall said, "There's this picture by Andrew Wyeth, with a girl in a field, and she's kind of got her foot at an angle, and she's sitting up, I mean, that's kind of the angle, oh, I'm not explaining this very well. . . ."

It was undoubtedly the first, and probably also undoubtedly the last, time that any witness in Courtroom A of the Justice Center in Fort Myers, Florida would answer a question about posture with an artistic allusion. But for those people in the room who were familiar with "Christina's World," Carol Lynn's posture at that moment was perfectly visualized.

A few minutes later, Brock brought her back to the point—what she had seen when she sat up.

Q. . . . did you become aware of the presence of any other person around you?

A. Just Steven.

Q. Okay. Where was it that you observed Steven?

A. He was standing on the walk.

Q. Okay. Do you specifically recall that he was *standing* on the walk?

A. Yes. . . . He was facing the Suburban.

Q. Do you recall what he was doing?

A. He was just staring straight ahead.

Q. Okay, what did you do after you became aware of his presence on the walk?

A. I couldn't understand why he wasn't coming over to help me.

Q. . . . I guess that was an impression that you had. Did you *say* anything?

A. No, I didn't.

Q. Okay, what's the next thing that you recall happening, after you observed Steven standing on the walk?

A. Steven's eyes opened really wide, and he seemed to react, to become, he'd been standing really still, not moving, at all, just staring straight ahead, and suddenly his eyes opened and his mouth dropped, and he turned around and raced back towards the house, or moved at a hurried speed, kind of ran, back towards the house.

This was not the end of Carol Lynn's testimony in answer to Mr. Brock's questions, but from her brother's point of view it might as well have been.

As direct examinations go, this one had been nearly perfect. If there were any flaws, they were the prosecutor's, for he seemed to stumble over his words at times, and his syntax was often awkward and blocky. He favored "during that particular point in time" over the simple "when." But there were those in and around the courtroom who knew Jerry Brock, and said that everything he did was calculated, part of an overall plan or strategy, and that he probably didn't mind one little bit looking and sounding clumsy in comparison with his highly articulate witness—or even in comparison with the lawyer who had the task of cross-examining Carol Lynn Benson Kendall.

Mike McDonnell didn't set out to bait Carol Lynn, or even, it seemed after a while, to take her on. Certainly, with two of southwestern Florida's highest-profile murder cases already under his belt (one win, one loss) he was experienced enough to know that she was a sympathetic witness, and he would bruise her at his client's peril.

Also, he was smart and experienced enough to know that she had done quite well on direct examination and that the prosecutor, and whoever (if anyone) had prepped her, had done a good job. It was also possible that Mike McDonnell is a nice man, and not a charter member of the rip-'em-up school of cross-examination.

Whatever the case, he started off slowly and politely, and if either one of them, the lawyer or the witness, could have been said to have an edge in his or her voice, it would have had to be the witness, Mrs. Kendall.

Even in response to questions that should not have caused such an intelligent witness to bristle, she often did. When he asked, "It is a fair statement, is it not, Mrs. Kendall, because of this tragic thing that happened to you, because of the physical nature of it, [to say that] you don't remember *every*thing that happened, do you?"

She had already admitted as much, or said so on direct examination, but her response was, "I don't really understand your question."

Q. For instance, you don't really remember the second explosion, I believe you said?

A. No, I do not.

Q. So therefore you don't remember all of the events, necessarily, of that morning?

A. [long pause] Could you be more specific, please?

It was a long time before he even laid a glove on her. Finally he raised some heat, perhaps more than he had wanted to raise.

They'd been discussing differences between her answers that day, and her answers to the same or similar questions back in September when he had taken her deposition. Pointing out such differences is central to proper cross-examination, and Mc-Donnell would have been remiss if he hadn't been pursuing this line of questioning—letting the jury know of such differences can make them question the witness's credibility, one of their prime responsibilities in weighing testimony to come up with the truth.

But Carol Lynn Benson Kendall, a woman who often mentions that she considers truthfulness probably her most important personal trait, even though she knows how the "game" is played, had no patience for that kind of suggestion. Unlike Kim Beegle before her, she was not going to shrug her shoulders and say, "I was confused"; she was going to give it right back. Thus, the following exchange:

Q. Do you remember this question and this answer, at that deposition?

"Question: And between the time you saw him on the walk, as you've described, and the blast, your eyes were continually on the walk in that area?"

"Answer: I couldn't say."

Did you say that?

A. [short pause] That's not the same question.

Q. Did you answer that question in that way? . . . Did you make that answer to that question?

A. If that's what you have down there, I have to assume that it's correct. But that question is almost completely the opposite of the one that you asked me first.

They fenced for a while longer, and McDonnell made a valiant effort to undo, or at least soften, her testimony about Steven turning and running back into the house after seeing his sister in dire need of help. More and more of an edge crept into her voice at these questions, and it is doubtful that her tone was lost on the jury.

They had a number of exchanges like the following:

Q. Now, you are certain that Steven had been sitting in the automobile?

A. I didn't say that. . . .

304 / John Greenya

That one actually led to a distinction being made as to how much of Steven's "buttocks," in McDonnell's phrase, had been in contact with the seat of the car. Carol Lynn would agree to "partially," but no more of her brother's buttocks than that.

Later, McDonnell clearly angered her, an anger that led to her expanding on her direct testimony to his client's disadvantage, by suggesting that something she'd said actually meant Steven was running to *help* their mother. She said she couldn't have meant that, because at that point she didn't even know if her mother had gotten out of the car or if she had "burned up while she was still inside it!"

It's possible that Mike McDonnell never saw the eruption coming, because when the witness blew, he looked genuinely surprised.

They had been going over the same ground, what the lawyers call "prior inconsistent statements," differences between her testimony in court and on her deposition, when something McDonnell said or did suddenly turned up the heat under what had been Carol Lynn's slow boil.

Q. May I ask you if you made that statement that is reflected there [he had given her his copy of her deposition]? Read as much as you want.

A. Before answering the question, I have to say that at the time that I——

Before she could finish what she was saying, McDonnell did what any competent trial lawyer would have had to do under the circumstances. He said, "Your Honor, I'd like the witness instructed to answer the question."

That did it for Carol Lynn, and she interrupted his interruption: "I *am* answering the question. I'm not going to have you," and here her voice rose, "*distort my answer* by not allowing me to answer the question completely."

McDonnell asked for a bench conference, but before that took place, Judge Hayes said to Carol Lynn, in his quiet manner, "Let me just advise the witness that she does have to answer the question at this point. If she wants to explain the answer, she can explain it after she has answered it."

"Please answer my question," said McDonnell, sounding like a schoolboy debater who had won a technical ruling but lost the point.

"Yes," she said, in a firm, take-this-answer-and-stuff-it kind of voice, "I did make that statement."

Around the courtroom, there were nods of approval for Carol Lynn's "victory" over the lawyer. And some spectators claimed to have seen quiet signs of approval from several members of the jury.

Carol Lynn Benson Kendall's testimony definitely helped the state's case against her brother. Early the next week, another Kendall took the stand. This one, Frank, was no relation to Carol Lynn or her former husband, but his testimony also turned out to be very damaging to Steven.

Frank Kendall was the fingerprint expert for the Bureau of Alcohol, Tobacco, and Firearms. He was the one who'd matched Steven's palm prints with those on the receipts for pipe and end caps from Hughes Supply Company, around the corner in east Naples from the Meridian trailer.

Under the slow, methodical questioning of the prosecutor, he explained his procedures and conclusions for Steven Benson's jury. McDonnell barely touched him on cross-examination.

Of course no one knew it at the time, but when the second Kendall left the stand, the prosecution was almost home.

For the Defense

The prosecution wound up its case against Steven Benson on Friday, July 25, 1986. During the two weeks it took to put on its case, the State presented almost fifty witnesses and introduced 180 items into evidence. Carol Lynn, the defendant's sister, had clearly been the most eagerly awaited, most news-generating witness. Whether she liked the terminology or not, she *had* been the State's "star witness" against her brother. But if she had worried that hers would be the only negative testimony from someone close to Steven, she could relax. During the second week of the State's case, there were several people whom Steven had once known well who took the stand and said terrible things about him.

Some of the most damaging information about Steven came from Wayne Kerr, Margaret Benson's lawyer and adviser, who had also counseled Steven and even, at times, Carol Lynn. More to the point, though, Wayne Kerr and Steven Benson were such close friends that he had once chosen Steven as his best man. If there had still been anyone in the courtroom who thought Steven was a proper businessman, he or she would have been disabused of that notion by the testimony of Wayne Kerr.

Assistant State's Attorney Dwight Brock, Jerry's younger brother and co-counsel in the Benson case, has an accounting background, so he examined witnesses who testified regarding finances. Dwight Brock resembles his older brother more in style than looks—he is shorter and stockier but displays the same sort of plodding persistence. He asked Kerr what he found when he finally got to examine the checkbooks for Steven's various Naples-based Meridian companies.

"Well," said the Pennsylvania lawyer, "I noticed that there was no balance forwarded on all the transactions. I noticed that there were items that had no payee and no amount." If that wasn't enough, he testified further. "There were certain canceled checks missing from the bank statements, there were items listed on the bank statements that were not found in the checkbook. There were checks that listed one amount but when I checked it [against] the bank statement, it listed another amount." In some cases, he could not figure out who the payee was.

"Did this cause any suspicion in your mind?" asked Dwight Brock, and Kerr replied that at first he thought it was only the bookkeeping. His implication? "We," he said, referring to himself and Margaret Benson, "saw symptoms of a problem that could be sloppy bookkeeping, could be misappropriation." The symptoms, he said, pointed in "several directions."

Initially, Wayne Kerr did not make a very strong impression. He is large, perhaps six-foot-three, and overweight, with the look of someone who does not care about his own appearance. His hair is long and the cut too young for a professional man nearing his mid-thirties. His thick glasses were smudged and dirty, and he sweated heavily in the air-conditioned courtroom.

Shortly after Kerr took the stand, a good-old-boy spectator said to the man next to him, in a too-loud voice that almost carried to the witness stand, "Jesus, ain't he a mess." Once Kerr began to testify, however, the image improved. He is, after all, a C.P.A. who later went to law school, finishing first, it is said, in his class at Penn.

McDonnell's cross-examination of Wayne Kerr was much like his cross-examination of many of the prosecution witnesses, whether or not they had been damaging: quiet, low-key, and not noticeably effective. He did, however, get Kerr to say that he had never confirmed his suspicions about whether Steven's bookkeeping proved that he'd been misappropriating funds. Perhaps of equal importance was Kerr's admission that he still considered Steven his friend.

The total impression, however, of Kerr's testimony was that Steven was a *terrible* businessman—and quite possibly also a crook who stole from his own mother.

The next two witnesses for the State were among the last they would put on. McDonnell did rather poorly with the first, but quite a bit better with the second.

The first was Steven Hawkins, who'd worked for Steven Benson at Meridian Marketing, the company the latter Steven had "hidden" from his mother. Hawkins, an earnest and good-looking man of about thirty with a strong voice and a manner to match, testified about a number of Steven's odd business practices, such as his habit of writing counter checks at the bank, and not telling anyone, thereby causing the company's regular checks to bounce, or telling Hawkins to put a dummy sign in front of the building so it would look like there were other businesses at the address.

Hawkins's most startling testimony brought quiet gasps from the spectators. He said that on July 9, 1985—which he called the day of "the tragic incident"—Steven Benson called him and told him about the explosions and deaths and asked him to bring Debby Benson to Quail Creek. When he got there, he confirmed that the first thing Steven asked him was, " 'Did we get any money in today?' "

Later that same day, he testified, he saw Steven remove boxes full of what looked to him like "financial records" from his mother's house.

Hawkins was memorable for another reason: he admitted to behavior that must have struck a common cord with many present in the courtroom. He said that after arriving on the scene, and seeing the vestiges of the tragedy, he felt "sick to his stomach" and asked a neighbor if he could use his restroom.

What did he think, asked the prosecutor, when Steven Benson asked him, first thing, if they'd gotten any money in that day? "It struck me as a little unusual," said Mr. Hawkins, in the understatement of the day.

He also testified that he stood as close as two feet from Steven Benson while they talked, and he did not notice any blood on him.

There were murmurs of anticipation when McDonnell walked over to cross-examine Hawkins, but within minutes they changed to mutters of disappointment. In a surprisingly short cross, McDonnell did little or nothing to soften the negative effect of Steven Hawkins's harsh testimony. The effort was so perfunctory that one had to wonder if the defense lawyer was getting overwhelmed by the State's case, despite his continually optimistic comments to reporters at the end of every court day. Or was he just playing possum?

Steven's lawyer did a much better job with the next prosecution witness, and it was a good thing he did, because the cumulative effect of her direct testimony was staggering.

The witness—yet another attractive woman with long blonde hair—was Dianna Galloway, an auditor with ATF who had studied the books from the various Meridian companies. She was offered as an expert witness in both auditing and accounting.

After she had been "qualified"—her credentials as an expert having been presented by the State, examined by McDonnell, and approved by Judge Hayes—and after the jury and everyone else had had a chance to listen to her wondrously slow southern accent, she was ready to begin testifying. The contrast was striking between her quiet and almost reserved manner and the grisly nature of the things she examines—business fraud, arson for profit, and, as in this case, bombings.

This expert had studied box upon box of business records, canceled checks, and bank statements from both Steven Benson (and his companies) and his mother. She presented her conclusions in a huge chart, with a series of backup documents, presented over more than three hours of direct testimony that began in late afternoon and lasted through an evening session that didn't conclude until ten o'clock.

She testified that in the fourteen months prior to his mother's death, Steven had received $247,132.67 from his mother and the various companies. ("But who's counting?" whispered a spectator.) After deducting certain "legitimate payments," there was still the amount of "$179,864.95" that had gone to Steven for no apparent "legitimate" business or personal reason. She pointed out, in her understated way, that during one six-week period Steven wrote $26,000 worth of counter checks!

McDonnell, in an equally painstaking cross-examination the next day, managed to cast doubt on a large part of that total, whittling it down, according to his figures, to less than half of the almost $180,000 total. But certain bits of her testimony were firmly embedded in the jury's mind, such as the mention that during the period she studied, she found that Steven had written $4,000 worth of checks that were returned marked "NSF"—not sufficient funds.

At 2:25 on the afternoon of Friday, July 25, 1986, the State of Florida rested its case against Steven Wayne Benson.

An hour and a quarter later Judge Hayes, in a thoughtful and rather lengthy explanation, denied the defense's motion for a directed verdict. He then let everyone go home until Monday. After court days that had run into nights, and even a Saturday session, it was most welcome.

"Getting out of here early is *so great*," exclaimed one of the young television crew members. "We will lift weights tonight!" His friends laughed, as if what he'd said had another meaning.

When Brenda Turnbull walked into the courtroom to testify, all eyes were upon her. It wasn't simply that she was an attractive young woman with dark red hair, wearing a nicely fitting white dress, but it was the bold way she strode over to the witness stand. Carol Lynn had walked a bit slowly, with her shoulders hunched over a little. Not Brenda Turnbull. She was there to stick up for her former boss, and she strutted up to the stand, her loyalty on display.

The next day, one young male reporter said to his cohort, regarding Turnbull and her initial appearance, "If I'd been McDonnell, I'd have had her dress real plain and act almost scared. But when I saw Brenda walk into court yesterday, my immediate thought was—'Bimbo!' " As unfair as that characterization undoubtedly is, it confirms that Turnbull definitely made an entrance.

As a first defense witness should be, she was immediately put to use rehabilitating Steven's reputation. An earlier witness had testified that Steven, at the service for his mother and Scott, made some comment about having constructed "bombs" as a kid. Had she heard that remark? Yes, she knew that that had been charged, but she was right there and she'd not heard him say it.

More important—potentially *most* important—she also testified that Steven was in his office at 3:25 on Friday, July 5 and again at 4:30 on Monday, July 8, the times that the police said he was out buying the pipes and end caps at Hughes Supply, a minute-and-a-half drive from the offices of Meridian Security on Domestic Avenue.

Unfortunately for Steven, on cross-examination, Brenda Turnbull had a lot of trouble with her memory, especially as it related to prior inconsistent statements; and eventually she began to cry.

She had to admit that previously she had given different answers. Several different answers.

She also exhibited something less than kindness toward Margaret and Carol Lynn. Asked if they were involved with the company, she replied that they didn't discuss business. What kind of decisions might interest them? "If they wanted a chandelier *here* or *there.*"

Brenda Turnbull had to use some form of the word "confuse" so often, that by the time she left the stand, several jury members had very doubting looks on their faces.

Shortly after she had left the stand, opposing counsel got into an argument, at the bench, over the defense's attempt to put on several surprise witnesses whom the prosecution had had no time to interview. Judge Hayes, up to this point a personification of judicial calm, lost his temper and, not realizing his microphone was still on, snapped, "This is bush-league practice of law . . . just damn bush."

One of the prosecutors then said something that angered Jerry Berry, McDonnell's partner, who said, in an angry voice, "I've represented him before and I don't like the implication. If you've got something, back it up!"

That seemed to make Judge Hayes even more upset. In a voice that quavered with his anger, he said, "The Florida bar would be glad to give you a hearing." There were other comments, harder to hear, and then he said, plainly, "Let's not make this system look any worse than it currently does."

For some time after that, there was a notable calm in the proceedings.

On the second day of the defense case, there was a stirring in the courtroom as two casually but very expensively dressed middle-aged men took seats in the spectator section. They wore tasteful amounts of gold, and one carried a handsome leather purse. Gossip quickly established that they were from Hollywood and were checking out the case as the possible subject of a movie. One of them, the tall one, it was said, had made "The Amityville Horror." He was friendly and had a joking manner: when a young reporter supplied the name of a movie he could not recall—"To Kill a Mockingbird"—the producer said, "Give that man a role!" His colleague, a somber man, watched the proceedings intently. They were picked up in front of the courthouse by a limo, and did not return after lunch.

The lawyers were back in the judge's chambers, presumably arguing about something, so the jury was not in and the spectators talked freely. People who had not seen the entire trial wondered whether the State was convincing the jury, but the consensus of the press, almost all of whom had been there from the very beginning, was that McDonnell was not mounting a strong enough defense and that Steven Benson was sure to be convicted.

It would become harder to argue with that opinion after the next witness, Dr. Bonnie Eads, a Naples optometrist, had testified. She was supposed to testify that Steven was "legally blind," and could never have gone into a store—such as Hughes Supply, as had been alleged—without his regular glasses, which he always wore. (The prosecution had introduced evidence that a man of Steven's general size and age, wearing "a cap and John Lennon-type sunglasses" had bought the materials at Hughes.)

But Jerry Brock, on cross-examination, so turned her around, by having her in effect dilute the definition of legal blindness, that when she left, more than one spectator commented that she'd seemed more like a *prosecution* witness than someone put on by the defense.

Jerry Brock seemed to be improving as the trial progressed. He even showed on occasion what might have been a touch of humor, such as when he asked Dr. Eads, "Can you get 'John Lennon' in a prescription?" (The answer was yes.)

Humor was definitely on the menu, though inadvertently, with the next defense witness. John Gargiulo, who lived across the street from Margaret Benson, was put on the stand to make the point that because a piece of metal, presumably from the blast, was still on the screen that covered his swimming pool, the police had not really done a thorough job of investigating the case.

He also testified that Buck, Scott's "attack-dog," did not always bark at noises. As proof, the neighbor said that sometimes Buck would be silent even when he shot at the raccoons that tried to get into his garbage cans.

With a sly smile, Jerry Brock asked Mr. Gargiulo what type of handgun he used to shoot raccoons.

"My .357 Magnum, loaded with buckshot."

All humor vanished with the next witness. Through a young attorney in the Frost and Jacobs firm, the same firm that was serving as personal representative of the estate, McDonnell introduced a portion of a tape the lawyer had found in Margaret Benson's home. On that tape were the voices of Margaret and Scott, in the middle of the vicious 1983 argument over Buck, the argument that had resulted in Margaret's calling the police and having Scott hospitalized for observation for five days.

Suddenly, after weeks of hearing testimony about two people who had been so horribly murdered, there were their actual voices, as if back from the dead, coming through the loudspeaker of a tiny tape recorder. The courtroom was very quiet, and Steven Benson, for only the second time since his trial had begun, showed some emotion. He cried.

And yet, as with so much of the defense's case, once the point had been made, one was tempted to say, "So what?" Granted Margaret and Scott had had their problems, and, yes, he sounded terrible when he told her the dog could rip her apart if he but gave the word. But what was there to tie that two-year-old emotion to the 1985 killings?

Even Joyce Quinn, one of Margaret's former secretaries who was there during the fight and testified that "Steven was more businesslike, but Scott was into tennis and partying," did not seem to provide the nexus. Something continued to be missing.

Perhaps the elements could have been supplied by the one

man everyone had been waiting to hear from since the trial be-
gan: the defendant, Steven Benson. What could he say about
Scott and drugs, clearly the implied line of defense in his case?
More to the point, what could or would he say about his own
actions in early July 1985? What would he say in his own defense?
What was *his* story?

Nobody ever found out. The defense concluded its case without calling Steven Benson to the stand.

The line to get into the courtroom began to form before 7:00 A.M.
on Wednesday, August 6, 1986, two hours before the lawyers were
to begin their closing arguments in the case of the State of Florida
vs. Steven Wayne Benson.

At 8:33, there was a rustle of movement and a swift turning of
heads as the bailiff led Harry Hitchcock and his daughter Janet
Lee into the courtroom and gave them front-row seats in the section reserved for family and friends—of the prosecution. Across
the aisle, the same seats were occupied by relatives of the defense lawyers. Steven's wife, Debby, had never attended the trial.

"The State may proceed," said Judge Hayes at 8:40, and Jerry
Brock got up to make his final argument.

It was almost immediately apparent that Jerry Brock was more
confident and more relaxed in making his final argument than he
had been in making his opening statement. He didn't talk any
more quickly—he never does—than he did at the beginning,
but he clearly felt more in control of his material, his message.

Methodically, he ticked off what he felt were the most important facts: Wayne Kerr's testimony about misappropriated funds;
Dianna Galloway's statement about $16,000 that ended up in Ste-
ven's bank account; Margaret Benson's discoveries in June and
July regarding Steven and money, such as his new house and the
presence of the car he'd told her he sold to make the down payment; and the use of a check on one of *her* accounts to make that
down payment.

After some minutes of this he said, simply, "These are the

events that led to the deaths of Margaret Benson, and Scotty, and almost to the death of Carol Lynn"; and at 9:01 he said to the jury, "I submit to you, ladies and gentlemen, that this defendant *knew* the pressure was building on him. . . . What does he do? . . . [He buys pipe and end caps], the first step in construction of these homemade explosives."

He got more histrionic as he went on, and he began to add gestures, even pounding on the lectern to emphasize a point— "And Margaret told him. 'You carry those books home and get them organized so we can go over them with Wayne in the morning!' "

Again and again he mentioned the palm prints. But he said, when he was close to the end, that they had so much evidence against Steven that they didn't even *need* the palm prints—"I submit to you that if he had left his *foot*print"—and here he walked over to the defense table and said, slamming his hand down on it to the great surprise of everyone in the courtroom, "we *still* would'a got him!"

McDonnell objected, but the point had already been made.

Brock closed by suggesting why Steven hadn't gone to the aid of Carol Lynn: "He was getting away from there because he knew the second bomb was fixin' to go off." And what kind of switch was used?—one like what they use in "burglar-alarm systems."

At 9:50, Jerry Brock was finished. Downstairs in the office of Joe d'Alessandro, Brock's boss—where a dozen people were crowded in front of a television screen, including Carol Lynn Kendall—there was a smattering of applause. Elsewhere in the area, tens of thousands of people sat or stood, watching television. The closing arguments were being carried live, and, as they say, "in their entirety."

During the break, some of the press got up and crowded around Harry Hitchcock, asking him for comments. Other members of the media hesitated. The door to the corridor had been opened and they didn't want to risk the loss of their seats. One male reporter did, and when he came back he found that a flashily dressed middle-aged woman, one of the regular cast of trial watchers who had been in court since the very first day, had vacated the seat she already had in order to come over and take his, because it afforded a better view.

"Hey," he said, startled, and on the spot, because the bailiff with arms like a stevedore had called for people to return to their seats. "You're in my seat."

"There's no saving seats," she told him.

"But I'm with the press."

"So what?" she said snidely, and then decided to add, "I have as much right to this seat as you do. Maybe more."

Now he had to move or he'd be out of the room. He looked at her with instant hatred. He said, to no one in particular, and with a snarl, "That bitch stole my seat!"

McDonnell, to the surprise of almost everyone, delivered a very quiet final argument. In fact, he spoke so softly to the jury that spectators at the far end of the courtroom missed most of what he said. After his almost whispered greeting to the jury, he went to the blackboard and wrote in big block letters, the word "SUSPICION."

He then began to talk about "stories," telling the jury that's what they'd just heard from Mr. Brock, a "story." It was a story, he said, "based on evidence not presented in this courtroom and before this jury." He called it "preposterous," and said it was based on suspicion, but in a court of law it didn't make any difference how suspicious things might be.

He told several stories himself, one of which was about a tailor, which he connected by saying, "And you too are being sold a suit that does not fit. . . ."

The other story was a well-told anecdote about seeing someone on the street you think you know. "But you can't be sure until you get up close—that's reasonable doubt."

"Now to the evidence," McDonnell said, and proceeded to go through the testimony of the various witnesses, dismissing each one as he went. Of Carol Lynn he said, "because of what she has been through, her testimony is unreliable." And he pointed out that what she *had* recalled, she recalled out of sequence.

He said that no one knew exactly how long Steven was gone, but a few minutes into this line of reasoning he tripped over his own verbiage, somehow getting "square peg" and "silk purse" into the same metaphor.

There were certain witnesses, however, that he did not mention.

As for Frank Kendall, the ATF print expert, McDonnell attacked him by saying there was no evidence that he was a *palm* expert and that "There's no evidence before you that anyone can identify Steven Benson, or anyone else, from a partial palm print."

That sounded good, but, as several reporters asked later, if it was true, why didn't the defense present a palm print expert of its own?

McDonnell also mentioned laughter, and suggested that nervous laughter is often only natural. He was apparently referring to Lieutenant Wayne Graham's testimony that on the day of the crime, when Debby Benson emerged from a bathroom in Margaret's house, she made an off-color joke (about what might have happened to her if she had been "on the can" when the bombs exploded), and Steven and Wayne Kerr had laughed.

Near the end, when he was whispering again, he said that while Steven was indeed a "sloppy businessman," his mother had "ratified" his actions by long inaction in correcting him.

As for Dianna Galloway, the arson-for-profit expert, he said she proved that it was easy to "make an assumption of guilt and work backwards."

And he called Brenda Turnbull "a lady who never wavered in any important detail."

"There are so many facts inconsistent with the State's case," he said when he was almost finished, "that it doesn't make sense." He then told one more story, apparently from the Bible, but he spoke so quietly only the jurors could hear everything he said.

Walking back to the defense table, he put his hand once again on the shoulder of his client, Steven Benson, and said to the jury, "I'm going to give him to you now. Take good care of him."

The jury listened intently to Jerry Brock's rebuttal argument, but one got the sense that they had already heard enough, and at twelve minutes after one in the afternoon, it was all over. Now it was up to them.

Six

The Verdict

"We Find the Defendant..."

In southwestern Florida in the summer months, it is unusual *not* to have an afternoon rainstorm. But the one that fell shortly after the jury left to begin its deliberations over the fate of Steven Benson was almost theatrical in its intensity. On cue, huge thunderheads rolled in, and the skies darkened as if some avenging angel were in charge of production. Then the rain fell in great swooping torrents. The scene was definitely set.

Before he sent them out, Judge Hayes had instructed the jury. During his instructions, a few of the jurors, undoubtedly at that moment even more mindful than ever of the terrible responsibility that awaited them, slid their eyes over toward the defendant. Steven Benson sat there, as impassive as ever, in his gray suit, white shirt with the collar slightly too big (from all the weight he'd lost in prison) and gray tie.

"No juror should be concerned," Judge Hayes had said, "that the defendant did or did not take the stand in his own defense." He also told them to remember that "the lawyers are not on trial," which caused a few jurors to smile. But they were all business

323

again a moment later when he explained that "prejudice, bias, or sympathy are not reasonable doubts."

At 2:05 P.M., Richard Cirace, Carol Lynn's lawyer, escorted Harry Hitchcock from the courtroom.

One minute later, the jury had the case.

At four o'clock, everyone in the still crowded courtroom was startled by a knock from inside the jury room.

It was not, however, a verdict. That would have been almost record time for the result of a four-week trial.

It was, however, the jury. The newly elected foreman said they would like to have testimony of two witnesses read back to them— some of Carol Lynn Kendall's, and all the testimony of Frank Kendall, the ATF print expert.

The testimony from Carol Lynn that interested them was her account of just where Steven was standing in relation to the Suburban when the first bomb went off. They also listened while the court reporter read her graphic account of the initial explosion.

Having heard it, along with Frank Kendall's testimony in its entirety, the jury returned to deliberate again. They left behind them some raised eyebrows. This was key testimony, and they had reached the point of debating it in a very short period of time. Perhaps they were having difficulty with the largely circumstantial nature of the case; and perhaps they were having hardly any. One could find either opinion, strongly held, with no trouble at all.

Almost five hours later, a surprise visitor walked into the quiet courtroom. Carol Lynn Benson Kendall, her attorney Cirace, and a few others who'd been eating and drinking at the Veranda restaurant half a block from the courthouse, had joined the crowd waiting for a verdict. The next day's papers carried pictures of her smiling, or at least looking anything but grim, as she had most of the time on the stand.

It was the first time that Cirace had let down his guard. He took full blame for it—"We'd all been eating, and having a few drinks, and I'm not a drinker, so the few I had probably affected my judgment, but when we left the restaurant and went back to the courthouse to wait for the jury to be excused for the night, and when the elevator stopped and they piled out, I went along. I had already walked into the courtroom before I turned and saw she was behind me. And then it was too late. But I don't think it hurt anything."

As Carol Lynn sat in the courtroom, her brother Steven was seated but a few feet in front of her. But his back was to her, and he may not even have known she was there. Whatever the case, he did not turn around.

At 9:02 P.M., the jury came in to announce that it had not reached a verdict. Judge Hayes told them to quit for the night and to start deliberating "anew" at nine the next morning.

At 11:14 A.M. on August 7, 1986, the jury knocked again. No verdict.

Out in the hallway, a reporter for the Miami *Herald* was interviewed by a television reporter. At issue was Mike McDonnell's characterization of that paper's coverage of the trial as being suitable for "the *National Enquirer* or even *Hustler*." The other reporters laughed, knowing that the prize-winning *Herald*'s coverage had been among the best from the start. One reporter suggested that what really irked the defense lawyer was that a sharp-eyed and equally sharp-penned *Herald* reporter had described the kindly white-haired woman who frequently sat behind Steven in the first row of spectator seats on the defense side as "Rent-a-Mom." The woman, it turned out, was the defense lawyer's mother-in-law.

But another reporter, a slightly older one, shook his head and muttered something about what was it all coming to, with the media interviewing the media for the media.

At 1:14, two hours after the last knock, there was another. Ten minutes later, Steven Benson was brought into the courtroom.

Mike McDonnell reached out and shook Steven's hand. Spectators whispered to one another that the gesture had to mean there was a verdict.

And there was.

At 1:30, Mr. Henning, the foreman, handed a slip of paper to the bailiff, who carried it over to Judge Hayes. The young judge read it, a somber look on his face but no change in expression that might indicate what the verdict was.

"Madam clerk," he said, "would you please read the verdict?"

She did, and it was guilty in the first degree on every count.

Aside from blinking fast, several times in a row, Steven Benson betrayed no emotion.

In the back of the spectator section, a woman said to an old man next to her, "They got 'im, and they got 'im good!"

Carol Lynn Benson Kendall was not in the courthouse when the jury brought in its verdict. She was not even in Fort Myers.

"Richard didn't think I should stay alone in the motel room waiting for the verdict to come in. He had gone up [to Fort Myers] in the morning, but I didn't want to go up, and he said that was okay, but he said he didn't think I should just stay in the room waiting for the verdict. And I'd let him know I didn't want to do that."

One of the problems was that her aunt and grandfather were there, and Carol Lynn and her aunt had been having a difference of opinion. "Janet Lee was really in favor of having him executed. She said that she hated him because he killed her sister and her nephew and he deserved to die. I just could not, did not, have the same feeling. To me, he was still my brother. It was a very difficult, stressful situation for me."

She went, with her lawyer's blessing, to have her hair done. "That probably sounds horribly callous, but the idea of sitting back there in the motel room with somebody who was waiting with bated breath to have Steven convicted was just not what I wanted to do. So Richard said it was okay if I went and got my hair done.

"There weren't many places where I was allowed to go, because Richard didn't want me out where I could be seen, but he said it was all right if I went to the hairdresser's, because it was the regular hairdressers where I went whenever I was in Naples. It wasn't as if I were walking into a strange place.

"Richard had said that if there was a verdict, he would have time to call me because they always notified everybody first before the jury was going to come in, and I'd have plenty of time to get home. So I left him the number at the hairdresser's."

Carol Lynn had her hair done, and was about to get in the car and head back to the motel when she noticed the sportswear shop across Third Street. The shop carried O.P., a brand of shorts and casual clothes that both of her boys liked, but which they had trouble finding in Boston.

She went across the street and, shopping quickly, found something for each of them. The store was not crowded, and she was the only customer at the counter when she went to check out.

"The clerk was a young man, and as he was about to take my credit card, he turned around and changed the station on the radio. I guess he didn't like what was playing and wanted to find a rock station. But the station he turned to had been interrupted, and they were broadcasting live from the courtroom."

Suddenly she heard the voice of the clerk reading out the verdicts, ". . . and on the count of murder in the first degree we find the defendant Steven Wayne Benson guilty . . ."

Carol Lynn says, "I almost fainted. I could feel the blood rush from my head, and I started to get sick. But I knew I had to get out of there and get home. I pushed the card across and *prayed* that he wouldn't recognize my name—or me. There I was, scars and all, with the same face that was in that morning's paper. But thank God he didn't, and I got out of there."

Concentrating, she was able to drive back to the motel, and get up to her room.

"I walked in the door and Janet Lee was *celebrating*! She said, 'Steven's been convicted, he's been convicted!' "

"I just looked at her, and said to her and to my grandfather, 'Please, please just leave me alone.' And I walked in my bedroom and locked the door."

Seven

The Aftermath

Reflections

Half of the jurors wanted to kill Steven Benson—or, rather, they wanted the state of Florida to execute him for what he had done—but absent unanimity, they did not get their wish. Under Florida law, given a six-to-six tie, the lesser penalty prevails. Depending on one's point of view, Steven was lucky.

In Florida, the jury in a murder case has a twofold function. It decides whether or not the defendant is guilty. If it returns a guilty verdict, then the jury goes back to deliberate again, this time on the question of a sentence. Should it be life, meaning a set number of years in prison, or death?

A Florida jury delivers an "advisory sentence" to the judge. The jurors can recommend death, or they can tell the judge they think the person they've just found guilty should be given X number of years in jail with no parole. A majority vote is required for the death penalty.

On Friday, August 8, 1986, the day after it found Steven Benson guilty, the jury returned its verdict—life in prison. Because several of the charges carried life sentences for set periods of time with no chance for parole, Steven Benson could be sentenced to a maximum of 100 years in prison.

The decision was up to Judge Hayes. As the term "advisory" suggests, he is not required by law to impose the sentence recommended by the jury. In fact, he had the power to sentence Steven Benson to death, even though the jury had not asked for the ultimate punishment. And a Florida judge has one more option. He can decide right away, or he can take some time.

Judge Hayes decided to take his time. It wasn't that he had any philosophical opposition to the death penalty. It was just that he wanted to offer the family one last chance to have some input in the punishment phase of the process by which Steven Wayne Benson had been convicted of killing Margaret and Scott and of attempting to murder his sister, Carol Lynn.

The jury had recommended twenty-five years without parole on each of the murder counts and twenty-two years for the attempted murder. The sentences could be run concurrently or consecutively. In other words, Steven could get twenty-five years without parole—or he could get fifty or seventy-two or, because of his convictions on the other counts, even 100!

Judge Hayes asked the family how it felt about the matter.

Janet Lee Murphy, responding by letter, said she favored the death penalty. Steven had killed her sister and her great-nephew, and he had almost killed her only niece. She wanted him to pay the ultimate price.

Harry Hitchcock told the judge he thought Steven should be put away for as long as possible. He told a Florida newspaper reporter, "I did not take a position on capital punishment because I did not want to be the one to pull the switch." However, said Steven's grandfather, "I wouldn't know whether the family would be safe with him on the streets. If he did it once, he could do it again. He deserves to be incarcerated and without his freedom for the rest of his life."

Carol Lynn, who had almost been the third fatality, had difficulty responding to the judge's request. On one hand, she would say to her lawyer, "He's still my brother, and you shouldn't want to see your own brother *executed*."

Prior to the trial, and in relation to a dramatic possibility, Carol Lynn had taken a somewhat different position. In the autumn of 1985, after Steven had been in jail for several months, his jailers uncovered a cache of sleeping pills in his cell. Reportedly, the medication had been prescribed by a doctor for Steven's insomnia. He had been given a pill each night with his dinner, but instead of taking the pills, he'd been hoarding them. He had saved more than enough to kill himself.

According to the police, when they informed Carol Lynn that they had confiscated the pills, she reacted with something close to disappointment. Asked about this a year later, she said, "The thought of being executed or spending one's life in jail was so horrible to me that I wanted him—strange as it may sound—to have that choice, that option: to take his own life. In another respect, I was actually angry. It would have been the honorable thing for Steven to do, because it would have spared the family the scandal of a public trial."

Back in August of 1986, Carol Lynn had a very practical reaction to the question of how long Steven's sentence should be: she didn't want him to get out while he would still be able to come after her and finish off the job he'd started on July 9, 1985.

Judge Hayes could rule the sentences be served concurrently, in which case, Steven, who was thirty-five, might get out of prison at the age of sixty. There were no guarantees that he would not attempt to kill Carol Lynn again. But even if he did not, the years preceding his release would be filled with anxiety for his sister.

As if matters weren't complicated enough for Carol Lynn Benson Kendall, she was trying to study the question from several different points of view. She even told Cirace that she was trying to figure out ". . . what my mother would want me to do."

Finally, with great reluctance, she made her decision. Unlike her aunt and grandfather, Carol Lynn would make no public statement, though Cirace told a reporter that she did not wish her brother to get the death penalty; that would be, he said, "another death that she would have to deal with." However, she asked Cirace to write the judge and tell him what her decision was. Cirace did so.

In a letter to the Department of Corrections official who was conducting the presentence investigation, Cirace wrote:

> Mrs. Benson Kendall expresses fear and grave concern for her personal safety and well-being, the safety and well-being of her children, and the safety and well-being of her other family members. She has come to realize and accept that her brother was not only capable but also did in fact kill her mother, kill her son, and attempt to kill her in a premeditated and deliberate fashion.
>
> For these crimes she asks the court to sentence the defendant to two consecutive, not concurrent, life sentences, one to the other, with additional consecutive sentencing on the remaining counts, in order to ensure that the defendant serve the maximum sentence possible. Moreover, Carol Lynn prays that Judge Hayes will give her the peace of mind in knowing that she is protected against any further attempts by the defendant on her life in the future.
>
> Although she is not recommending that the defendant be put to death, Carol Lynn implores Judge Hayes to sentence the defendant to the maximum sentence, so as to allow her to live her remaining years without being in fear of bodily harm to herself and her family.
>
> Steven Benson has inflicted severe personal and emotional injuries on my client. He has left her with severe scarring and burns over her face and body. He has caused her to endure the pain and suffering associated with skin-grafting and reconstructive surgery. And she will forever have to endure the loss of her mother and her son.
>
> It is virtually impossible for Mrs. Kendall to go forward with

her life if she lives forever in the shadow of fear—thinking about Steven Benson's possible release during her lifetime. Asking her to live with this anguish would be to further victimize this woman who is already a tragic figure. . . .

On September 2, 1986, Judge Hayes sentenced Steven Benson to serve a minimum of fifty years without parole. That meant he could not get out of prison until he was almost eighty-five years old. Her attorney reported that Carol Lynn felt "relieved." More than anything else, she says today, that relief was simple gratitude that it was over.

Days later, Steven Benson was transferred from the Collier County jail and moved to Lake Burton, where the state maintains an induction center for people about to enter the mainstream of Florida's prison life. After spending several days there, he was moved to Raiford, one of the toughest prisons in Florida, where he is to serve his sentence.

He will not be eligible for parole until the year 2036.

A few days after the trial was over, assistant state's attorney Jerry Brock, the "victor," allowed as yes, he did feel a certain disappointment. "Before the case, things are building," he told a reporter, "then while it was going on the adrenaline gets pumping. When it's all over you feel a letdown."

In November, three months after the trial, he had not changed his feelings. Had he become "famous"? A polite man, he tries not to laugh at the question.

"There's no thanks or acclaim in this job for doing what you're supposed to do. People don't care what you did yesterday. They want to know what you're going to do tomorrow."

In general agreement is the man who presided over the trial of Steven Benson, Collier County Circuit Court Judge Hugh Hayes.

An even-tempered and unusually candid man, especially for a judge, Hugh Hayes thinks Jerry Brock did an excellent job.

Nonetheless, he remembers that at certain points of the trial, especially at the beginning, Jerry Brock had definitely not yet hit his stride.

During the first hearings at which the defense tried to get the county to pay for Steven's defense on the grounds that he was an indigent, "I had serious doubts about the 'indigency' but the State wasn't asking the right questions. And it got to the point where I had to make a decision, sitting on the bench, [that] you can't be the lawyer for the State. . . . I couldn't be the attorney for the state and sit up on the bench, too. But I *could* arrive at justice, and that's my fundamental purpose."

One of the agreements between the two sides that least pleased Judge Hayes was the legal fiction of the "pass-through" by which money went to Steven Benson, who then waived all rights to it so that it could go to his children. Judge Hayes reflects a very commonsensical view: "How can you pass the money through Steven Benson and not say he got it? I mean how can he say, 'I waive any right I have to it and I give it to my kids, and we're going to set up a guardianship account for my kids and we're going to play this pass-through game'? You can't 'pass through' like that. I don't think the IRS will buy that . . . and I didn't either."

What bothered the judge then, and clearly still bothered him three months after the trial, was that the trial of Steven Benson could not be simply a criminal matter. The wills and the estate kept getting in the way. "That was an irritant to me as I proceeded on the criminal charge, because I had to second-guess everything these guys did, because [even though] I knew they were doing it for the benefit of the estate and of the people involved, I couldn't let that control the case."

Having been the person who decided what the jury could and could not hear in the way of direct evidence, Judge Hayes got to see the total picture. As a result, his theories as to just what happened in front of Margaret Benson's house on the morning of July 9, 1985, are probably as well informed and likely to be true as anyone else's. For example, he wonders about the testimony indicating that Steven Benson showed grief when he viewed the results of the first blast.

"It was my theory at the time that it doesn't make any difference whether he ran into the house or behind the van, because— and only he would know—once the blast went off he could have been standing there looking at her and *then* run into the house, realizing, 'I didn't get her! She's going to survive this thing!' "

Told that Fred Merrill (one of the first witnesses on the blast scene) holds a very similar view, Judge Hayes says, "I don't have any doubt, personally, after listening to all the evidence and testimony, that that's exactly what happened. I actually think that the only reason he stood there and his mouth dropped wide open was—it was the classic reaction—'Oh *shit*, she's alive!' It's not the shock of the carnage and the death, but the shock of life!"

During his opening statement, Steven's defense lawyer had described Steven as the "substitute father" in the Benson family. If that were true, asks Judge Hayes, "If he were this conscientious, responsible young man, then why is it that nowhere in the testimony is there [anything] to reflect that he ever attempted to render any aid, to check the pulse or vital signs of *anybody*? . . .

"Why wouldn't you go to the aid of your sister? I think the normal reaction would be not only shock, but to *do* something. But just to call 911, or tell someone else to, and then do nothing— it didn't add up."

As for the fact that so much of the evidence was circumstantial, the judge says, "Circumstantial evidence cases can be lost if you try to rest your case only on one event in the transaction. . . . True, it was a circumstantial evidence case, but what the jury used to convict was the only *direct* evidence in the case, Carol Kendall's eyewitness testimony and the palm print. That's what got him. And the jury honed in on the only direct testimony in the case. That's what convinces me that they made their decision on sound judgment and sound evidence. They weren't buffaloed by the bullshit."

Judge Hayes says that, for all the secondary issues, important as they may have been, he could never lose sight of the nature of the crime for which the defendant was on trial. Four months after the trial, as he sat in his office during an interview, he searched his copy of William Blackstone's *Commentaries on the Laws of England* until he found what he was looking for—the great legal scholar's words on "parricide."

"In book IV, chapter 14, page 202, he says, 'By the Roman law, parricide, or the murder of one's parents or children, was punished in a much severer manner than any other murder or homicide. After being scourged, the delinquents were sewed up in a leather sack, with a live dog, a cock, a viper, and an ape, and cast into the sea.' And that," says the judge with a burst of hearty laughter, "is heavy shit!"

One nonlegal aspect of the case continues to fascinate Judge Hayes. "If you look at the size of those cannisters, and figure the amount of gunpowder that had to be in there, and see the remains of the Suburban, it is truly *unbelievable* that anybody could have survived that blast. Even the first one, much less the second one. But how Carol Kendall is alive is beyond even your imagination.

"Why she survived is a question that no one will ever figure out. Unless you believe that Steve Benson just was fated to be caught, and somebody had to survive, and God picked her. If you believe in the kind of supernatural law that you can't kill your mother and get away with it, and God will get even with you, then Carol Kendall was definitely the avenging angel.

"There is no legal, medical, or scientific reason why she survived. It was more than luck. It gets into the other world, without a doubt. This is not something that the normal mind of man can comprehend. It leads you to believe in the supernatural. I don't believe in it that much myself, but I guarantee you, if I was Carol Lynn Kendall I wouldn't have any problem with it. Why she survived is a real enigma. Luckily for her she did, but 'unfortunately' for Steve.

"Looking at it realistically, if she had died—even with Steven's not-so-ingenious planning, buying the pipe where he did and all that—if she had not survived, I think he would have gotten away with it."

Judge Hayes takes this a step further, by speculating on what might have happened, or not happened, had Carol Lynn died.

"If no one had survived the blast, then Steven would have been the best source of information for the investigators, and as a result I don't think they would have found the palm print, because he would never have led them in that direction. The obvious track to take them on would have been the drug investigation. Steven would have been able, basically, to steer them [by saying], 'These witnesses will tell you that Scott was a druggie.' " And then the jury could logically have assumed that the Bensons had been the victims of a drug war or vendetta.

Two women who knew Steven, though from different vantage points—and both of whom testified at his trial—find their reaction to his conviction tempered by their positive memories of him. They are Kim Beegle, Scott's girlfriend, and Ruby Caston, Margaret Benson's housekeeper.

"Steve was always really nice to me," said Kim, in a March 1987 interview. "And something else nobody seems to mention—he had a good sense of humor. I think Steven was a really nice guy. Me and Steven got along really well."

Kim smiles as she begins to recount one particular memory. She and Scott had driven to the airport to pick up Steven, and as he walked toward them they both noticed that he was sporting a new hairdo.

"Steven had gotten a perm. I didn't even recognize him. I just burst out laughing—try to picture Steven in a curly perm!

"Scott goes, 'Shh. Don't say anything about his hair.' He knew I was always busting on somebody. But Steven looked at me, and he started smiling, and he said, 'What do you think?'

"I said, 'Steven, do you really want to know?' And he goes, 'Yeah, what do you think?'

"And I said, 'It looks like they made you ride on the wing of the plane.'

"Steven started laughing, but Scott was so embarrassed. Later, in the car, Steven was in the back of the Jaguar, and Scott whispered to me, 'I can't believe you said that to my brother!' Scott would never say anything like that to Steven. But Steven just laughed. He had a great personality."

Kim remembers Steven as always being on a diet. "The poor guy was always trying to lose weight. When I saw him at the trial," after he'd been in jail for a year, "I commented to my mom, 'Steven finally lost the weight he wanted to lose.' "

At one point, Scott and Kim helped Steven and Debby move, and Kim noticed that Steven—like his father before him—had a passion for buying in volume. "He had *cases* of Raid," she says, "and cases of soap and bleach, and things like that. Cases and cases!"

That was after Debby had returned with the children and she and Steven had been reconciled. Kim met Steven in 1982, when he was still separated. "When I first moved in with Scott in Port Royal, Debby and Steven were not seeing each other. She had taken the kids and left. Scott had told me about [it]—told me [Steven] was having problems with his wife. Scott said Steven was really upset . . . when Debby left, because [Steven] really loved his babies."

Kim Beegle relates that Scott, "told me everything about the family. Just before he was killed he told me, 'Mom's really upset with Steven. He bought a brand new house in Fort Myers, and he was supposed to sell a car and didn't and he was using a lot of the business money to buy the house.' "

Kim Beegle describes her own relationship with Margaret Benson as one that changed frequently. "When she was around her kids, she would treat me like I was the little poor kid on the block, but when she wasn't around her kids she liked me. She was wonderful, at times. But she was always either mad at Steven or she was mad at Scott. She couldn't be with both of them or all of them. Either she liked Carol Lynn that week, and she hated Scott and Steven. Or she liked Steven that week, and couldn't get along with Scott."

Kim once made the mistake of answering the phone at the Benson home. "It was Debby. I knew she was Steven's wife, even though I had never seen her." She asked where Steven was and Kim told her. "As I was talking to her, I looked at Mrs. [Margaret] Benson, and she was looking at me like she was ready to jump off her chair. And so when I hung up the phone, she said, 'If you want to pretend you're a secretary, do the job right.'

"I just looked at her, and she said, 'If that woman ever calls here again, you don't give her any information other than that Steven's not here.' And I said, 'But that was Debby!' and she said, 'I know who it was!' And, I thought, God! And I said, 'Well, I'm not going to answer the phone then.' I was very upset."

Shortly after Steven's trial, Kim consented to a television interview in which she said, in effect, that the family had forgotten about her, and that she felt somewhat abandoned. In a March 1987 interview (at the Gold Spike, the restaurant and bar her mother runs in Naples) Kim Beegle seemed to have moved away from that point, and spoke fondly—if not uncritically—of all the family members, and especially of Steven. Near the end of the interview she said, suddenly, "Steven was such a doll."

Three days after that interview, Kim called her interviewer long distance to say there was something she wanted to add. "My mother and I talked it over, and we decided I should tell you something else. In August of 1984, I had an abortion. It was Scott's baby. It was Steven's idea that I get the abortion, and he arranged everything with the doctor in Fort Lauderdale, and he paid for it.

"Steven said, 'If my mother finds out you're pregnant, she'll cut Scott out of the will. Whatever you do, don't tell her.' So I had the abortion."

Kim Beegle says that in general she remembers Margaret Benson with affection. But she definitely feels that she was a woman who attempted to control her children through her money. Kim recalls that Margaret "used to walk around the house clutching her purse. Sometimes Scott would grab it away from her if she wouldn't give him money." Both Kim and her mother say the reason Margaret's projected dream house was so huge was that she hoped, somehow, someday to bring all her children back under one (very large) roof.

"Originally, she was going to build on to her house in Quail Creek and have Scott and me stay in the kitchen side, and then she would live in a new wing she was going to build above that. She was getting all this tile and stuff, and she'd say," and Kim Beegle slips easily into an almost affectionate mimicking of Margaret Benson, " 'Now, honey, I want you and Scott to look through this stuff and see what color tile you'd like. It's going to be *so* pretty. I just can't wait. I'm so excited about it.' "

Another woman who has good memories of Margaret *and* Steven Benson is Ruby Caston, who was Margaret's housekeeper for the last two years of her life.

Asked, almost two years after the bombings, to give her impressions of Steven, she says, simply, "Steve was my friend. He was always there for me when I needed him. We had a lot of good times together. We talked a lot."

Ruby Caston says that both Steven and Debra loved their children, and that Debby may even have been "a little overprotective."

After a discussion of the "bad blood" that she agrees existed between Margaret Benson and her daughter-in-law, Ruby Caston says, "Steve was under quite a bit of pressure."

How did Ruby feel about the possibility of Steven's guilt? "When I saw Steve on the day of the murder, he put his arms around me, and put his weight on me, and I had no idea it could have been him. I didn't even *think* that."

About a month later, however, Ruby Caston had an experience that, she says, "shocked me." She saw Steven in his lawyer's office a few days before his arrest, and suddenly he said to her, " 'Don't ever hurt anybody.' And he had never said anything to me like that. He was different that day. It was like he was trying to tell me something."

And she says that at the trial she had to admit to a different belief. "The day I knew he did it was the day I took the stand and Steve wouldn't look at me. He just kept his eyes on the floor. Then I knew he was guilty."

Ruby agrees with Carol Lynn that Steven changed during the year or so before the murders: "It was like he worried more, and he didn't care how he looked or dressed. 'Course he was never what you would call a dresser. He was totally in love with his wife. Mrs. Benson told me he threatened to commit suicide one time about Debra before she came back home."

Ruby Caston says that Steven and Debra's children are "real sweet kids," and adds, "I love those kids, and I hate that I won't be able to see them again. I don't think any of the family will. I think that's cruel."

Mrs. Caston adds that when she says Steven helped her out a lot, she does not mean just financially. "He gave me a lot of moral support. He would talk to you for a long time," if you came to him with a problem. "Steve was a good talker.

"And he was a giggler, too. He had a good sense of humor and could make you laugh. He'd come to the house and have every-body giggling. Yeah."

She remembers one time in the last year they were discussing Scott, who, she says, "Used to do a lot of weird things." She asked Steven what they could do about Scott, and he said, " 'Well, I guess he's too big to send away to camp.' We laughed it off. And that wasn't too long before the accident."

Ruby says, "Everybody depended on Steven. Mrs. Benson looked up to her son. Before talking to Wayne, her attorney, she would talk to Steve. They used to lock up in her room and talk, all the time."

Ruby says that these sessions seldom if ever included Carol

Lynn. "I always felt about Carol Lynn like they didn't give her a chance. And she had it rough with the boys. She did so much for her mom, businesswise, and going and helping out. She was always good to her mom. Everybody gets mad with their mom, but Carol Lynn was always, 'Yes mother.'

"She never talked back to her. If she did it, it was behind her back, and I used to do my mom like that when she'd make me mad. It was always, 'Yes mother, no mother.' And every time her mother needed her, Carol Lynn would be there."

After mentioning that, by 1985, Carol Lynn was coming down to Naples more and more often, Ruby Caston adds an intriguing observation: "I think Steve felt a threat there. They hated it when Carol Lynn came. It was like, 'Oh, wow, is she coming?' Scott too. Scott would move out."

Ruby also had a great fondness for Scott, though she would never call him a "teddy bear," because she had seen him push Carol Lynn around and even knock her down—once, just after she'd come out of the shower wearing only a towel, so that she ended up naked.

Carol Lynn agrees with Ruby Caston that Scott could be violent. She says there were times—several times—in Scott's last few years when he attacked her with such violence that she thought he might injure her seriously.

"Once I made a flip remark to my mother, something about how much money Scott would have if she were dead, and suddenly he came running, from another room, and shouted, 'Don't you ever say anything like that!' He knocked me down with his forearm, onto a bed, and started to choke me. My mother screamed and hit him on the back until he quit.

"I finally came to the conclusion," she says now, "that Scott must have known, after all, that I was his mother. And I think it is very possible that Steven told him. I can see now why Scott was so violent with me—he must have been filled with so many strange and conflicting emotions."

Ruby Caston also saw Scott threaten Margaret. Of course, Ruby says, he would be contrite and feel terribly guilty within minutes.

"I even asked him to leave several times after he'd pushed his mom [Margaret]. I never saw him knock *her* down, but I sure saw him push her and call her dirty names, really bad names."

Ruby verifies that Margaret had all but given up on disciplining Scott, especially as regarded his girlfriend's sleeping with him in her house. "She hated that because she didn't think it was proper, but she was supporting Scott and she was supporting his girlfriend. She told me Scott'd been doing it ever since he was thirteen, fourteen years old. She said if she told him he couldn't bring them in, he'd bring them in anyway, and sleep with 'em right there in the house.

"Scott was a baby. His mother used to call him a teenager, even when he was twenty-one, he was still her teenager."

Still, Ruby acknowledges that Scott "cared a lot about" Kim. "He used to come home bloody [after fights with her], and they'd be together the next day. He told me he wasn't going to marry her because he knew she wasn't what his mother wanted, and that she was no good for him. He said to me, 'But she's got good sex, Ruby!' That's what he told me."

Ruby Caston believes that while Scott most likely did not know Carol Lynn was his mother, he did know that Margaret Benson was not. "He hated Carol Lynn. He'd say, 'Oh, that bitch's coming, I'm moving out.' I walked out of there the day he had that big fight with her and knocked her down buck naked. I mean he had her by the hair, and it was like he had somebody in the street that he didn't give a shit about. It was real weird.

"I left that day. I said, the hell with all of them. But Mrs. Benson called me, and said, 'Ruby, I'm sorry I got the kind of kids I got. I can't help it.' I never would have quit her, but, God, I could have. I stuck with her because she was lonely. Mrs. Benson was a lonely woman."

Ruby Caston feels that Debby and Steven Benson were a most unusual couple. They lived oddly, she feels, citing as an example the time she and a girlfriend helped them move, and found Debby's diamond ring. Debby, she says, reacted in a decidedly ho-hum fashion. "It didn't excite her."

Ruby says they found something else—bunches of uncashed checks! "We found all kinds of checks in the garage just lying around—three thousand, a thousand here and a thousand there. Old checks, lying around in the garage with the trash. I said, 'Oh, God, it must be nice to be rich!' "

Ruby says that while Debby was very particular about her children, she showed more concern for the inside of her house than for her husband, at least as far as feeding him was concerned. "It was like she didn't prepare him dinners. I used to feed him whenever I could.

"I went over there one night [to baby-sit] and she didn't want to leave her kids because they would cry. She just kept playing games at the door. I said, 'Why don't you get in the car and get the hell gone? The babies are going to cry for a second, but they'll be just fine.' I know. I've got four kids. But I went all the way over there that one particular night and they never went out because she couldn't stand to see her babies cry. And they had a date, to be out with friends, but she wouldn't leave."

Ruby mentions a wild scene she witnessed in Lancaster on a day when she'd been working, helping Margaret clean out the warehouse. Apparently, at the end of the day everybody was to get together for dinner, even Steven and Debby and their children, but they weren't there for long when a huge fight erupted. Ruby walked out of the house to find Steven sitting on the pavement, Debby having left with the kids.

"I said, 'What's the matter, Steven?' and he said, 'I don't know. I don't know, Ruby.' "

Harry Hitchcock and Janet Lee had arrived, apparently at the invitation of Debby, who was staying with her children at Margaret's house, in what turned out to be her last appearance there. When those who had been working in the warehouse showed up, tired and dirty, Debby had, for some reason, changed her mind. She told her mother-in-law to call Harry Hitchcock and Janet Lee and tell them not to come. Margaret refused, and when they arrived, Debby, kids in tow, stormed out and took a cab to a hotel. The next day she went back to Florida. She had insisted that Steven accompany her, but for once he held out.

Another incident, which preceded the one recounted above, involved a chance remark made by one of Steven and Debby's children in an earlier visit to Margaret's house.

As Ruby Caston recalls it, "The baby must have said, 'Grandmother,' [to Margaret Benson] and Debby said, 'That's not your grandmother. Don't call her that.' It was really mean. I said, 'Debby, you shouldn't teach the kids that.'

"Mrs. Benson heard that, and it must have hurt her. But she said, 'It's not the first time she's done that, Ruby.' But that really upset Boppa that day. I've never seen him upset like that before. I think that's the first time he saw that side of Debra."

Finally she had to ask herself, "Why does Steven love her so much?"

Ruby Caston's conclusion about Steven and Debby Benson is simply that "They should have gotten out and worked for themselves."

Told that some people have suggested that Carol Lynn Benson Kendall actually *enjoyed* her central role in the case, Ruby disagrees strongly. "Oh, God, you couldn't enjoy seeing your brother up there like that. Carol Lynn loves her brother too. She told me in [the hospital in] Boston to tell Steve that she still loves him, but she would never forgive him for what he did. But she loved him because he was her brother.

"We cried together that night. We were by ourselves, and we just got really into it, and it was the first time that she ever really cried."

The events of July 9, 1985, changed the lives of many people, not all of whom were featured, or even mentioned, during the trial in 1986. Two of the people whose lives were affected are Kurt and Travis Kendall, Carol Lynn's sons.

In recent interviews, one and a half years after the bombings, they talked about their extended families, as those families existed both before and after the tragedy.

Kurt, is a tall, trim seventeen-year-old high school senior. His smile, when it comes, is unexpectedly friendly. Recently elected most valuable player by his fellow swim-team members, he has applied to several Ivy League schools, and hopes to be accepted at Princeton. "I want a school," he says "that will push me." He shares his mother's ability in science and math, and they have friendly competitions over achievements past and present—"She got better grades, but my board scores were higher."

Protective of his mother, Kurt Kendall is direct about saying he was not particularly fond of his grandparents, because, basically, they treated him and his mother and brother as second-class relatives. As for Steven Benson, "He was just my uncle. If he and my grandfather [Edward Benson] were talking about something, Travis and I would have to leave the room."

He recalls fighting with his grandmother over something she'd said to his mother, and being scolded by his grandfather, Edward Benson: "He was so mad I thought he wanted to kill me. . . . I just didn't know him. We lived either around the corner or across the street, but we never had any person-to-person talks, nothing like that. He was a person you didn't want to cross. He was just totally 'adult.'"

As for Scott, the uncle who became a half-brother, Kurt Kendall says that while he was fun when he was younger, "After fifteen, he had his life and I had mine." Kurt was not impressed with the way Scott Benson chose to live that life. And, he has a vivid memory of Scott fighting with Carol. "My mother," he says, "had a lot of resentment toward her parents in regard to Scott, both for the way they adopted him and for the way they raised him."

He does have a fond youthful memory of one relative, though. Janet Lee Murphy, his great aunt. "We liked going over to her house. She had a Ping Pong table, and she gave us Cokes." And he expresses great fondness for "Boppa," his great-grandfather.

Kurt Kendall's description of his reaction to the violent deaths of his grandmother and Scott make him sound somewhere between stoical and unfeeling. He had been speaking of how he felt when his grandfather, Edward Benson, died, saying, ". . . it really wasn't anything major," and then he added, "when *any* of them died, it wasn't, it didn't really bother me a lot." Though, he says, it bothered him "at the funeral." By contrast, his younger-by-one-year brother, Travis, reacted very emotionally. As Kurt put it, "He was crying all over the place." But then Travis had been very close to Scott.

"She hated our guts," is his blunt appraisal of Margaret Benson's feelings for him and his brother. "She took me to Disney World once, but that was because she was upset with Travis."

But weren't there at least *some* times when she was nice to them? "She was never nice, the way you picture a grandmother being nice—I don't think ever. It just didn't happen. She was civil with us, and yet she wasn't civil with us [because] she'd always yell at us. If anything went wrong, we were always blamed."

On July 9, 1985, Kurt got the news of the tragedy from his younger brother by phone. "Travis called and said, 'Mom's been blown up.' I said, 'Funny joke,' and he said, 'No.'

"I think I knew immediately that Scott was dead, that my grandmother was dead, and that my mom was injured. That was it. Through the entire thing, even while she was in the hospital, I had no feeling that she was going to make it or not. It was like, if it happens, it happens; there's absolutely nothing I can do about it. And I was trying to resign myself to that."

And how did Kurt feel when Carol Lynn told him—after the bombings—that Scott was also her son?

"It didn't bother me. I was completely neutral on the subject. It didn't really matter, because it didn't change anything at all. My feelings for him as a person were already settled, and his being my brother didn't really matter one way or the other."

According to his mother, ever since he was old enough to understand what was going on between grown-ups, Kurt Kendall had been his mother's protector. She tells of the time when Kurt, all of three or four, stood up to his grandparents (in his Dr. Dentons) and said, "Don't you make my mommy cry!" While he feels Carol Lynn showed great strength during her ordeal, which culminated, at least publicly, with the trial, he still has those protective feelings.

Asked if he felt his mother was a strong person, Kurt answered, "Yes and no. I think she's very emotionally dependent on my brother and me. I don't know. There are times when she's very much bothered by it, by the whole situation, it really bothers her." And sometimes, he says, his mother gets upset about *his* feelings about the situation.

"She feels really sorry for Steven, and she gets upset when I make crude remarks. I said I didn't care what happened to Steven, even if he got the electric chair.

"I mean, people come up to me and say, 'I hope Steven gets the electric chair.' I've never had anybody come up to me and say they hope he doesn't.

"People don't understand—the lawyers and everything. Nobody knows what's going on, all these lawsuits and things. The lawyers always say, 'Well, I'm just doing this for the kids.' And my answer is, "If you're just doing it for the kids, then why don't you take less than forty percent?

"I don't think anyone knows that Steven's kids are getting money from the estate. I don't think anyone would believe that, it seems so absurd. It doesn't make sense that you kill someone and then you get the money for it."

As a result of all of this, says Kurt Kendall, he has almost no respect for lawyers. "I think they're in it for all the money they can get out of it. They don't care for the people."

Asked if he shares his mother's sense of family, her feeling of all of them being part of a Benson "clan," Kurt Kendall says, "Not to the extent that she does," but he says that, in a way, the family is now closer. "I get along really well with everybody left

BLOOD RELATIONS / 351

in my family. All the people I didn't get along with are now in jail or have died."

Unlike his older brother Kurt, Travis Kendall spent some time with their Uncle Steven and his wife Debby. As a result, he says, he "kind of" liked them. "I stayed in their house in Florida a few times," he says. Mindful of how his mother feels about Debby Benson, he says, cautiously, "She was nice, but I wasn't really paying attention."

On the question of Edward Benson, he is clearly in sync with his brother Kurt. A one word description? "Strict." But the problems he and his brother encountered, in particular the one-sided, least-favored-nation treatment, were, he said, ". . . not so much my grandfather. It was more my grandmother. And that was because, I would say, she felt more toward Scott."

Reminded of an incident in which he was accused by Margaret Benson of having put nails in his pocket and scratching the piano bench, Travis shakes his head and points to Buck—once Scott's dog—at his feet. "It was that fellow there," he says, with a smile.

How does he remember his grandmother? "As an extension of my grandfather. Strict in her own ways, but still nice. I believe."

In general, the sandy-haired, athletic Travis Kendall was closer to the rest of the family than was his older brother Kurt. And of all the family members, the one he was closest to was Scott Benson, the uncle who turned out to be his brother, and the relative—in fact—he most resembles.

"I liked to do more of the things that he liked to do, like going fishing"—and riding around in fast cars. Indeed, Travis claims to have been in the Lotus with Scott on one of the times Scott drove it 160 miles an hour. And he is well aware of the tale of Scott getting caught by the state police, whom he left in the dust of I-75 but didn't shake entirely because he slowed down rather than drive his car into a puddle.

"He was just that way," he says, talking happily about "Uncle Scott," and forgetting for a moment that Scott was his brother, "A lot of times I'd clean his car, just because I like to work on cars, and he'd appreciate seeing it nice and clean. He knew that if he went through [the generally puddled entrance to Quail Creek] fast, he would have thrown off water, so he'd drive maybe one mile an hour through it, and then drive slowly for a little bit for the tires to dry, and then he'd go fast on the other side."

Travis said he and Scott often got into "serious conversations," especially in the later years, and in one of them, Scott said, " 'If anything ever happens to me, I want you to know that I want you to take care of my dog,' and then, I forget what it was, but something to do with Kim, and the third thing was 'Make sure my car doesn't get sold.' "

Travis says the conversation had nothing to do, as far as he knew, with any hint on Scott's part that his days might be numbered. Rather it was, as Travis puts it, "saying it just to say it." As of March 1987, Scott's beloved Lotus is still parked in the estate—along with the other Lotus, Margaret's Porsche, and several more automobiles. But Buck, Scott's dog, now lives with the Kendalls in Boston.

Carol Lynn says she has discovered an odd, and somewhat unsettling, coincidence. To the dog, Travis's voice apparently sounds just like Scott's. While the animal is able and willing to ignore the other two people in the house, whenever Travis speaks, Buck's ears perk up and he bounds off in search of his master. "Until I got used to it," she says, "it kind of gave me the creeps."

Travis was in Lancaster—having gone down to visit a friend, and *not* having checked in with his aunt or his grandfather ("because I knew then they'd make me stay with them and I'd have to be in early")—and had been walking to that friend's house, from the Lancaster Country Club, when the news of the bombing deaths was broadcast. By the time he arrived at his friend's, they knew.

"They called me into the living room, and they said, 'There's been a problem.' They said, 'a problem with your mother.' They said, 'but your mother's okay. Your mother's okay, but your Uncle Scott and your grandmother were killed.'

"I stood up and just walked outside. At that point my grieving was definitely more for Scott than for my grandmother."

Several days later, Travis rode away from the funeral in a car with Steven and Debby. His most vivid recollection was that Steven made a point of complaining about the people who had been asked to be pallbearers for Margaret. "Just," says Travis, "for who they were. He was reading the list in the paper and swearing about it."

The sixteen-year-old, who was then fifteen, also found Debby's reactions on the day of the double funeral to be other than what he had expected. "She didn't cry," he says, "throughout the whole afternoon." It seemed to him that Debby was "getting along fine."

Like his brother, Travis Kendall says that while he realizes that "at one time there was a very large chance [Carol Lynn] might die, I knew her well enough to know what she could put up with."

Is she strong? "Yeah," he says smiling, "she's pretty strong."

Carol Lynn Benson Kendall may need to be strong. As of April 1987, with very little light at the end of the legal tunnel, she fears an economic result that could be as cataclysmic as the original crime.

"It is very possible," she said twenty-one months after the killings, "that I could end up with no home, no money, and owing the lawyers several hundred thousand dollars *more*."

The estate breaks down this way: of the original estate (and Carol Lynn says that the oft-cited ten million dollar figure is too high by possibly as much as three million dollars) four million was paid in taxes. As of April 1987, the remaining assets include cash and a variety of noncash assets, such as a mortgage on the Ridge Road house in Lancaster, five vehicles (Margaret's Porsche, the two Lotuses, a VW van, and a Chevrolet Silverado pick-up) and

354 / John Greenya

personal effects and furniture in storage in Lancaster and Naples.

What so complicates the estate is a lingering, but vitally important legal question: how many legitimate heirs are there?

The paternity suit, which is scheduled to be heard in May 1987, is the first part of a legal proceeding known as a "Petition to Determine Beneficiaries." Once they have settled the question of whether or not Tracy Mullins's little girl is also Scott Benson's, the court and the parties can move on to the issue of the rights of Steven's three children.

According to Carl Westman, the Naples attorney chosen by Richard Cirace to act as personal representative of Margaret Benson's estate, even though Steven Benson has been found guilty of murdering Margaret (and Scott), and even though the Killer Statute says he cannot inherit, his children are Margaret Benson's legal heirs. (Others dispute that view, saying the law is not at all clear on this central point.)

He explains that there is a full $750,000 set aside for Scott Benson's alleged heir, should Tracy Mullins win her paternity suit. Equal shares were set aside for Steven and Carol Lynn. Carol Lynn has received almost all of hers, and about half of Steven's has been paid to his children's guardian. The guardianship has paid some of that money out to cover pretrial legal expenses, and (under court order) to the guardians of Steven's children and to Debra Benson.

Carol Lynn says that from that $750,000 she has put aside $200,000—"It's the last money I have in the world, and it's my and my children's future." The rest, $550,000, has already been spent: she says, "at least $400,000 has gone for legal fees and expenses; $50,000 in health-related expenses; and the rest, approximately $100,000, has gone for living expenses and costs directly related to the trial."

Carl Westman and Richard Cirace have a more optimistic view—though one to which she takes *strong* exception—of Carol Lynn's financial future. "There is," says Westman, "$115,000 in cash set aside for her right now, with an additional $76,000 in transition. That's in addition to the $750,000 she has already received. Even if you take a worst-case scenario of the value of the rest of the estate and the outcome of the Petition to Determine Beneficiaries, Carol Lynn would still end up with $1.2 to $1.5 million. Taking a *best*-case scenario, she could receive $3.5 to $4 million."

"That," says Carol Lynn, "is flat out *ridiculous*! For that to be true, there would have to be at least another million dollars somewhere in the estate, and it just isn't there, using his own figures."

What worries her, she adds, is that "I may have as much as $400,000 in taxes to pay, and who knows how much more in legal fees on top of the almost half a million I've already paid."

Carol Lynn is struck by the irony that she is caught up in a dispute with attorney Westman when neither she nor her mother wanted a lawyer as personal representative. Margaret Benson had dropped Wayne Kerr as administrator in her final will.

Both Carl Westman and Richard Cirace say that Carol Lynn has been kept fully informed as to the progress of her mother's estate. The extent to which Carol Lynn disagrees with that position is reflected by the fact that in February 1987 she retained a Lancaster attorney to provide her with what she calls an accounting of Carl Westman's handling of her mother's estate.

Carl Westman says, "I'm very sorry that Carol Lynn feels that way, but everything that has been done is recorded on all the forms and documents with which I've been supplying her—the drafts of the accountings, the copies of the investment accounts, and the Federal Estate tax forms. As Florida law requires, we will be filing a final accounting prior to termination of the estate proceedings."

In late March 1987, Richard Cirace sent Carol Lynn Benson Kendall his formal notification of withdrawal as her attorney. He says he considered her hiring of the Pennsylvania attorney an indication of her lack of faith in his judgment. And he says he disagrees with "her assessment of the fees she has paid, and her concerns as to the outcome of the estate. Carl Westman has always provided me with copies of all documentation and I have always made them available to her and I have asked her to come in and discuss them at all times. At no time has anybody ever kept *any* information from her.''

Carol Lynn, who calls this statement disingenuous, citing ''a minimum of $216,000 in cancelled checks to Cirace marked fees, and $48,000 to a Naples lawyer who served as his local counsel,'' continues to feel that the lawyers did not keep her properly informed as to the details of her mother's estate: ''I'm tired of being in the position of hearing them say that they're the two lawyers and they know everything, and who am I but some dumb little woman.''

As of March 1987, only the formal notice of appeal had been filed by the defense in the case of *Florida vs. Steven Wayne Benson.* No brief had been written and no court date had been set for argument of his appeal. There was talk of bringing in Alan Dershowitz, the Harvard law professor and appellate ace who had won a new trial for Claus von Bülow in Rhode Island. But there was, as defense attorney Michael McDonnell pointed out succinctly, no money. There were rumors that Steven had been in contact with a Miami lawyer and that he might drop McDonnell. But for once there was really no news.

McDonnell told the Naples *Daily News* that he might ask to be released as Steven's attorney. That could enable Steven to qualify for legal assistance from a public defender, and, perhaps, for an appeal paid for by the State.

A friend of Steven's from junior high school days back in Lancaster, who asked that neither his name nor his occupation be used, says he writes Steven and talks with him on the phone fairly regularly.

He says Steven told him he had wanted to take the stand in his own defense, but that ''the lawyers'' would not let him. The friend said that Steven would have simply denied everything, but that, as far as he could tell, Steven had no new information or explanation to impart. He also said that Steven Benson complained that during the year he was in prison in Naples, his defense lawyer had visited him only seven times. Steven, the friend added, was depressed and "probably scared."

Steven Benson had good reason to be scared. Raiford is a real prison, not the kind of place where white collar criminals are incarcerated. For the most part, the men behind bars there are the kind of men from whom society most needs protection.

The horrible reality of this was brought home to Steven Benson at Christmastime of 1986, when he found himself the object of an argument between several inmates over whose "wife" he was. When it was over, he needed medical treatment, including rectal stitches, as a result of being beaten and raped.

Debra Franks Benson still lives in the small Wisconsin town of Westby, the hometown to which she returned not long after Steven was arrested. It is not known whether she or the children have had any contact with him since that time. She has refused all requests for interviews.

A spokesperson in McDonnell's office says that the defense lawyer made "a reluctant decision" to keep Debby Benson away from her husband's trial because of "the negative effect that all the publicity would have on her and the children."

Another lawyer in contact with Debby Benson says her only desire is to "shield her children from all of this."

Let Hugh Hayes, the man who presided over the trial of Steven Wayne Benson, have the last word.

"Two hours after the jury had convicted Steven Benson, I suggested to both sides that they prepare to argue the death penalty right away, to do it that same day. But they both, the prosecution and the defense, pleaded mental and emotional exhaustion. So it was put off until the next day.

"Frankly, I now think the jury was ready, or at least *enough* of them were ready—say seven to five, or eight to four—to vote for death. But by giving them the night to think it over, I think it saved Steven's life.

"For whatever reasons, Steven Benson looked at his family and rationally decided that they were not fit to live and that, somehow, it was all right for him to kill them, and take and spend the money as he saw fit.

"I think he was guilty, and I do not think that he was insane, unless one takes the view that anyone who commits such a crime is insane, but then the whole system of criminal justice would be rendered meaningless.

"In trying to understand his personality and motivation, you can read whatever you want, from Freud to Locke and Hobbes, but I, for one, keep being struck by the question of how far we have come—or not come—from the jungle."